D0209497

EDUCATION REFORM IN THE '90s

370.973
F497

EDUCATION REFORM IN THE '90s

Edited by

Chester E. Finn, Jr., and Theodor Rebarber

Macmillan Publishing Company
New York

Maxwell Macmillan Canada
Toronto

Maxwell Macmillan International
New York   Oxford   Singapore   Sydney

LIBRARY ST. MARY'S COLLEGE

190719

The opinions expressed herein are solely those of the authors in their private capacities, and are in no way to be construed as reflective of the policies or positions of the U.S. Department of Education.

Copyright © 1992 by Vanderbilt University, Educational Excellence Network

All rights reserved. No part of this book may be reproduced or
transmitted in any form or by any means, electronic or mechanical,
including photocopying, recording, or by any information storage
and retrieval system, without permission in writing from the
Publisher.

Macmillan Publishing Company
866 Third Avenue
New York, NY 10022

Maxwell Macmillan Canada, Inc.
1200 Eglinton Avenue East, Suite 200
Don Mills, Ontario M3C 3N1

Macmillan Publishing Company is part of the Maxwell
Communication Group of Companies

Library of Congress Catalog Card Number: 91-27033

Printed in the United States of America

printing number
1 2 3 4 5 6 7 8 9 10

Library of Congress Cataloging-in-Publication Data

Education reform in the 90s / edited by Chester E. Finn, Jr. and
    Theodor Rebarber.
        p.   cm.
    Report of a three and a half day summer institute held on the
Vanderbilt campus during July, 1990.
    Includes bibliographical references and index.
    ISBN 0-02-897095-0
    1. Educational change—United States.   2. Education—United
States—Parent participation.   3. Education and state—United
States.   I. Finn, Chester E., 1944-.   II. Rebarber, Theodor.
LA217.2.E38   1992
370'.973—dc20

The paper used in this publication meets the minimum requirements of
American National Standard for Information Sciences—Permanence
of Paper for Printed Library Materials. ANSI Z39.48-1984.

LIBRARY ST. MARY'S COLLEGE

Contents

Foreword

We are near the beginning of what some call the "second wave" of education reform since the release of *A Nation at Risk* in 1983. In unusually strong language, the authors of that epochal report warned that the sorry state of American education endangered our standing in the highly competitive global economy as well as our domestic peace and civic culture, and likened the situation to an "act of war" by a hostile power. Most states responded to this clarion call with sincere efforts to enhance the quality of their public schools. Those "first wave" reforms focused primarily on raising standards through such traditional means as stricter graduation requirements, higher teacher's salaries, and minimum competency tests for teachers and students.

Nearly a decade later we find that these efforts, although well-intentioned, had scant impact. What reliable measures we have of student achievement show little or no improvement. The important question, of course, is why. For many observers, the inadequacies of the first reform wave stemmed from an overly rigid response by central authorities at the state and local levels, a response that failed to recognize the wide variety of school conditions and needs. In light of these and other concerns, new reform proposals addressing more fundamental aspects of the current system are now under discussion in education policy circles, not least in many state legislatures.

This volume is the final product of a two-year project whose goal was to assist legislators in getting ahead of the curve on some of the major education reform topics currently under debate. Entitled "Better Education Through Informed Legislation," the project was co-sponsored by the National Conference of State Legislatures, a nonprofit, nonpartisan organization serving the country's state legislatures and their staffs, and Vanderbilt University's Educational Excellence Network, an association of more than 1,700 reform-minded educators, scholars, policymakers, journalists, and others interested in improving education.

Throughout this project, proposals aimed at improving educational quality have been grouped into three broad categories:

- *Restructuring reforms:* ways of altering educational administration to encourage flexibility and professionalism are discussed in the second section of this book entitled "Revamping the System."
- *Accountability systems:* mechanisms that measure progress toward explicit educational outcome goals and create incentives for success in achieving them are examined in the third section, "Accountability for Results."
- *Parent-enabling programs:* methods intended to help families become more effective participants in their children's education are analyzed in the fourth section, "On the Home Front."

The project was begun with an intense three-and-a-half-day summer institute held on the Vanderbilt campus during July 1990 for key legislators from fifteen states. Participants are listed later in this book. Attendees heard panel discussions by nationally known educational experts and legislative leaders and participated with them in small groups on education issues of interest to their respective states. The "faculty" included such noted scholars and practitioners as Francie Alexander, John Chubb, G. Alfred Hess, Michael Kirst, Gene Maeroff, Joseph Murphy, Thomas Payzant, and Terry Peterson, whose contributions to this collection are much appreciated. A trio of highly regarded legislators—Representatives Ken Nelson of Minnesota, C. Arthur Ollie of Iowa, and Kim Peery of Washington—also served as faculty members and provided an invaluable link between the world of education theory and the realities of legislative action. During the course of the institute, participants also heard presentations by Floretta McKenzie, managing partner of the McKenzie Group and former superintendent of the District of Columbia public schools, and by testing critic John J. Cannell, author of *Nationally Normed Elementary Achievement Testing in America's Public Schools: How All Fifty States Are Above the National Average* (the "Lake Wobegon" report).

After the summer institute, technical assistance sessions were held in each of the fifteen participating states, providing further education and training to legislators regarding education issues on their agenda in the 1991 session. Three legislative handbooks corresponding to the project's key categories—restructuring, accountability, and parent enabling—and two videos were also produced and distributed to lawmakers and others with an interest in education policy.

The emphasis in this volume on reform at the state level reflects a shift in the focus of educational policy-making that began in the late 1970s and early '80s. Although ample room remains for innovation and initiative at the local level, most observers agree that the states will provide much of the policy direction for reform in the '90s.

Although their roles are not always fully understood, state legislators are central figures in state education policy-making. Whether wrestling with substantive issues or funding issues, legislatures are critical components of any serious reform effort. While actions of a few, well-publicized "education governors" have been more apt to catch the media's eye, there has never been a governor who enacted major reforms without the legislature's approval. In fact, the primary initiative for reform has often come from the legislative institution.

The essays contained in this book represent a variety of perspectives on some of the most fundamental and contentious issues of education reform. Taken together, they are intended as a resource for busy elected officials, their aides, and other interested citizens trying to make sense of complex issues and of the policy options available to them.

Many people deserve special acknowledgment for their untiring efforts in connection with this project. John L. Myers, NCSL's Education Program Director, oversaw the entire enterprise from conception to final realization. The NCSL education staff that has worked on this project—including Connie Koprowicz, Tim Storey, Julie Bell, Terry Whitney, and Veronica White—showed unwavering commitment as well as great ability in attending both to the largest responsibilities and to the most minute details. Chester E. Finn, Jr., and Theodor Rebarber of the Educational Excellence Network have exceeded our highest expectations with this fine and useful volume, the imaginative design of the summer institute, and the handbooks and other parts of the project on which they have worked. Other network staff members who helped in these endeavors—Andrew Forsaith, Matthew Gandal, and Courtney Uhler—deserve our gratitude. Carol Sergent and Ann Houston of Houston-Sergent Consulting are also worthy of acknowledgment for a fine job handling many of the on-site logistics for the institute.

Finally, none of this would have been possible without generous funding from four foundations committed to improving the education of our nation's children: the Donner Foundation, the Gates Foundation, the Joyce Foundation, and the John D. and Catherine T. MacArthur Foundation.

John Martin
President, National Conference of State Legislatures
Speaker, Maine House of Representatives
March 1991

Introduction

Chester E. Finn, Jr.

Where We Stand in 1991

From one source after another, for the past decade we've been receiving evidence that American education is doing a mediocre job, one that ill-serves this country and our children. What is most alarming is that after a sustained period of valiant reform effort—and no small investment of resources—in the 1980s, we have so little to show for our labors and our money.

Test scores remain flat or declining. International comparisons continue to show us near the back of the pack. Remedial education is the fastest-growing activity on many college campuses. Employers say they still cannot find competent workers. The quality of our civic and political life erodes.

To be sure, American education can boast some remarkable accomplishments over the decades. We have done well at constructing a universal and flexible system in which just about anyone can have just about as much education as he or she wants, pretty much whenever they want it. We have also made commendable progress in opening classroom doors to minorities, immigrants, and the handicapped. We are pretty good at recognizing student differences and trying to respond to them through the schools. Ours is an adaptive and fairly forgiving system in which it is never too late to try again.

We have hugely widened people's access to higher education, too, such that we are the only country in world history where more than half of those who complete secondary school go on to further study. (How many of them wind up with a college degree is another, and far gloomier, story.)

All true and all good. But these accomplishments cannot mask the bad news, above all the weak intellectual skills and knowledge possessed by our average high-school graduate, and the widening gap between those skills and knowledge and the levels required for the kinds of jobs we are creating in the United States today, the kinds of jobs we have to be able to fill with qualified individuals if we are to be economically strong, not to mention culturally vibrant, civically alert, and internationally secure.

Wholesale and Retail

We cannot yet pass final judgment on the efforts of the 1980s. American education is vast, decentralized, ponderous, and slow to change. Youngsters still take seventeen years to reach their seventeenth birthday, and they need twelve or thirteen of those years to pass through the schools. Some of the boldest reform plans—such as those in Chelsea and Chicago, in Milwaukee and Kentucky—are just commencing. There may be progress in the making that has not yet shown up in the outcomes data. We all hope so.

The odds improved somewhat in mid-1991 when President George Bush unveiled his "AMERICA 2000" education reform strategy, developed by his dynamic new Secretary of Education (and former Tennessee governor) Lamar Alexander. A wide-ranging and long-term plan for changing some of the country's basic education values and priorities, for catalyzing bold action at the state and local levels, and for enlisting the private sector in these endeavors, it enhances the possibility that we may actually achieve our ambitious national education goals by decade's end.

Yet I remain glum in the face of the challenges ahead. The main sources of my dismay are the clues that people probably are not changing their actual behavior at what we can term the "retail" level of education not withstanding the valiant reform efforts already undertaken since the nation was declared "at risk" in 1983. There is a kind of widespread schizophrenia in which people seem, on the one hand, to acknowledge that we have a grave country-wide education problem but also seem, on the other hand, to be reasonably content with their own and their children's education and with their local schools. The nation may be at risk, but "I'm all right, Jack."

Most children think they are doing well, even when they are not (Lapointe et al. 1989; Stevenson 1987). Most parents give high marks to the schools attended by their own youngsters while panning schools in general (Elam on Gallup 1990). Students and parents alike are far more easily satisfied with their performance (and with their schools) than are their Asian counterparts (Stevenson 1987). Teachers, while critical of many features of current public schooling, nonetheless tell pollsters that the schools in which they teach are providing students with a good education (Harris 1990). School administrators agree. An Allstate Insurance Company survey reported in January 1990 that 91 percent of principals and superintendents think American public education today is doing an excellent, very good, or good job at turning out an educated population A group of business executives, asked the same questions, checked in at just 23 percent. (Ritchie and Abbott, 1990).

Consider the implications for education reform: If children think they are doing satisfactorily, if parents think their daughters and sons are doing well, if people think their local schools are doing okay, and if the teachers and administrators in those schools agree with this appraisal, why should anyone feel inclined to alter his or her actual behavior, to demand different results from themselves or their children, or to agitate for significant changes in the schools their children attend?

Yet if the actual behavior of actual people does not actually change in millions of individual cases, there is no reason whatsoever to expect our averages and aggregates to change. Our outcomes will remain flat. And that, I suggest, has at least something to do with why the results of our reform efforts to date have not been more positive. It also says to me that any education improvement plan that does not deal directly with the "complacency problem" is doomed to failure.

Why have we managed to raise the nation's consciousness about its wholesale education problem but failed to get the message across at the retail level? I can only speculate. Americans tend to be optimists to start with: We think pretty well of ourselves; we don't much like bad news; we are inclined to believe that things tend to get better, not worse.

We also have what Dr. John J. Cannell calls the "Lake Wobegon" effect of current state and local testing programs—the phenomenon that finds virtually everyone to be performing above the "national average"—and we have a flood of upbeat press releases pouring from state and local education agencies, nearly always asserting that results are good and getting better (Cannell 1987).

Our elected officials have also let us down by not looking us in the eye and saying "When I talk about educational meltdown, Mr. and Mrs. Abernathy, I'm talking about *your* Johnny and Janet and the school they attend, *not* about somebody else's children, the schools across town, or the towns on the other side of the state."

But another possible explanation also worries me greatly. There is some evidence that young Americans are behaving "rationally" when they do not study very hard or learn much in school.

Outside the yuppie elites clawing their way into Amherst and Stanford, it turns out that few Americans actually reap significant rewards from studying hard and learning a lot. Children ordinarily get promoted from one grade to the next regardless of how they do. Report cards customarily consist of good news and cheery, upbeat comments, no matter the actual level of performance. High-school graduates entering the work force earn the same salary (for as long as ten years out of school) whether they take hard courses and earn high grades or enroll in gut classes and get C's (Bishop 1989). Their employers merely ask whether they received a diploma; nobody looks at their transcripts, let alone compensates them differently according to their school record (Commission on Skills of American Workforce 1990).

Higher education is just as unhelpful. Admission to most colleges and universities requires merely that you be able to walk through the door and write a check; only a tiny fraction of prospective students seek admission to competitive campuses. For most people, entry to the nearby state university is a sure thing, no matter what their high-school record shows.

Think about it. If we do not differentially reward high achievers—or penalize low performers—why *should* youngsters study hard and learn a lot, particularly when they have so many enticing distractions and short-term gratifications? Remember, they and their parents think they are doing satisfactorily in school. So, in the main, do their teachers and principals.

Swept Under the Rug?

Widespread retail-level complacency is not the only issue that has bedeviled efforts thus far to revitalize American education. We have slighted some others, too.

First, we have not been paying attention to the truism that people learn things in rough proportion to the amount of time they spend studying. The time factor has barely been touched in the course of our reform efforts. As a result, American youngsters spend less time engaged in academic learning than any other youngsters in the industrial world. We have shorter school days and years; our children do less homework. They are also more apt (at the secondary level) to spend their after-school hours working at jobs. Is it any wonder that they wind up knowing less than their age-mates in other lands? A 1990 study finds U.S. high-school students engaged in academic work only half as many hours a week as their counterparts in Japan (Juster and Stafford, 1990). I suspect that any reform scheme that fails to deal with the time factor will make scant difference in the outcomes of American education.

Second, until very recently, we have not been clear about our goals, about what an adequately educated young American would actually look like. Not long ago, Ernest Boyer compared education to "an industry that's unclear about its product, and thus is hopelessly confused about quality control" (Quoted in Finn, 1990). The governors and President George Bush have begun to correct this situation, with the six big (and to my eye commendable) national education goals that they set forth in early 1990. But few states have yet embraced these, and most do not have explicit goals of their own. No state yet requires all its youngsters to take the full array of academic high-school courses that the National Commission on Excellence in Education termed the "new basics" in 1983: four years of English; three years each of math, science, and social studies; two years of a foreign language; and half a year of computers. This is a nontrivial matter. Only when we all understand the direction in which we are traveling do we have a prayer of getting where we want to be.

Third, it is not just that we have not known where we are heading; we also have not known enough about the progress we are making. Our information feedback and accountability systems are unequal to the task at hand. We do not really know how well our children are learning or how well our institutions are doing at the many levels where we need such information: the individual youngster, the classroom, the school building, the local school system, the state, and the entire nation. People take seriously only that which is measured and reported. Student-learning outcomes at these six levels have not been satisfactorily measured *or* reported. Most of the testing programs that provide child-specific results also yield false good news. Instruments that generate more trustworthy data, such as the SAT exam, are meant to gauge aptitude, not achievement —that is, to tell us what our young people are capable of, not how much they have learned or how effective their schools are. Few testing programs permit valid comparisons to be made between schools, districts, or states. None is anchored to a world standard. Most overrely on multiple choice formats, and those that use more sophisticated techniques are accessible only to honor students (Advanced Placement exams) or administered just to small samples of the population (National Assessment).

Fourth, even if we had a shared sense of direction and better forms of accountability, we would need a system whose normal functioning inclines people to do that which they should be doing. As we have seen in the Soviet and Eastern European economies, systems in which people seem consistently unable to achieve reasonable objectives or to generate high productivity rarely fail because of individual culpability. Instead, people have been saddled with unworkable ground rules that doom practically all efforts to do things better or faster or more efficiently. American education is similar. That is why any true reform must include thorough restructuring of basic operating procedures and incentive arrangements.

Fifth and finally, we have not tapped the enormous potential of parents as partners in the education enterprise. By the time they complete secondary education, American children have spent less than 10 percent of their lives in school. Both in motivating their children outside school and working with them directly to reinforce their schooltime experiences, parents have a huge impact. Today we are beginning to see choice policies that engage parents in thinking about the most appropriate education for their children and that encourage schools to reach out and be more responsive to their concerns. Policymakers are also beginning to experiment with programs and activities to bridge the gap between school and home and engage parents in worthwhile activities with their children. But what a long way we still have to go.

Lessons for the 1990s

The 1990s offer us a chance to learn from our experience, to address some of the fundamental issues that we began to identify in the '80s. This means, in essence, that we need shrewder, more thoroughgoing and comprehensive—one might say more radical—reforms, the kinds that alter the underlying rules, organizational dynamics, power relationships, and incentive structures of the education system.

In the nine essays that follow, some of the nation's foremost analysts put their minds and pens to the honorable if not always cheerful tasks of explaining how we have come to the situation in which we find ourselves and distilling some lessons and advice for reformers of the 1990s.

The book is organized into five sections. In the first of these, Vanderbilt professor Joseph Murphy provides a systematic discussion of school restructuring, a favorite term of contemporary educators and policymakers but one that has had nearly as many meanings as users. Murphy's examination should prove especially helpful to legislators and other state officials who wonder how to get a satisfactory purchase on so elusive yet popular a concept.

The second—and much the longest—section is also about education restructuring in a broad sense but examines it from four very different perspectives. In Chapter 2 Stanford's Michael Kirst thoughtfully discusses the contemporary state role in wholesale education reform, blending practical advice with much-needed caveats, as well as some timely

observations on coordinating nonschool services for children. In Chapter
3 John Chubb of the Brookings Institution and Terry Moe of Stanford
summarize the central arguments of their celebrated book, *Politics, Markets,
and America's Schools*, concluding that the political process, by its very
nature, cannot cure what ails our education system and that the incentives
and dynamics of the marketplace must instead be brought to bear; they
also outline the kinds of changes they believe states should make and
respond to some of the more frequently voiced objections to their
proposals. In Chapter 4 G. Alfred Hess of Chicago's Panel on Public
School Policy and Finance provides a lively case study of one of the most
remarkable education reforms visible in the United States today, the
radical decentralization and parent empowerment now under way in
Chicago. The section closes with Chapter 5, a careful account of school
reform in San Diego written by that city's dynamic and erudite superintendent, Thomas W. Payzant. His role at the 1990 summer institute in
Nashville was to comment—and bring a dose of realism to bear—on each
of the major themes of the project, and his chapter serves much the same
purpose in this volume.

The third section consists of a pair of chapters on accountability,
featuring case studies of two very different states. Chapter 6 is written by
Terry Peterson of South Carolina's Business-Education Subcommittee, a
veteran of that state's ambitious school reform efforts who also led an
important federal study of state-level accountability systems. From both
those perspectives, he sheds considerable light on the requisites of
workable accountability strategies, from goal-setting through the development of reliable indicators to the rewards and interventions that put the
stuffing into what otherwise too often resembles an empty cushion cover.
Francie Alexander formerly bore responsibility for curriculum and assessment in California, a state that is justifiably admired for its pioneering
pupil-assessment program as well as for its tireless effort to align what is
taught and measured with what state officials hope that students will
learn. Her Chapter 7 essay capably describes those efforts and the
reasoning that undergirds them.

In the book's fourth section, Gene Maeroff of the Carnegie Foundation
for the Advancement of Teaching takes up the crucial matter of parent
involvement. Without sacrificing the moral passion that makes him an
effective writer and speaker, Maeroff extends our understanding by
subdividing this sprawling topic—and Chapter 8—into three parts: the
nonschool aspects of children's lives that strongly but indirectly affect
their educational success; activities that parents can engage in outside
school that bear directly on their children's schoolwork; and the several
genres of direct participation by parents in the life of the schools, ranging
from teacher conferences to full-fledged governance.

Last but perhaps not least, coeditor Ted Rebarber and I reflect upon the evolving politics of education reform, particularly at the state level. In the book's concluding chapter, we endeavor to explain the revolutionary nature of certain of the changes we have observed in this policy arena, with respect both to the character of some of the decisions being made and the identity of those making them. Yet we also find that there is sometimes less to these changes than meets the eye; radical terminology can mask mild reforms with scant prospect of outcomes better than those achieved in the '80s.

As John Martin notes in the Foreword, this book is the result of a joint venture undertaken by the Educational Excellence Network and the National Conference of State Legislatures (NCSL), supported by a quartet of private foundations that shared our view that any important and powerful changes to be made in American elementary-secondary education in the years ahead are apt to be forged in the committee rooms and chambers of the fifty state legislatures. The members and staffs of those key lawmaking bodies have been our primary audience from the outset— and they are anything but passive in that role! Throughout the project, our thinking has been challenged, sharpened, and refined as a result of the experiences they have related, the insights they have volunteered, and the questions they have raised. If, as we hope, this book sheds some light that others will also find beneficial, it is due in no small part to the lively collaboration we have enjoyed with hundreds of individual legislators as well as with their exemplary organization. A number of NCSL officials and staff members have been wonderful partners from the beginning of this venture. Among the many earning our respect and gratitude, special mention is due to John L. Myers, whose low-key manner conceals a tough intellect, a stalwart character, a tireless capacity for work, and an authentic commitment to the betterment of American education. Even as we write, John and his associates continue to see the project through in the form of technical assistance to policymakers in fifteen states. Our overriding objective, after all, was not just to produce a video or write a book. It was—and remains—to do all we can to strengthen the effectiveness and productivity of the education provided to boys and girls in the fifty states that constitute this great but not-quite-perfect land.

References

BISHOP, JOHN H. 1989. "Why the Apathy in American High Schools?" *Educational Researcher* 18 (1):6–10.

CANNELL, JOHN JACOB. 1987. *Nationally Normed Elementary Achievement Testing in America's Public Schools: How All Fifty States Are Above the National Average.* Daniels, W.V.: Friends for Education.

COMMISSION ON SKILLS OF AMERICAN WORKFORCE. 1990. *America's Choice: High Skills or Low Wages.* Rochester, N.Y.: The National Center on Education and the Economy.

ELAM, STANLEY M., and GALLUP, ALEC M. 1990. "22nd Annual Gallup Poll of the Public's Attitude Toward the Public Schools." *Phi Delta Kappan* 72(1):41–55.

FINN, CHESTER E., JR. 1989. "Norms for the Nation's Schools." *Washington Post,* July 16:p. B7.

HARRIS, LOUIS and ASSOCIATES, INC. 1990. *The Metropolitan Life Survey of the American Teacher 1990.* New York: Author.

JUSTER, THOMAS, and STAFFORD, FRANK P. 1990. *The Allocation of Time: Empirical Findings, Behavioral Models, and Problems of Measurement* Survey Research Center, Institute for Social Research. Ann Arbor: The University of Michigan.

LAPOINTE, ARCHIE E.; MEAD, NANCY A.; and PHILLIPS, GARY W. 1989. *A World of Differences: An International Assessment of Mathematics and Science.* Princeton, N.J.: Educational Testing Service.

RITCHIE, ROBERT, and ABBOTT, WENDY E., ET AL. 1989. "Reactions to the American Public Education System." Study prepared for the American Association of School Administrators and Allstate Insurance Company.

STEVENSON, HAROLD W. 1987. "The Asian Advantage: The Case of Mathematics." *American Educator* 11:26–31, 47.

STEVENSON, HAROLD W.; CHEN, CHUANSHENG; and UTTAL, DAVID H. 1990. "Beliefs and Achievement: A Study of Black, White, and Hispanic Children." *Child Development* 61:508–23.

U.S. DEPARTMENT OF EDUCATION. 1989. *Digest of Education Statistics,* 25th edition. National Center for Education Statistics. Washington, D.C.: U.S. Government Printing Office.

EDUCATION REFORM IN THE '90s

THE CHANGING NATURE OF SCHOOL REFORM

Restructuring America's Schools: An Overview

Joseph Murphy[1]

> President Bush and the nation's governors walked away from last week's educational summit with an unprecedented agreement to establish national performance goals and to engineer a radical restructuring of America's education system. (Miller 1989, p. 1)

Today the world is being bombarded with proposals to alter dramatically the landscape of American schooling. Restructuring has become the term of art for a wide-ranging series of endeavors to improve education by introducing fundamentally different methods of school governance and significantly different ways of organizing schooling, particularly the work performed by teachers and the teaching-learning process unfolding in classrooms.

We begin this chapter by placing restructuring within the context of the larger reform movement that burst upon the education world in the early 1980s. Next, we examine the foundations of the more radical recent efforts to change schooling and the infrastructure that underlies them. We also unpack the main principles of restructuring in the second section. Collectively, these principles suggest that we may be poised on the brink of a paradigm shift in our views of schooling. In the third part of the chapter, we map the major features of restructuring—the actors, components, strategies, and metaphors of transformational change. Finally, we

[1]Support for this research was provided by the National Center for Educational Leadership (NCEL) under Department of Education Contract No. R 117c8005. The views in this report are those of the author and do not necessarily represent those of the sponsoring institution nor the universities in the NCEL Consortium—the University of Chicago, Harvard University, and Vanderbilt University.

3

turn our attention to what state policymakers can do to facilitate the restructuring of American public schooling.

Reform as Prelude to Restructuring

In the early 1980s a concerted effort to reform American education began. The impetus was primarily economic. People from all walks of society concluded that America was on the verge of being displaced as a major player in the world economy. The belief that we were falling behind other industrial powers in development, productivity, and quality was a leitmotiv of the various education reform reports and proposals of the period (for example, the Carnegie Forum on Education and the Economy 1986; the Education Commission of the States 1983; the National Commission on Excellence in Education 1983; and the National Governors' Association 1986; for a review see Murphy 1990). It did not take policymakers long to draw a connection between this economic impotence and the educational system. Nor was the potential for schooling to restore America's economic preeminence ignored:

> Sinking economic productivity, national debt, international commercial competition, trade deficits, and a declining dollar placed the nation in increasing economic jeopardy. Schooling was seen as part of the problem and part of the solution. (Guthrie and Kirst 1988, p. 4; see also Association for Supervision and Curriculum Development 1986; Kearnes 1988a, 1988b)

Once the failure of schools to produce literate and numerate graduates was documented (Murphy 1990) and linked to our declining economic position in the world marketplace, investigators began dissecting the education system in search of explanations. The fundamental conclusion of these analyses (for example, Boyer 1983; Chubb 1988; Goodlad 1984; Powell, Farrar, and Cohen 1985; Sedlak, Wheeler, Pullin, and Cusick 1986; Sizer 1984) was that schools were characterized by intellectual softness, a lack of expectations and standards, inadequate leadership, a dysfunctional organizational structure, conditions of employment that were inconsistent with professional work, and the absence of meaningful accountability arrangements. When laid open to review in this fashion, the system's basic infrastructure was found to be in need of serious repair. The luster was wearing off the educational enterprise.

The concern flowing from this analysis, joined to the original economic fears, launched the most widespread, intense, comprehensive, and sustained effort to improve education in our nation's history (McCarthy 1990; Odden and Marsh 1988). Fueled by national and state reform reports, attempts to strengthen the quality of public education began to unfold in states, districts, and schools throughout the nation. Initially, these efforts focused on restoring quality by fixing the existing education system. The conceptual structure of early suggestions for repair was highly mechanistic in nature, composed mainly of centralized controls and standards (Boyd 1987; Sedlak et al 1986). The assumptions embedded in this approach suggest that the conditions of schooling contributing to poor student-outcome measures are attributable to the poor quality of school workers and the inadequacy of their tools and that these problems are subject to revision through mandated, top-down initiatives—especially those emanating from the state. Use of the bureaucratic model to institute improvement proposals led in turn to the emphasis in early reform efforts on policy mechanisms such as prescriptions, tightly specified resource allocations, and performance measurements that focused on repairing faulty components of the system (for example, writing better textbooks) and raising the quality of the work force by telling employees how to work (for example, specifying instructional models; see Coombs 1987; Hawley 1988). A dizzying array of initiatives was discussed in reports and studies and subsequently passed into law by the various states.

Criticism of these early efforts to reform schooling was quickly forthcoming (e.g., Chubb 1988; Cuban 1984; Elmore 1987; Purpel 1989; Sedlak et al 1986; Sizer 1984). The main thrust of critics of wave 1 reform measures was that they were taking educators down the wrong road—the road of the quick fix—and were using inappropriate policy tools to improve schooling, especially mandates from the top. These reformers argued that fundamental revisions were needed in the cultural institutions of the larger society, in the ways that education systems were organized and governed, in the roles adults played in schools, and in the processes used to educate America's youth. The belief that the current system was beyond repair began to take root. Analysts called for a complete overhaul of the education system—a comprehensive attempt to reweave the basic fabric of schooling or a restructuring (rebuilding, reinvention, reformation, revolution, rethinking, or transformation) of the education enterprise.

Restructuring Schools: The Foundation

Not surprisingly, reformers who argue for a major transformation in American education have built their ideas on different foundations and constructed their edifices with different materials than those employed in the early and mid-1980s. Embedded in their views of education are the seeds for a paradigm shift in schooling (Finn 1990).

Restructuring: The Infrastructure

The philosophical foundation of wave 2 reformers is that education improvement hinges upon empowering teachers to work more effectively with students (Carnegie Forum on Education and the Economy 1986; Holmes Group 1986). A less central but persistent theme is that real change also depends upon empowering parents (Chubb 1988; Kearnes 1988a, 1988b). The major policy mechanism employed in wave 2 reforms has been "power distribution"—a strategy that

> assume[s] that schools can be improved by distributing political power among the various groups who have legitimate interests in the nature and quality of educational services. Reforms that seek to reallocate power and authority among various stakeholders are based on the belief that when power is in the right hands, schools will improve. (Association for Supervision and Curriculum Development 1986, p. 13)

Unlike the approaches of the earlier era of school reform, this change model is designed to capitalize on the energy and creativity of individuals at the school level. As education analyst J. Green explains,

> the individual school is the focus of the second wave of reform. While previous reports called for leadership, it was generally at the state level; now the cry is for local involvement and reforms that improve what happens in the classroom itself. (Green 1987, p. 4)

In the words of veteran analysts Denis Doyle and Terry Hartle, "Putting policy changes into effect—actually implementing what the reformers have called for—is a responsibility that will fall on local schools. That is where the leadership must come from if the promise of education reform is to be realized" (Doyle and Hartle 1985, p. 24).

Underlying almost all second-wave proposals is the belief that the problems in education can be ascribed to the structure of schooling—"that the highest impediment to progress is the nature of the system itself" (Carnegie Forum on Education and the Economy 1986, p. 40). The bureaucratic infrastructure of education has been subjected to close scrutiny and has been found to be failing (Clark and Meloy 1989; Frymier 1987):

> We are learning, for instance, that deeply ingrained "ways of organizing," often written into statues and legally binding regulations, are more clearly attributable to educator self interest, prevailing prejudice, and the deeply ingrained mythology of schooling, than to any firm knowledge base. (Erickson 1979, p. 9)

It is not surprising that the focus of improvement in this era of reform has been on the professionals who populate schools and the conditions they need to work effectively, including basic changes in the organizational arrangements of schooling—a shift from mechanistic, structure-enhancing strategies to a professional approach to reform and from "regulation and compliance monitoring to mobilization of institutional capacity" (Timar and Kirp 1988, p. 75). Nor is it surprising that reformers who consider the basic structure of schools as the root of education's problems should propose more far-reaching and radical solutions than their predecessors, who believed that the current system could be set right (Boyd 1987; Perry 1988):

> We recommend nothing less than a revolution in the role of the teacher and the management of schools in order to upgrade the quality and professionalism of the U.S. teacher work force. (Committee for Economic Development, cited in the Carnegie Forum for Education and the Economy 1986, p. 36)

Restructuring: Paradigm Shift[2]

Our attempts to reinvent schooling augur fundamental shifts in our view of education. Restructuring begins with a basic change in our view of the relationship between the school and its environment. Historically ingrained notions of schools as sheltered monopolies, or delivery systems, are breaking down under the incursions of a market philosophy into education (see Boyd 1990; Boyd and Hartman 1988). The traditional dominant relationship between schools (and professional educators) and the public is being reworked in favor of more equal arrangements—i.e., partnerships (Seeley 1980, 1988). For the first time in our history, the business of schooling is being redefined in relation to its customers. Restructuring is facilitating unprecedented inroads of market forces into the governance and organization of schools.

Consistent with this change are efforts to develop new forms of school organization and management. The hierarchical, bureaucratic organizational structures that have defined schools over the past one hundred years are giving way to more decentralized (Guthrie 1986; Murphy and Hart 1988) and professionally controlled systems (David 1989; Houston 1989) —systems that "can be thought of as a new paradigm for school management" (Wise 1989, p. 303). In these new postindustrial organizations (see Beare 1989), labeled "heterarchies" by Maccoby (1989), there

---

[2]The remaining subsections in this part of the chapter are based on material taken from Joseph Murphy, *Restructuring Schools: Capturing and Assessing the Phenomena.* (New York: Teachers College Press, copyright © 1991 by Teachers College, Columbia University. All rights reserved.)

are found "very basic changes in roles, relationships, and responsibilities" (Seeley 1988, p. 35): traditional patterns are altered (Conley 1989), authority flows become less hierarchical (Clark and Meloy 1989), role definitions are both more general and more flexible (Corcoran 1989), leadership is connected to competence for needed tasks rather than to formal position (American Association of Colleges for Teacher Education 1988; Angus 1988; Maccoby 1988, 1989), and independence and isolation are replaced by cooperative work (Beare 1989). In addition, a traditional structural orientation is overshadowed by a focus on the human element. The operant goal is no longer maintenance of the organizational infra-structure but rather the development of human resources (Mojkowski and Fleming 1988). Developing variegated learning climates through organiza-tional adaptation is substituted for the more traditional emphasis on uncovering and applying a single best model of performance (Clark and Meloy 1989; McCarthey and Peterson 1989). The changed metaphors being applied to these restructured schools—for example, from principal as manager to principal as facilitator, from teacher as worker to teacher as leader—nicely illustrate these fundamental revisions in our views of organizations and our conceptions of management. They reveal a shift in the transformation of schools from control to empowerment.

At the same time, better understanding of the education production function has begun to be translated into what William Spady terms "dramatically different way[s] of thinking about the design, delivery, and documentation of instructional programs" (1988, p. 8). Underlying these changes are radically different ways of thinking about the "educability of humanity," in David Purpel's phrase (1989, p. 10). Schools originally designed to produce results consistent with the normal curve, to sort youth into the various strata corresponding to our economic tiers, are being redesigned to ensure equal opportunity and success for all learners (see Miller and Brookover, 1986). David Seeley (1988, p. 34) astutely notes the importance of this change when he comments that "it represents a significant shift in the goals of our educational system, and a fundamental component of a new vision, since all other components gain motive force from this shift in goals." New views about what is worth learning are also emerging in restructuring schools. In classrooms, the traditional emphasis on content coverage and rote learning of basic skills is being challenged by deeper treatment of fewer topics and an emphasis on higher-order thinking skills (Carnegie Council for Adolescent Development 1989). As attention is turned to active learning, our century-old concern for indepen-dent work and competition is slowly receding in favor of more cooperative learning relationships (David 1989).

Underlying these changes is an evolution in the sacred values of education (see Lortie 1975; Corbett, Firestone, and Rossman 1987) and strategies for improvement (see Murphy 1990 for an analysis). Alterations in roles and responsibilities are being accompanied by changes in beliefs and values, and more comprehensive reform efforts are replacing the earlier wave of discrete programs and separate approaches (David 1989; see also Lindquist and Muriel 1989; Seeley 1988). Discussions about the purpose of schooling itself have been reopened (Elmore 1988) as the needs of the economy have changed. Teacher egalitarianism and isolation are beginning to crack under the new organizational imperatives for differentiated roles and collegial work. And school success is no longer defined primarily in terms of providing services (processes) but rather in terms of product quality, namely student learning outcomes (Murphy and Hart 1988).

Restructuring: Capturing the Phenomena

Education restructuring generally encompasses systemic changes in one or more of the following: institutionalized and governance structures, work roles and organizational milieu, core technology (the teaching-learning process), and connections between the school and its larger environment. Restructuring also involves fundamental alterations in relationships among key players in the education process. Figure 1-1 depicts these changes in organizational elements and relationships. This framework guides our work on restructuring at the federally supported National Center for Educational Leadership (for a fuller treatment see Murphy, in press). The boxes represent key *actors*—for example, parents and teachers. The lines connecting the various players are designed to explicate some of the predominant *components* of restructuring. The concepts in the circles—school-based management, teacher empowerment, voice/choice, and teaching for understanding—represent the four most prevalent *strategies* employed under the rubric of restructuring to transform schools. The italicized phrases—for example, teachers as leaders—are the new *metaphors* of restructuring.

Even a cursory review of the framework in Figure 1-1 shows the complexity involved in transforming schooling. It should also be obvious that restructuring can begin in a variety of places and employ a number of different strategies, depending upon the specific objectives being sought (see Elmore 1989). The framework is also designed to signal clearly that real education transformation will require the involvement of all the key players, work on all components of the system, and simultaneous use of four distinct but interrelated restructuring strategies. To date, most efforts at reformation have emphasized only one or two of these strategies. Teacher empowerment held center stage at the outset of the restructuring movement. More recently, attention has shifted to school-based management and parental choice/voice. Considerably less work has been devoted

FIGURE 1-1.   Restructuring Schools: A Conceptual Framework

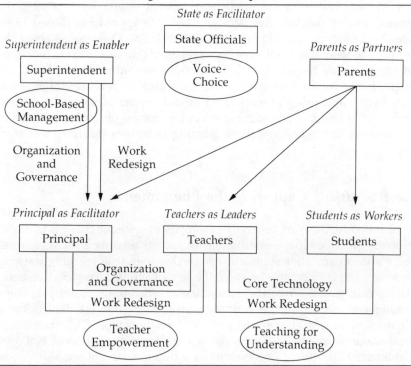

SOURCE: J. Murphy, *Restructuring Schools: Capturing and Assessing the Phenomena*. New York: Teachers College Press, in press.

to teaching for understanding, or to redefining the teaching-learning process, although rumblings of early movements in these areas are becoming more and more audible (see Murphy and Evertson 1990). We look briefly at each of these four strategies below.

School-Based Management

School-based management (SBM) has been defined in a number of ways. When we analyze these definitions and descriptions, we discover that two concepts—structural decentralization and devolution of authority— characterize much of what has been written. Structural decentralization generally entails the dismantling of larger organizational units into smaller, and presumably more responsive, ones. This strategy is typically employed in larger, more heavily centralized districts, such as Milwaukee, New York, and Chicago. These structural changes are usually accompanied by a reduction in the number of levels in the hierarchy and in the number of middle-management personnel. Employees who once occupied these middle-management portions are sometimes reassigned to support functions in individual schools. In other cases, the money used to fund these positions is freed up to support new initiatives at the school site level. In addition, individual schools in structurally decentralized systems may acquire the freedom to sidestep the remaining hierarchical system. As Beare (1989, p. 20) correctly notes, this structural decentralization is, by and large, "modelled upon the modern corporation, the flexible conglomerate which keeps central control of the essential and strategic areas but allows entrepreneurial freedom to the operating units" that constitute the corporation.

Devolution of authority is the fundamental concept in school-based management (Lindquist and Muriel 1989). Under this system of governance schools, in effect, become deregulated from the district office (Beare 1989; Murphy and Hart 1988). We see "sweeping alterations in the basic authority-and-accountability relationships," explain Chester Finn and Stephen Clements (1989, p. i). The basic principle of this system is expanded local control and influence, with schools being given greater responsibility for their own affairs (Beare 1989; Watkins and Lusi 1989). The strategy of improvement is change from the bottom up. Many benefits are expected from devolving authority to the school site and making schools the masters of their own fates. These include enhanced concern for equity issues (Mojkowski and Fleming, 1988), stronger educational programs, and improved student performance (Lindquist and Muriel 1989; Mojkowski and Fleming 1988), and greater satisfaction among school personnel and constituents (Lindquist and Muriel 1989).

Teacher Empowerment

Efforts to empower teachers are designed to improve schooling by professionalizing their work. The goal is to move away from treating teachers as hired hands (Sizer 1984) or assembly-line workers (Purpel 1989) to a situation in which change is teacher-driven, not authority-driven. While various approaches have been tried, two general strategies have received the greatest attention—providing teachers with formal decision-making authority and other avenues of influence and redesigning their work.

We noted above that school-based management is primarily an alteration in the organizational function of school districts. Authority and influence pass from higher to lower levels of the organization. To redistribute authority between organizational levels is one thing, however, while reallocating newly acquired influence among actors at the site level is quite another (see Lindelow 1981). Hence, teachers and administrators in schools and districts that are working to professionalize teaching are developing vehicles that enable teachers to assume control over decisions that have historically been the province of others. Team approaches to school management and governance are particularly good examples of enhanced teacher participation in decision-making.

Reformers concerned with teacher empowerment also envision comprehensive changes in the work performed by teachers in restructured schools. A number of analysts contend with Smylie and Denny (1989) that the "development of new leadership roles for teachers" is "on the crest of the wave" of restructuring (p. 2). We have already noted one major change in teacher work—expanded responsibilities in the decision-making arena. Teachers in some schools are also beginning to play new professional roles as well—for example, master teachers. In these and related cases, the basic teaching role itself is altered. Finally, redesigning the work of teachers in restructured schools may include the development of career opportunities —through the creation of differentiated staffing, for example—that permit teachers to advance in the profession without leaving their classrooms.

Voice/Choice

Parents are portrayed in Figure 1-1 as key players and voice/choice as one of the main restructuring strategies. Changes in governance structures and authority flows, in turn, sit at the center of new relationships between schools and their constituents. Such changes are usually expressed in three ways. First, restructured schools empower parents and community members (Murphy and Hart 1988). Parents are thus able to exercise greater influence over school decision-making processes than is currently the norm (Academic Development Institute 1989; U.S. Department of Education 1989). This enhanced decision-making responsibility is usually formalized in new governance arrangements.

Second, the partnership metaphor includes efforts to expand the school community—to unite parents, professional educators, businesses, universities, foundations, and the general populace into a collective force dedicated to the improvement of schooling for all children. There is an explicit recognition that successful policies must simultaneously address the needs of two generations—the parent and the child—for these are interdependent (Jennings 1990). Embedded in the idea of expansion are two related concepts: enhanced community involvement in schools—by parents, business people, and other adults—and schools serving as community centers, providing a variety of services for parents and children (see Bradley 1989; David 1989; Schmidt 1989).

Third, the principle of parental choice informs many discussions about transforming the relationship between schools and their constituents.

Advocates argue that only by breaking the privileged monopoly status enjoyed by public schools will significant improvement be possible. Thus, many restructuring proponents clamor for the adoption of a market philosophy in education (U.S. Department of Education 1989), accompanied by open-enrollment patterns and choices for parents and students.

Teaching for Understanding[3]

Of the four restructuring strategies pictured in Figure 1-1, teaching for understanding has received the least attention, both in reform reports and in state-, district-, and school-level efforts. We know from the limited amount of work done under this rubric to date, however, that curriculum, instruction, and organizational arrangements for learning look dramatically different in schools that have focused on restructuring classroom activities and processes. From these early initiatives and from the writings of various educational reformers, we can develop a fairly clear concept of teaching for understanding.

Curricula in restructured schools are characterized by both greater complexity and greater cohesion. Seven changes are often found:

1. expanded use of a core curriculum,
2. an increase in the interdisciplinary nature of content,
3. emphasis on depth of coverage,
4. use of more original source materials,
5. greater focus on higher-order learning skills,
6. expanded methods of student assessment, and
7. additional teacher choice (Murphy in press).

Instructional changes in schools that restructure their educational processes will also be comprehensive and radical. The most fundamental revision is a shift from teacher-dominated to learner-centered pedagogy. The emphasis is on the student, not on the delivery system. Acquiring information is subordinated to the ability to use knowledge. Teachers, Spady says, will no longer be "in the coverage business but in the learning success business" (1988, p. 7). They will act as facilitators, modelers, and coaches who invest students with more power and responsibility for their own educational benefit (McCarthey & Peterson 1989; Spady 1988; Sizer 1984; Elmore 1988). The standardized teacher-directed model of instruction that has dominated traditional classrooms (see Goodlad 1984; Powell, Farrar, and Cohen 1985; Sizer 1984) gives way to a greater variety of

---

[3]For a fuller discussion, see Evertson & Murphy, in press.

approaches when teaching for understanding is stressed. Instruction becomes less generic and more personalized. Rather than being suppressed, the complexity of teaching is recognized and used as a foundation in initiatives to revise the core technology of education. Cooperative approaches to learning in which students work together in teams are stressed (David 1989).

Significant alterations in the structures used to deliver educational services constitute the final component of teaching for understanding. Such changes seem to underscore the centrality of human relationships in schools, to replace program isolation with connectedness, and to promote personal engagement in the teaching-learning process. They represent a fundamental reconceptualization of the school climate away from an emphasis on its physical factors and toward a focus on its human elements. At the heart of these calls for organizational change is mounting disenchantment with impersonal, time-based, calendar-dependent learning arrangements. For schools concerned with restructuring educational processes, learning theory and student needs take precedence over the custodial interests of parents, administrative convenience, and employee interests (that is, the need to protect adult jobs in the workplace) in the creation and reshaping of structures to house teaching and learning (Sizer 1984; Spady 1988). Calendar-based school organizations give way to structures founded on three powerful concepts: mastery (or outcome)-based learning, developmentally based learning, and personalized learning.

The State Role in Restructuring

In this era of school restructuring, the roles of state policymakers as well as the perspectives they bring to school improvement look significantly different than in the past. We see a shift away from the state's historical role as monitor of educational process. In its stead, a new tripartite set of responsibilities is emerging. First, state actors tend to assume the lead role in working with all stakeholders in the educational process to establish a new vision of education and to translate that vision into desired student outcomes.[4] Second, they try to support—through as wide an array of methods as possible—efforts at the district, school, and classroom levels to empower parents and professional educators, to nurture the evolution of new forms of governance and organization, and to develop a new core

[4]The work of the Southern Regional Educational Board is an excellent example of state-level activity in this area.

technology for classrooms. Third, they hold schools and school systems accountable for what they accomplish. Operating in this fashion, state policy actors are less involved in the micro-level management of the educational enterprise. Instead, they will play a key role in charting the course and in assessing the results rather than in monitoring processes or effort. Parents, professional educators, and students in each school in turn become freer to direct their own destinies.

In a 1990 article in *Education Week,* Jane Armstrong of the Education Commission of the States (ECS) summarized the comments of more than three hundred participants from two workshops sponsored by the ECS and the National Governors' Association. She listed thirteen steps that policymakers can take to facilitate school restructuring. These constitute an excellent framework for state policymakers:

1. Develop a vision of desired student outcomes and a vision of a restructured education system.
2. Build a coalition of business, community, education, and political leaders.
3. Gain public and political support.
4. Provide flexibility, encourage experimentation, and decentralize decision-making.
5. Shift state and local education agency roles from enforcement to assistance.
6. Restructure teacher and administrator education.
7. Provide ongoing development opportunities for every teacher and administrator.
8. Hold the system accountable.
9. Give all students every chance to learn and contribute.
10. Use policies as catalysts to promote and support restructuring.
11. Identify pilot restructuring sites.
12. Reallocate existing resources for restructuring.
13. Use technology to support restructuring.

A similar set of "state actions to launch restructuring" has been described by Jane David and her colleagues in the National Governors' Association's 1990 report, *State Actions to Restructure Schools: First Steps.* They recommend that policymakers promote a vision, spread the word, build statewide support for restructuring, invite school and district participation, provide support (flexibility, time, and assistance), shift the state role (away from compliance and toward objectives, assistance, and outcomes), focus on results, and maintain visibility. In addition, unlike the reforms of the early 1980s, they remind us that for each state, the beginning steps of restructuring are exploratory. This is uncharted territory with no road maps. Inside schools, districts, and state agencies, leaders and educators are learning by experimenting. (David 1990, p. 35)

Summary

Efforts are afoot to change schooling significantly in every state in the country. To date, most of these restructuring moves have focused on empowering teachers and parents, changing governance structures and management patterns, and altering the roles and work of teachers. Incipient efforts are also afoot to transform the teaching-learning process itself. Collectively, these strategies represent new ways of thinking about education and schooling.

The reconstruction of schooling means new ways of conducting business for all the actors in education, including stakeholders at the state level. It is important, therefore, that policymakers understand school restructuring and be able to assess likely impact on the educational enterprise. Accustomed roles should be discarded. Greater attention should be devoted to the discussion of what the new school should look like, to helping others see its possibilities, to framing a picture of the new dwelling, and to providing key workers—parents, teachers, students, and administrators—with the support they need to complete the facility. Much less attention will need to be provided to establishing detailed construction specifications, to specifying building materials, and to micro-managing the construction process itself.

References

ACADEMIC DEVELOPMENT INSTITUTE. *Building the Value-based School Community.* 1989. Chicago: The Institute.

AMERICAN ASSOCIATION OF COLLEGES FOR TEACHER EDUCATION. 1988. *School Leadership Preparation: A Preface for Action.* Washington, D.C. The Association.

ANGUS, L. 1988. *"School Leadership and Educational Reform."* Paper presented at the annual meeting of the American Educational Research Association, New Orleans.

ARMSTRONG, J. 1990. "A Road Map for Restructuring Schools." *Education Week,* March 28: p. 24.

ASSOCIATION FOR SUPERVISION AND CURRICULUM DEVELOPMENT. 1986. *School Reform Policy: A Call for Reason.* Alexandria, Va.: The Association.

BEARE, H. 1989. *"Educational Administration in the 1990s."* Paper presented at the national conference of the Australian Council for Educational Administration, University of New England, Armidale, New South Wales, Australia, September 25.

BOLIN, F. S. 1989. "Empowering Leadership." *Teachers College Record* 91 (1): 81–96.

BOYD, W. L. 1987. "Public Education's Last Hurrah? Schizophrenia, Amnesia, and Ignorance in School Politics." *Educational Evaluation and Policy Analysis* 9(2): 85–100.

BOYD, W. L. 1990. "Balancing Control and Autonomy in School Reform: The Politics of 'Perestroika.'" In J. Murphy (ed.), *The Reform of American Public Education in the 1980s: Perspectives and Cases.* Berkeley, Calif.: McCutchan.

BOYD, W. L. and HARTMAN, W. T. 1988. "The Politics of Educational Productivity." In O. Monk and J. Underwood (eds.), *Distributing Educational Resources Within Nations, States, School Districts, and Schools.* Cambridge, Mass.: Ballinger.

BOYER, E. L. 1983. *High School: A Report on Secondary Education in America.* New York: Harper and Row.

BRADLEY, A. 1989. "Coca-Cola Joins Growing List of Education Benefactors." *Education Week*, November 15: pp. 1, 20.

CARNEGIE COUNCIL FOR ADOLESCENT DEVELOPMENT. 1989. *Turning Points.* Washington, D.C.: The Council.

CARNEGIE FORUM ON EDUCATION AND THE ECONOMY. 1986. *A National Prepared: Teachers for the 21st Century.* Washington, D.C.: The Forum.

CHUBB, J.E. 1988. "Why the Current Wave of School Reform Will Fail." *The Public Interest* 90:28–49.

CLARK, D. L., and MELOY, J. M. 1989. Renouncing Bureaucracy: A Democratic Structure for Leadership in Schools. In T. J. Sergiovanni and J. A. Moore (eds.), *Schooling for Tomorrow: Directing Reform to Issues that Count.* Boston: Allyn and Bacon.

CONLEY, S. C. 1989. "Who's on First? School Reform, Teacher Participation, and the Decision-making Process." Paper presented at the annual meeting of the American Educational Research Association, San Francisco, March.

COOMBS, F. S. 1987. "The Effects of Increased State Control on Local School District Governance." Paper presented at the annual meeting of the American Educational Research Association, Washington, D.C. April.

CORBETT, H. D.; FIRESTONE, W. A.; and ROSSMAN, G. B. 1987. "Resistance to Planned Change and the Sacred in School Cultures." *Educational Administration Quarterly* 23 (4): 36–59.

CORCORAN, T. B. 1989. "Restructuring Education: A New Vision at Hope Essential High School." In J. M. Rosow and R. Zager (eds.), *Allies in Educational Reform.* San Francisco: Jossey-Bass.

CUBAN, L. 1984. "School Reform by Remote Control: SB813 in California." *Phi Delta Kappan* 66(3): 213–15.

DAVID, J. L. 1989. *Restructuring in Progress: Lessons from Pioneering Districts.* Washington, D.C.: National Governors' Association.

DAVID, J. L.; COHEN, M.; HONETSCHLAGER, D.; and TRAIMAN, S. 1990. *State Actions to Restructure Schools: First Steps.* Washington, D.C.: National Governors' Association.

DOYLE, D. P., and HARTLE, T. W. 1985. "Leadership in Education: Governors, Legislators, and Teachers." *Phi Delta Kappan* 67 (1): 21–27.

EDUCATION COMMISSION OF THE STATES. 1983. *Action for Excellence.* Denver: The Commission.

ELMORE, R. F. 1987. "Reform and the Culture of Authority in Schools." *Educational Administration Quarterly* 23(4): 60–78.

ELMORE, R. F. 1988. *Early Experience in Restructuring Schools: Voices from the Field.* Washington, D.C.: National Governors' Association.

ELMORE, R. F. 1989. "Models of Restructured Schools." Paper presented at the annual meeting of the American Educational Research Association, San Francisco, March.

ERICKSON, D. A. 1979. "Research on Educational Administration: The State-of-the-Art." *Educational Researcher* 8: 9–14.

EVERTSON, C., and MURPHY, J., 2. "Beginning with Classrooms: Implications for Restructuring Schools." In H. H. Marshall (ed.), *Redefining Student Learning: Roots of Educational Change.* 5:Ablex.

FINN, C. E. 1990. "The Biggest Reform of All." *Phi Delta Kappan* 71(8): 584–92.

FINN, C. E., and CLEMENTS, S. K. 1989. *Reconnoitering Chicago's School Reform Efforts: Some Early Impressions.* Washington, D.C.: Educational Excellence Network.

FRYMIER, J. 1987. "Bureaucracy and the Neutering of Teachers." Phi Delta Kappan, 69 (1): 9–14.

GOODLAD, J. I. 1984. *A Place Called School: Prospects for the Future.* New York: McGraw-Hill.

GREEN, J. 1987. *The Next Wave: A Synopsis of Recent Education Reform Reports.* Denver: Education Commission of the States.

GUTHRIE, J. W. 1986. "School-based Management: The Next Needed Education Reform." *Phi Delta Kappan* 68(4): 305–309.

GUTHRIE, J. W., and KIRST, M. W. 1988. *Conditions of Education in California 1988.* (Policy Paper No. 88-3-2.) Berkeley, Calif.: Policy Analysis for California Education.

HAWLEY, W. D. 1988. "Missing Pieces of the Educational Reform Agenda: Or Why the First and Second Waves May Miss the Boat." *Educational Administration Quarterly* 24(4): 416–37.

HOLMES GROUP. 1986. *Tomorrow's Teachers.* East Lansing, Mich.: The Group.

HOUSTON, H. M. 1989. *"Professional Development for Restructuring: Analyses and Recommendations."* Paper presented at the annual meeting of the American Educational Research Association, San Francisco, March.

JENNINGS, L. 1990. "States Should Require Schools to Craft Family-support Plans, Chiefs Propose. *Education Week,* February 14: p. 8.

KEARNES, D. L. 1988. "A Business Perspective on American Schooling." *Education Week,* April 20: pp. 32, 24.

KEARNES, D. L. 1988b. "An Education Recovery Plan for America." *Phi Delta Kappan* 69(8): 565–70.

LINDELOW, J. 1981. "School-based Management." In S. C. Smith, J. A. Mazzerella, and P. K. Piele (eds.), *School Leadership: Handbook for Survival.* Eugene, Oreg.: ERIC Clearinghouse on Educational Management.

LINDQUIST, K. M., and MURIEL, J. J. 1989. "School-based Management: Doomed to Failure?" *Education and Urban Society* 21(4): 403–416.

LORTIE, D. C. 1975. *Schoolteacher.* Chicago: University of Chicago Press.

MACCOBY, M. 1988. "A New Model for Leadership." *Research Technology Management* 31(6): 53–54.

MACCOBY, M. 1989. *"Looking for Leadership Now."* Paper prepared for the National Center for Educational Leadership conference, Harvard University, Cambridge, Mass., December 14–15.

McCARTHEY, S. J., and PETERSON, P. L. 1989. *"Teacher Roles: Weaving New Patterns in Classroom Practice and School Organization."* Paper presented at the annual meeting of the American Educational Research Association, San Francisco, March.

McCARTHY, M. M. 1990. "Teacher Testing Programs." In J. Murphy (ed.), *The Educational Reform Movement of the 1980s: Perspectives and cases.* Berkeley, Calif.: McCutchan.

MILLER, J. A. 1989. "Educational Summit's Promise: Social Compact for Reforms." *Education Week,* October 4: pp. 1, 10.

MILLER, S. K., and BROOKOVER, W. B. 1986. "School Effectiveness Versus Individual Differences: Paradigmatic Perspectives on the Legitimation of Economic and Educational Inequalities. Paper presented at the annual meeting of the American Educational Research Association, San Francisco, April.

MOJKOWSKI, C., and FLEMING, D. 1988. *School-site Management: Concepts and Approaches.* Andover, Mass.: Regional Laboratory for Educational Improvement of the Northeast and Islands.

MURPHY, J. 1990. "The Educational Reform Movement of the 1980s: A Comprehensive Analysis." In J. Murphy (ed.), *The Reform of American Public Education in the 1980s: Perspectives and Cases.* Berkeley, Calif.: McCutchan.

MURPHY, J., and EVERTSON, C. 1990. *Restructured Schools: Looking at the teaching-learning process.* Nashville, Tenn.: National Center for Educational Leadership, Peabody College of Vanderbilt University.

MURPHY, J. In press. *Restructuring Schools: Capturing and Assessing the Phenomena.* New York: Teachers College Press.

MURPHY, M. J., and HART, A. W. 1988. "Preparing Principals to Lead in Restructured Schools." Paper presented at the annual meeting of the

University Council for Educational Administration, Cincinnati, Ohio, October.

NATIONAL COMMISSION ON EXCELLENCE IN EDUCATION. 1983. *A Nation at Risk: The Imperative of Educational Reform.* Washington, D.C.: U.S. Government Printing Office.

NATIONAL GOVERNORS' ASSOCIATION. 1986. *Time for Results.* Washington, D.C.: The Association.

ODDEN, A., and MARSH, D. 1988. "How Comprehensive Reform Legislation Can Improve Secondary Schools." *Phi Delta Kappan* 69(8): 593-98.

PERRY, N. J. 1988. "The Education Crisis: What Business can Do." *Fortune*, July 4: pp. 38-41.

POWELL, A. G.; FARRAR, E.; and COHEN, D. K. 1985. *The Shopping Mall High School: Winners and Losers in the Educational Marketplace.* Boston: Houghton Mifflin.

PURPEL, D. E. 1989. *The Moral and Spiritual Crises in Education: A Curriculum for Justice and Compassion in Education.* Granby, Mass.: Bergin and Garvey.

SCHMIDT, P. 1989. "Foundation Formed to Spur Partnerships to Create Business-school Academies." *Education Week*, November 22: p. 14.

SEDLAK, M. W.; WHEELER, C. W.; PULLIN, D. C.; and CUSICK, P. A. 1986. *Selling Students Short: Classroom Bargains and Academic Reform in the American High School.* New York: Teachers College Press.

SEELEY, D. S. 1980. "The Bankruptcy of Service Delivery." Presentation delivered before the Foundation Lunch Group: Panel on Children, at the Edwin Gould Foundation for Children, New York City, February.

SEELEY, D. S. 1988. "A New Vision for Public Education." *Youth Policy* 10(2): 34-36.

SIZER, T. R. 1984. *Horace's compromise: The Dilemma of the American High School.* Boston: Houghton-Mifflin.

SMYLIE, M. A., and DENNY, J. W. 1989. "Teacher Leadership: Tensions and Ambiguities in Organizational Perspective." Paper presented at the annual meeting of the American Educational Research Association, San Francisco, March.

SPADY, W. G. 1988. "Organizing for Results: The Basis of Authentic Restructuring and Reform." *Educational Leadership* 46(2): 4-8.

TIMAR, T. B., and KIRP, D. L. 1988. "State Efforts to Reform Schools: Treading Between a Regulatory Swamp and an English Garden." *Educational Evaluation and Policy Analysis* 10(2): 75-88.

U.S. DEPARTMENT OF EDUCATION. *Educating Our Children: Parents and Schools Together.* Washington, D.C.:

WATKINS, J. M., and LUSI, S. F. 1989. "Facing the Essential Tensions: Restructuring Schools from Where You Are." Paper presented at the annual meeting of the American Educational Research Association, San Francisco, March.

WISE, A. E. 1989. "Professional Teaching: A New Paradigm for the Management of Education." In T. J. Sergiovanni and J. H. Moore (eds.), *Schooling for Tomorrow: Directing Reforms to Issues that Count.* Boston: Allyn and Bacon.

REVAMPING THE SYSTEM

2

The State Role in School Restructuring

Michael W. Kirst

School restructuring is a complex set of interrelated concepts and procedures that should lead to increased pupil attainment. While momentum is building for restructuring at the local level, there has been less clarity about the potential state role in it. This chapter will help define the state role, but it begins with some further definitions of restructuring itself. It also raises some unanswered questions about restructuring and the problems of accountability in a restructured school. Although the state cannot mandate or force restructuring, the state role is crucial in many contexts. State leaders have been struggling to see how their activities can enhance restructuring and how restructuring can be integrated with prior state reform objectives, such as mandated higher standards and equity policies. A key theme is that state policy should be coherent and restructuring cannot be a set of projects unrelated to each other or to existing state policies.

Concepts of Restructuring

Restructuring has many definitions and entails concepts that could mislead policymakers to begin a series of disconnected initiatives. This chapter does not address the arguments for restructuring, since this has been covered by many other authors (David 1989). There is no single approach or recipe for restructuring. Indeed, Jane David has presented an instructive graphic of the "puzzle of restructuring" and how any one set of policies must affect others (Figure 2-1). State policies must therefore be designed to address numerous areas simultaneously.

Figure 2-2 presents the types of state policies that must be articulated to enhance restructuring. The most acute disease inhibiting restructuring is state "projectitis" (that is, a failure to mount a comprehensive or coherent strategy). For example, state teacher preservice programs are rarely linked to school restructuring. The second major problem has been an inattention to curriculum, instruction, and pupil attainment, as discussed in the next section.

FIGURE 2-1.   The Puzzle of Structural Change

SOURCE: Bay Area Research Group, Palo Alto California.
Copyright © 1990 by Jane L. David.

FIGURE 2-2.   State Policies to Enhance Local Coherence

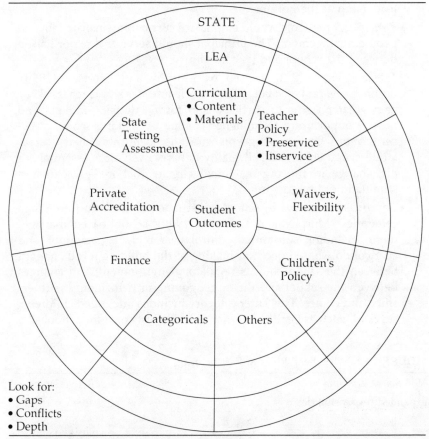

SOURCE: Prepared by author Michael W. Kirst.

Murphy and Evertson (1990) usefully outline the major local components of restructuring this way:

> • *Work redesign.* Change is required in the relationships among
> superintendent, principal, and teachers. This entails interdepen-
> dence and cooperative work teams that trade assignments. Superin-
> tendents and their top staff act as coordinators and enablers rather
> than directors and controllers. Their mission is to serve and assist
> schools, manage by exception, and focus on parts of the organiza-
> tion that experience difficulty. The resulting organization is flatter,

with less hierarchy, in which the role of the top is to nurture leadership at the bottom.

- *Principal.* A new role would emphasize curriculum, instruction, and people management. The principal should serve as a major liaison between the school and its community.
- *Teachers.* Figure 2-3, devised by Murphy and Evertson (1990), outlines several key changes in the role and work of teachers. They gain greater rights to participate in formal decision-making and greater opportunity to influence change by making school structures more flexible. Concepts such as mentor teachers, career ladders, and enhanced collegiality fit here. Even more essential is a big change in the organizational climate that makes schools a stimulating place to work.
- *Governance.* changes in school governance divide into four broad categories (Murphy and Evertson, 1990): school-based management, including substantial control over budget, personnel, and curriculum; shared decision-making at the building level; changes between the school and its regulatory environment; and changes between the school and the larger community, including partnerships and choice. This latter category includes integrated children's services (such as health, day care, juvenile justice) at the school site.

FIGURE 2-3.   Teachers' Roles in Restructuring

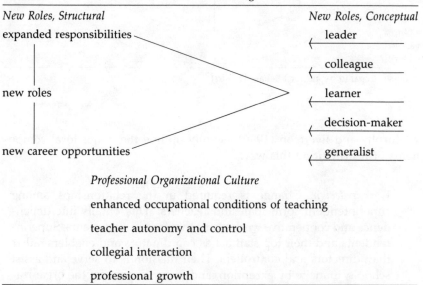

New Roles, Structural	*New Roles, Conceptual*
expanded responsibilities	leader
	colleague
new roles	learner
	decision-maker
new career opportunities	generalist

Professional Organizational Culture

enhanced occupational conditions of teaching

teacher autonomy and control

collegial interaction

professional growth

SOURCE: Joseph Murphy, *Restructing Schools: Capturing the Phenomena* (New York: Teachers College Press, 1991).

Linking Restructuring with Instruction and Pupil Outcomes

Issues of curriculum and instruction have often received the least attention from restructuring advocates. Few reform reports have touched on the core of the education process—for example, changed processes of more effective learning that should flow from rich conceptions of teaching and learning and that should *precede* restructuring of other aspects of schools (Sykes and Elmore 1989). We must recognize that the research literature has yet to validate the linkage between restructuring components and student outcomes. State policymakers cannot advocate such restructuring features as school-based management or teacher collegiality by citing evidence that enhanced pupil attainment will certainly result. The jury, in that sense, is still out.

Much of the restructuring activity is still in an experimental phase, but there is no doubt that it must begin with attention to revisions in subject matter, teaching strategies, higher order skills, and assessment. The state wields major influence upon such areas as interdisciplinary curricula, school periods longer than fifty minutes for science labs, and authentic pupil assessments that stress problem-solving, synthesis, analysis, and inference. Today many state assessment systems are overwhelmingly oriented to basic skills and ignore these complex operations, but the states have considerable leverage to change these conditions. For example, curricular frameworks can alter traditional concepts of science education so that the familiar "layer cake" curriculum (biology in tenth grade, chemistry in eleventh, and so forth) is replaced with one that provides some physics and chemistry concepts to all pupils every year throughout grades 8–10.

States must begin their restructuring strategies with an explicit notion of how changes in school structure, regulations (and waivers), and financial incentives will lead to improvements in instruction and then in pupil outcomes. In sum, the major components of restructuring are presented below, roughly in sequential order:

1. curriculum and instruction
2. authority and decision-making
3. roles and responsibilities
4. accountability and assessment
5. integrated children's services beyond education

Table 2-1 depicts the major components of restructuring.

TABLE 2-1. The Main Components of Restructuring

CURRICULUM AND INSTRUCTION must change to:
- Actively engage students in learning
- Promote understanding and application of skills and knowledge
- Create curricular goals that embody challenging learning tasks
- Stimulate synthesis, inference, problem-solving, and analysis

AUTHORITY AND DECISION-MAKING must:
- Decentralize so important educational decisions are made at the school site
- Increase flexibility so there are decisions left to be made by schools
- Provide the authority and knowledge to make and carry out decisions

ROLES AND RESPONSIBILITIES must change up and down the system
- Create new, more flexible roles for teachers and principals with built-in time for acquiring new knowledge and learning
- Encourage new roles for the community—parents, business, senior citizens
- Shift role of district and state administrators from rule-making and monitoring to helping school faculties create stimulating learning environments

ACCOUNTABILITY
- Focus on results, not procedures
- Use assessment instruments that measure valued goals well
- Put authority and accountability at same level (school)
- Create culture in which educators use information to assess how they are doing (and model this for students)

BEYOND EDUCATION
- Create links with social and health service agencies
- Ensure all students are ready for schools

SOURCE: Bay Area Research Group, Palo Alto, California. Copyright © 1990 by Jane L. David.

Smith and O'Day (1991) thoughtfully suggest that statewide restructuring begin with an "instructional guidance system" that includes a coherent state curricular framework, assessment, teacher training, and staff development. State guidance would outline what students need to know but would not be a specific curricular blueprint that teachers must follow weekly. States should not suppose that a single component like school-based management is all there is to restructuring. Nor should states adopt a simple recipe or definition.

Implementing the State Role

Restructuring must flow from bottom-up commitment at the local level, so the state role needs to include technical assistance and financial support for

- incentives to change
- provision of time and access to knowledge about restructuring
- flexibility and removal of state impediments
- revisions in state policy that conflict with restructuring (for example, basic skills–only assessment systems and the imposition of Carnegie unit requirements on high-school graduates by state universities)
- staff development to strengthen the abilities of teachers, principals, and others engaged in restructuring

States need to encourage more diversity in local school policy and practice and then to build on this diversity. The dominant state policy instrument is "capacity building" for localities interested in restructuring. States can then create networks of restructuring schools that can learn from each other and attract more members. Capacity building is a strategy wholly different from mandates and highly specified incentives such as payments for longer school years (Elmore 1988).

In carrying out this capacity building role, states should be sensitive to local preconditions for restructuring. There needs to be a local understanding of the strengths and weaknesses of school sites. Localities need time and technical assistance to discover what they like or do not like about their schools. They need a vision of high-quality curriculum, instruction, and student attainment such as states like California and Connecticut are now beginning to provide. This entails agreed-upon systems for measuring local results that are compatible with concepts in the state assessment system.

The planning phase should be followed up by a significant investment in staff training and school site team-building. Restructuring entails new staff attitudes and skills. Sometimes a specific school improvement proposal results from site team-building. The central office must also spend time and resources rethinking its role and providing more authority and flexibility to the school sites. All this is difficult without harmonious labor relations and a collaborative union/management ethos as well as discretionary money to spend on these start-up activities.

States must realize from the outset that myriad existing routines are embedded deeply in local school cultures. Teachers, for example, are doing what they were taught in preservice preparation. Consequently, state policies involving teacher training need to be revamped as part of a coherent strategy.

A number of state policies should reinforce each other (for example, state assessment and local curricular changes), but there is no need to mandate the same teaching practices for all students. For instance, the state instructional guidance responsibility could be an assessment system in grades 4, 8, and 12 that provides school site data on what pupils know

TABLE 2-2.   State Actions to Launch Restructuring

What	How
Promote a vision.	Create a vision of the future with help from a task force, consultants, or existing knowledge.
Spread the word.	Hold statewide and regional conferences to inform educators and the public about the problems and define restructuring.
Build statewide support for restructuring.	Maintain regular communication between executive and legislative branches of state government, the business community, and statewide education associations.
Invite school and district participation.	Start small, with a pilot or demonstration project, based on informed decisions to participate.
Provide flexibility.	Offer blanket waivers or provision to request waivers from state rules and assurance of local support.
Provide time.	Acknowledge that restructuring places extra time demands on school staff and that it takes time for the results of restructuring to be visible.
Offer assistance and know-how.	Provide help and new knowledge directly or through brokering and networking.
Begin shifting state role.	Slowly shift state philosophy and behavior from mandates and compliance to goals and assistance.
Focus on results.	Hold schools accountable for meeting their goals for students and align state accountability.
Maintain visibility and focus.	Promote the vision through the media, public relations, and open lines of communication.

SOURCE: Jane David, et al. *State Actions to Restructure Schools: First Steps* (Denver: National Governors' Association, 1989), p. 36.

and can do. This state instructional guidance system provides accountability benchmarks for local restructuring. The launching process is summarized by the National Governors' Association in Table 2-2.

Potential Problems with State Policies

States that have tried to enhance school restructuring have encountered several pitfalls.

1. They start too small and move too slowly; pilot programs are not expanded or networks of adherents built.

2. They develop incoherent "projectitis," making isolated changes that are not related to each other.

3. They rely too much on rewards and sanctions that are oriented to low-level basic skills tests.

4. They fail to realize that restructuring involves the whole system, not just the individual school. For instance, restructuring is much more than school-based management.

5. They put too much stock in state waivers of regulations as the prime strategy for change. Local school systems tend to see waivers as only temporary. In any case, restructuring entails much more than waivers.

6. Impatience develops, since states do not realize that restructuring takes a long time (5–10 years).

Despite these hazards, some states have changed the rhetoric surrounding education reform and have mounted comprehensive approaches. The Kentucky statewide reform is a noteworthy example, and the Illinois legislature's decision to decentralize the Chicago public schools is another.

The State Role in Restructuring

Several states—including California, Massachusetts, and Washington—have begun small demonstration projects that provide planning and seed money for local restructuring. States face some dilemmas in framing criteria for choosing among local competitors. States want to stimulate creativity and innovation and not be too prescriptive. On the other hand, they want to convey some key ideas that local planners should adopt. Schools may confuse restructuring with merely intensifying the existing school system, or see the state restructuring program as just another funding source.

Some potential restructuring criteria that states might use should include negative considerations, too (California State Department of Education 1991). Proposals will *not* be approved if, for example, they are

- tinkering on the edges or proposing only small changes in the existing structure
- changing only one feature or program of the school

- fragmented and piecemeal, without an overall comprehensive strategy
- providing neither coherence nor linkage with curricular content goals or outcomes
- dominated by a top-down model of making change at the school or district level
- adopting a model from somewhere else that does not appear to meet the school site's needs or local context

States can also emphasize that certain district-wide policies and technical assistance are crucial for effective school-based restructuring. The district role in assisting sites might include

- specifying curriculum content and achievement outcomes for all pupils
- providing staff development to assist the schools in meeting their restructuring goals
- providing schools with flexibility to meet their restructuring goals through waivers or rules and regulations
- providing an accountability system that will provide outcome measures of progress
- encouraging the use of federal and state categorical funds as part of a restructuring program
- assisting school sites in making linkages with universities, businesses, and parents

The importance of intensive staff development is often overlooked in state restructuring programs. States assume that the site capacity exists and that teachers are able to restructure. There is a lot more to restructuring, however, than merely the removal of central constraints and then hoping that many different creative and novel ideas will be generated locally. States can provide fiscal support for the time and expertise required to help school sites rethink their procedures. Some states have gone further, entering a joint venture between the Education Commission of the States and the Coalition for Essential Schools led by Theodore Sizer of Brown University. This is a promising development for sharing concepts and delivering technical assistance across state boundaries.

States must realize that restructuring takes time and must be patient before demanding specific pupil outcomes. There is always a danger of teacher burnout and gradual loss of enthusiasm for the hard work of making changes. Consequently, states need a strategy to sustain the restructuring process as well as to start it.

Restructuring and Integrating Children's Services

States have a major role in extending restructuring to include collaboration with public and private children's services providers in such areas as health, parent education, child protective services, and juvenile justice (Kirst 1991). Some restructuring proposals start from the view that schools can still do it all, but increasingly educators are seeking alliances with other children's agencies.

The answer is not as simple as expanding existing programs like Head Start, which was featured at the September 1989 Charlottesville "Education Summit." What is needed is a complete overhaul of children's services, bringing together public and private organizations to meet the needs of children, youth, and parents in a comprehensive fashion. Schools should provide part but not all of a coordinated network of comprehensive children's services.

At a time when funding for services is down, some children receive redundant services for various overlapping problems while others get no help at all. A youngster with multiple problems typically receives a single label—substance abuser, delinquent, dropout, teen parent—that oversimplifies the nature of the troubles and obstructs a real evaluation of what is going on and needs to be done. As he moves from one level of care to another—from home to juvenile hall, or from inpatient psychiatric hospitalization to residential treatment—he moves in and out of various departmental jurisdictions, encountering different groups of service providers protective of their turf.

Fragmentation prevents professional interveners from seeing the cumulative impact of their intentions. Because problems are defined as short-term and single-issue, there is no "permanent record" that shows what happened to a child over the long haul; there is no joint assessment by the drug counselor, school nurse, welfare eligibility worker, and special education teacher. Most resources go to reacting to acute problems and emergencies; prevention is slighted.

Only an alliance of parents, social service agencies, and educators can make a big difference for children with multiple needs and dysfunctional families. For example, some schools have become "hubs" for integrated social services, including health, child care, children's protective services, juvenile justice counseling, and parent education. They stay open from 7 A.M. to 7 P.M. and provide breakfast, snacks, recreation, child care, and a variety of social services. But these schools are rare, and there is no federal or state policy to increase them.

Attempts to patch the current system often display the syndrome of "projectitis," whereby one of the delivery systems (such as schools) obtains a grant to coordinate all the others. This merely multiplies the number of separate projects in an already overloaded system replete with agencies guarding their professional domains. The coordination game degenerates into superficial reorganization, such as an "office for children" that placates child advocates but does not change actual service delivery or support parents.

Policy makers should reverse the current pattern and provide services that emphasize prevention, continuity, comprehensiveness, equity, and accountability. State government has a major role in funding local planning and providing start-up capital for the integrative efforts sketched above. But the states also need to get their own houses in order. State legislature jurisdictions should be merged, and a new state mechanism for waiving regulations should be created for health, social services, juvenile justice, education, and other areas.

Conclusion

There is no road map to "correct" state policy in restructuring, but lasting reforms tend to create organized constituencies committed to their maintenance. The tendency for each successive state administration to launch a new program inhibits long-term constituency building.

Restructuring is not free. States may need to provide localities with funds for planning, technical assistance, network formation, staff development, waivers, and new assessment techniques. There will be other state costs for restructuring but not for the familiar standardized staff development packages created by consultants. Instead, outlays are needed for more responsive local capacity building.

Both content and process are crucial. Local initiatives for restructuring may begin in the principal's office, teacher organization, central office, or another part of the system. State leadership, which needs to be opportunistic as well as coherent, should provide direction, resources, and support to restructuring movements arising from localities. The state role, however, will vary according to the state's historical political culture. More centralized systems, such as those in South Carolina and Georgia, will differ in approach from those in traditionally less aggressive states, like Wyoming or New Hampshire.

No matter the approach, education remains a state responsibility. Trends in recent decades that have resulted in states providing the largest share of education funding have underscored this responsibility, as voters increasingly look to state capitals for an accounting of how their children are faring, how their education dollars are spent, and how well their schools are working. Practically as well as legally, therefore, it is up to state policymakers to find the restructuring approach that works best in accordance with the norms and traditions of education in their state.

References

CALIFORNIA STATE DEPARTMENT OF EDUCATION. 1991. *Proposed Criteria for Senate Bill 1274 Restructuring Grants*. Sacramento, Calif.: The Department.

DAVID, JANE.1989. *Restructuring in Progress: Lessons from Pioneering Districts*. Washington, D.C.: National Governors' Association.

DAVID, JANE, ET AL. 1989. *State Action to Restructure Schools: First Steps*. Denver: National Governors' Association.

ELMORE, RICHARD. 1988. *Early Experience in Restructuring*. Washington, D.C.: National Governors' Association.

KIRST, MICHAEL. 1991. "Improving Children's Services: Overcoming Barriers, Creating New Opportunities." *Phi Delta Kappan* 72 (April): 615–618.

MURPHY, JOSEPH. In press. *Restructuring Schools: Capturing and Assessing the Phenomena*. New York: Teachers College Press.

SMITH, MARSHALL, and O'DAY, JENNIFER. 1991. *"Systemic School Reform."* in Susan Fuhman (ed.), *Politics of Education Association Yearbook, 1990*. Philadelphia: Taylor and Francis.

SYKES, GARY, and ELMORE, RICHARD. "Making Schools More Manageable." In Jane Hannaway and Robert Crowson (eds.), *The Politics of Reforming School Administrations*. New York: Falmer, 1989.

3

Educational Choice: Why It Is Needed and How It Will Work

John E. Chubb and Terry M. Moe

For America's public schools, the last decade has been the worst of times and the best of times. Never before have they been subjected to such savage criticism for failing to meet the nation's educational needs, yet never before have governments been so aggressively dedicated to studying the schools' problems and finding the resources for solving them.

The signs of poor performance were there for all to see during the 1970s. Test scores headed downward year after year. Large numbers of teenagers continued to drop out of school. Drugs and violence poisoned the learning environment. In math and science, two areas crucial to the nation's success in the world economy, U.S. students fell far behind their counterparts in virtually every other industrialized country. Something was clearly wrong.

During the 1980s, a growing sense of crisis fueled a powerful movement for educational change, and the nation's political institutions responded with aggressive reforms. State after state increased its spending on schools, imposed tougher requirements, introduced more rigorous testing, and strengthened teacher certification and training. And, as the decade came to an end, creative experiments in various forms—from school-based management to magnet schools—were launched around the nation.

We think these reforms are destined to fail. In a recently published book, *Politics, Markets, and America's Schools* (1990), we find that current reforms simply do not get to the root of the problem. After analyzing a sample of some 500 schools and 22,000 students, teachers, and principals—the most comprehensive survey of American high schools ever assembled—we conclude that the fundamental causes of poor academic performance are not to be found in the schools but rather in the institutions by which the schools have traditionally been governed. Reformers fail by relying on these institutions to solve the problem—when the institutions are the problem.

The key to better schools, therefore, is institutional reform. What we propose is a new system of public education that eliminates most political and bureaucratic control over the schools and relies instead on indirect control through markets and parental choice. These new institutions naturally function to promote and nurture the kinds of effective schools that reformers have wanted all along. Our purpose here is to summarize the evidence that leads us to this conclusion and to outline how a new system of public education could work. While our analysis and suggestions are national, the bold changes we contemplate would best be undertaken by individual states.

Schools and Institutions

Three basic questions lie at the heart of our analysis. What is the relationship between school organization and student achievement? What are the conditions that promote or inhibit desirable forms of organization? And how are these conditions affected by their institutional settings?

Our perspective on school organization and student achievement agrees with the most central claims and findings of the "effective schools" literature, which served as the analytical base of much education reform throughout the 1980s. We believe, as most others do, that how much students learn is not determined simply by their aptitude or family background—although, as we show, these are certainly influential—but also by how effectively their schools are organized. By our estimates, the typical high-school student tends to learn considerably more, comparable to at least an extra year's worth of study, when he or she attends a high school that is effectively organized rather than one that is not.

Generally speaking, effective schools, be they public or private, have the organizational characteristics that the mainstream literature would lead one to expect: sturdy leadership, clear and ambitious goals, strong academic programs, teacher professionalism, shared influence, and staff harmony, among other things. These are best understood as integral parts of a coherent syndrome of organization. When this syndrome is viewed as a whole, moreover, it seems to capture the essential features of what people normally mean by a school team—principals and teachers working together, cooperatively and informally, in pursuit of a common mission.

How do such schools take root and develop? Here again, our perspective dovetails with a central theme of educational analysis and criticism: the dysfunctions of bureaucracy, the value of autonomy, and the inherent tension between the two in American public education. Bureaucracy vitiates the most basic requirements of effective organization. It imposes goals, structures, and requirements that tell principals and teachers what to do and how to do it, denying them the discretion they need to exercise their expertise and professional judgment, as well as the flexibility they need to develop and operate as teams. The key to effective education rests with unleashing the productive potential already present in schools and their personnel. It rests with granting them the autonomy to do what they do best. As our study of U.S. high schools documents, the freer schools are from external control, the more likely they are to have effective organizations.

Only at this late stage do we begin to part company with the mainstream. While most observers can agree that the public schools have become too bureaucratic and would benefit from substantial grants of autonomy, it is also the standard view that this transformation can be achieved within the prevailing framework of democratic control. The implicit assumption is that the very institutions that have acted in the past to bureaucratize can now be counted upon to reverse course, grant the schools autonomy, and support and nurture a new population of autonomous schools. Such an assumption, however, is not based on a systematic understanding of how these institutions operate and what their consequences are for schools.

Political Institutions

Democratic governance of the schools is built around the imposition of higher-order values—of the community, the state, and the nation—through public authority. As long as that authority exists and is available for use, public officials will come under intense pressure from social groups of all political stripes to use it. And when they do use it, they cannot blithely assume that their favored policies will be faithfully implemented by the heterogeneous population of principals and teachers below, people whose own values and professional views may be quite different from those being imposed. Public officials have little choice but to rely on formal rules and regulations that tell these people what to do and hold them accountable for doing it.

These pressures for bureaucracy are so substantial in themselves that real school autonomy has little chance to take root throughout the system. But they are not the only pressures for bureaucracy. They are compounded by the uncertainty inherent in all democratic politics: Those who exercise public authority know that other actors with different interests may gain authority in the future and subvert the policies they worked so hard to put in place. This knowledge gives them additional incentives to embed their policies in protective bureaucratic arrangements—arrangements that reduce the discretion of schools and insulate them from the dangers of politics.

These pressures, arising from basic properties of democratic control, are compounded further by another special feature of the public sector. Its institutions provide a regulated, politically sensitive setting conducive to the power of unions, and unions protect the interests of their members through formal constraints on the governance and operation of schools—constraints that strike directly at schools' capacity to build well-functioning teams based on informal cooperation.

All the major participants in democratic governance—including the unions—complain that schools are too bureaucratic. And they mean what they say. But they are the ones who bureaucratized the schools in the past, and they will continue to do so in the future, even as they tout the great advantages of autonomy and professionalism. The incentives to bureaucratize are built into the system.

Market Institutions

This kind of behavior is not something that Americans simply have to accept, like death and taxes. People who make decisions about education would behave differently if their institutions were different. The most relevant and telling comparison is to markets, since it is through democratic control and markets that American society makes most of its choices on matters of public importance, including education. Public schools are subject to direct control through politics. But not all schools are controlled in this way. Private schools—representing about a fourth of all schools—are subject to indirect control through markets.

What difference does it make? Our analysis suggests that the difference is considerable and that it arises from the most fundamental properties that distinguish the two systems. A market system is not built to enable the imposition of higher-order values on the schools, nor is it driven by a democratic struggle to exercise public authority. Instead, the authority to make educational choices is radically decentralized to those most immediately involved. Schools compete for the support of parents and students, who in turn are free to choose among schools. The system is built on decentralization, competition, and choice.

Although schools operating under a market system are free to organize any way they want, bureaucratization tends to be an unattractive way to go. Part of the reason is that virtually everything about good education—from the knowledge and talents necessary to produce it to what it looks like when it is produced—defies formal measurement through the standardized categories of bureaucracy.

More fundamentally, however, bureaucratic control and its clumsy efforts to measure the unmeasurable are simply *unnecessary* for schools whose primary concern is to please their clients. To do this, they need to perform as effectively as possible—which leads them, given the bottom-heavy technology of education, to favor decentralized forms organization that take full advantage of strong leadership, teacher professionalism, discretionary judgment, informal cooperation, and teams. They also need to ensure that they provide the kinds of services parents and students want and that they have the capacity to cater and adjust to their clients' specialized needs and interests, which this same syndrome of effective organization allows them to do exceedingly well.

Schools that operate in an environment of competition and choice thus have strong incentives to move toward the kinds of "effective-school" organizations that academics and reformers would like to impose on the public schools. Of course, not all schools in the market will respond equally well to these incentives. But those that falter will find it more difficult to attract support, and they will tend to be weeded out in favor of schools that are better-organized. This process of natural selection complements the incentives of the marketplace in propelling and supporting a population of autonomous, effectively organized schools.

Institutional Consequences

No institutional system can be expected to work perfectly under real-world conditions. Just as democratic institutions cannot offer perfect representation or perfect implementation of public policy, so markets cannot offer perfect competition or perfect choice. But these imperfections, invariably the favorite targets of each system's critics, divert attention from what is most crucial to an understanding of schools: As institutional systems, democratic control and market control are strikingly different in their most fundamental properties. As a result, they structure individual and social choices about education very differently, and they have very different consequences for the organization and performance of schools. Each system puts its own indelible stamp on the schools that emerge and operate within it.

What the analysis in our book suggests, in the most practical terms, is that American society offers two basic paths to the emergence of effective schools. The first is through markets, which scarcely operate today in the public sector but which act on private schools to discourage bureaucracy and to promote desirable forms of organization through competition and choice. The second is through "special circumstances"—homogeneous, relatively problem-free, usually suburban environments—which, by minimizing the trio of political pressures just discussed, prompt democratic governing institutions to impose less bureaucracy than otherwise. Private schools therefore tend to be effectively organized because of the way their system naturally works. When public schools happen to be effectively organized, it is in spite of their system; they are the lucky ones with peculiarly nice environments.

The power of these institutional forces is graphically reflected in our sample of U.S. high schools. Having cast our net widely to allow for a full range of institutional factors that might reasonably be suspected of influencing school autonomy, we found that virtually all of them fall by the wayside. The extent to which a school is granted the autonomy it needs to develop a more effective organization is overwhelmingly determined by its sectoral location (public or private) and the niceness of its institutional environment.

Viewed as a whole, then, our effort to take institutions into account builds systematically on mainstream ideas and findings but, in the end, puts a very different slant on things. We agree that effective organization is a major determinant of student achievement. We also agree that schools perform better the more autonomous they are and the less encumbered by bureaucracy. But we do not agree that this knowledge about the proximate causes of effective performance can be used to engineer better schools through democratic control. Reformers are right about where they want to go, but their chosen institutions cannot get them there.

The way to get schools with effective organizations is not to insist that democratic institutions should do what they are incapable of doing. Nor is it to assume that the better public schools, the lucky ones with nice environments, can serve as organizational models for the rest. Their good fortune is not transferable. The way to get effective schools is to recognize that ineffective performance is really a deep-seated institutional problem that arises from the most fundamental properties of democratic control.

The most sensible approach to genuine education reform is therefore to move toward a true institutional solution—a different set of institutional arrangements that actively promotes and nurtures the kinds of schools people want. The market alternative then becomes particularly attractive, for it provides a setting in which such organizations take root and flourish. That is where "choice" comes in.

A Proposal for Real Reform

We propose that state governments create a new system of public education—based on the market principles of parental choice and school competition—with the following properties:

- The state will set minimal criteria—e.g., graduation, health and safety, and teacher eligibility requirements—that define what constitutes a "public school" under the new system. Any group or organization that meets these criteria must then be chartered as a public school and granted the right to accept students and to receive public money.
- Existing private schools will be among those eligible to participate, and their participation should be encouraged, because they constitute a ready supply of often-effective schools. Our own preference is to include religious schools, too, since they constitute the majority of all private schools. But states may address the issue of religious school participation as they wish, so long as they recognize the need for an expanded supply of public schools and the right of schools not run by local districts to operate.
- School districts can continue running their present schools. But districts will have authority over only their own schools and not over any of the other public schools chartered by the state that may operate within their borders.
- The state will set up a choice office in each district, which, among other things, will maintain a record of all school-age children and the level of funding—the "scholarship" amounts—associated with each child. This office will directly compensate schools based on the specific children they enroll. Public money will flow from funding sources—local, state, and federal—to the choice office and then to schools. At no point will it go to parents or students.
- Districts may retain as much of their current governing apparatus— superintendents, school boards, central offices, and their staffs—as they wish. But they have to pay for them entirely out of the revenue

they derive from the scholarships of those children who voluntarily choose to attend district-run schools. Aside from the governance of these schools, which no one need attend, districts will be little more than taxing jurisdictions that allow citizens to make a collective determination about how large their children's scholarships will be.

• As it does now, the state will have the right to specify how much, or by what formula, each district must contribute for each child. We prefer an equalization approach that requires wealthier districts to contribute more per child than poor districts and that guarantees an adequate financial foundation to students in all districts. Although we would not prohibit districts from exceeding their required contributions and thereby spending more than other districts after state equalization funds are counted, we would prohibit parents from supplementing scholarships with personal funds. This new public system is to be fully publicly funded.

• Scholarships will also take into account special educational needs —arising from economic deprivation, physical handicaps, and other disadvantages—that can be effectively met only through costly specialized programs. At-risk students should be empowered with larger scholarships than others, making them attractive clients for all schools—and stimulating the emergence of new specialty schools.

• Each student will be free to attend any public school in the state, regardless of district, with the student's total scholarship flowing to the school of choice.

• Insofar as tax revenues allow, every effort will be made to provide transportation for students who need it. This provision is important to help open up more alternatives to all students, especially the poor and those in rural areas.

• To assist parents and students in choosing among schools, the state will provide a parent information center within each local choice office. This center will collect comprehensive information on each school in the district and will distribute and collect school applications. Its parent liaisons will meet personally with parents to help them judge which schools best meet their children's needs.

• The application process must take place within a framework that guarantees each student a school, as well as a fair shot at getting into the school he or she most wants. We suggest that the parent information center be responsible for seeing that all applications are submitted by a given date. Schools will then be required to make their admission decisions within a set time, and students who are accepted into more than one school will be required to select one as their final choice. Students who are not accepted anywhere, as well as schools that have yet to attract as many students as they want, will then participate in a second round of applications, after which unaccepted students (there should be few) will be assigned to schools by the choice office.

- The state must grant each school full authority to determine its own governing structure. A school may be run entirely by teachers, even by a teachers' union. It may vest all power in a principal. It may be built around a committee that guarantees representation to the principal, teachers, parents, students, and members of the community. Or it may do something completely different.

- The state will do nothing to tell the schools how they must be internally organized. The state will not set requirements for career ladders, advisory committees, curriculum, textbook selection, staff training, preparation time, homework, or anything else. Each school will be organized and operated as it sees fit.

- Statewide tenure laws will be eliminated, allowing each school to decide for itself whether or not to adopt a tenure policy and what the specifics of that policy will be. This change is essential if schools are to have the flexibility they need to build a well-functioning team. Some schools may not offer tenure at all, relying on pay and working conditions to attract the teachers they want while others may offer tenure as a supplementary means of compensating and retaining fine teachers. Teachers, meantime, may demand tenure in their negotiations (individual or collective) with schools—and, as in private colleges and universities, the best teachers are well positioned to get it, since they can take their valued services elsewhere. School districts may continue to offer district-wide tenure, along with transfer rights and seniority preference and whatever other personnel policies they have adopted in the past. But these policies apply only to district-run schools and the teachers who work in them.

- Teachers will continue to have the right to join unions and engage in collective bargaining, but the bargaining unit will be the individual school or—as in the case of a district government—the larger organization that runs the school. If teachers in a given school wish to join a union or, having done so, want to exact financial or structural concessions, that is up to them. But they cannot commit other teachers and schools, unless they are in other district-run schools, to the same things, and they must suffer the consequences if their victories put them at a competitive disadvantage in supplying quality education.

- The state will continue to certify teachers, but its requirements will be minimal—corresponding to those that many states have historically applied to private schools. In our view, individuals should be certified to teach if they have a bachelor's degree and their personal history reveals no obvious problems. Whether they are truly good teachers will be determined in practice, as schools determine whom to hire, observe their own teachers in action over an extended period of time, and make decisions about merit, promotion, and dismissal. The schools may, as a matter of strategy, choose to pay attention to certain formal indicators of past or future performance, such as graduate degrees, completion of a voluntary teacher certification program at an education school, or voluntary certification by a national board. Some schools may choose to require one or more of these, or perhaps to reward them in various ways. But that is up to the schools, which will now be able to look anywhere for good teachers in a much larger and more dynamic market.

- The state will hold the schools accountable for meeting the criteria set out in their charters, for adhering to nondiscrimination laws in admissions and other matters, and for making available to the public, through the parent information center, information on their mission, their staff and course offerings, standardized test scores (which we would make optional), parent and student satisfaction, and anything else that would promote informed educational choice.

- The state will not hold the schools accountable for student achievement or other dimensions that call for assessments of the quality of school performance. When it comes to performance, schools will be held accountable from below, by parents and students who directly experience their services and are free to choose.

Questions and Answers

The kind of basic reform we are recommending inevitably raises many questions. Is it practical? Are its results predictable? Aren't markets fraught with as many problems as politics—for example, inequity, deceptive advertising, and uninformed choice? Over the past several years, as we have written and spoken about educational choice, we have been asked these questions and many, many more. We cannot answer all or even most of those questions here. But we can briefly address a number of important issues that are frequently raised.

Given that the system of education we recommend has never been fully tested, how can we be confident that its far-reaching changes will work as predicted?

Predicting the consequences of major reform can never be an exact science. But there are several distinct and substantial sources of support for the predictions we make. The first is theory. There can be little doubt that a market environment is more conducive than a political environment to the development of many qualities of successful schooling. As we explained, markets discourage educational bureaucratization and thereby encourage effective school organization. Except under special circumstances—in which school systems are small, politically homogeneous and trouble-free, for example, as we find in certain suburbs—politics breeds bureaucracy and impedes leadership, professionalism, and a clear focus on academics.

Nor are these the only important differences between politics and markets. Markets provide stronger incentives than politics for schools to reach out to parents, to involve them in school activities, and to gain their parental support in the home. Schools know that when parents are free to leave, they must find ways to satisfy parents. When parents lack this freedom, as they generally do today, they become just another interest group whose involvement may conflict with the interests that boards, superintendents, and other political authorities represent. Politics is also less likely to get students fully engaged in schools. In a market setting, students will seek schools responsive to their interests and needs and in which they want to be enrolled. Students will consequently tend to be better motivated than when their schools are not to their liking. Schools will tend to reinforce the benefit of self-selection by recruiting staff and developing programs that fit distinctive missions and appeal to particular clienteles. In a political setting, where public authorities create schools in response to innumerable pressures and where students must accept whatever these schools offer, students and schools are less likely to be well matched and students less apt to be fully motivated.

All this provides strong reason to expect better performance from schools controlled by competition and choice than from schools controlled by politics and bureaucracy. Considerable evidence supports this reasoning further. Our research, as we have said, reinforces what many other researchers have concluded about school performance: It is hindered by excessive bureaucracy and facilitated by effective organization. Our research extends these conclusions by linking them to politics and markets: When all else is equal, autonomy, organization, and achievement are significantly better in private schools than in public. But while our research is the first to demonstrate just how far-reaching the differences between politics and markets can be, it is hardly the first to indicate that private schools outperform public schools academically when the two kinds of schools are working with similar students.

Public-private comparisons do not provide the only evidence of how education markets will work, moreover. There are now a number of efforts underway to create reasonable facsimiles of such markets in the traditional public sector. These efforts are commonly called public-school choice programs. Although these efforts are often too new to yield firm conclusions, they suggest that educational choice can have the kinds of effects we believe it promises. District 4 in East Harlem, New York, created a choice system for middle-school students based on autonomous, teacher-directed alternative schools, that helped raise the test scores of that district's highly disadvantaged students from last place in New York City to the middle of the distribution. Cambridge, Massachusetts, has created a thoroughgoing choice system for elementary schools that has succeeded in winning back large numbers of families from private schools and has boosted test scores. Minnesota has operated a statewide system of open enrollment since 1989 that is just beginning to promote student mobility and school competition. Since 1985, it has also allowed high-school students to opt for local colleges and universities instead of their regular high schools. This program, which now has more than ten thousand participants, has stimulated such school improvements as sharp increases in advanced placement offerings. Yes, choice has been tried and occasionally failed to produce promised changes. But in every such instance, such as Alum Rock, California, the choice program was so severely constrained that it represented politics as usual and not reform through markets.

Even if educational choice has an edge over politics in promoting educational excellence, aren't markets likely to undermine educational equity—to provide the poor and less-competent choosers with schooling that is grossly inferior?

In our view, there is little question that the poor and the less competent would be far better off under a choice system than they are now. In the first place, people with money already have lots of educational choice. They can move to areas with good schools or can pay for private schools. The poor, however, are trapped, usually in inner cities with deplorable schools. The current education system, in other words, is profoundly inequitable. The system we propose eliminates the financial and legal barriers that now constrain the choices of the poor and thereby promises to be more equitable—not less.

In addition, schools that now suffer most from the political and bureaucratic nightmares that we find to be so disruptive are located in large cities and attended disproportionately by the poor. The greatest beneficiaries of choice—and the autonomy it entails—are not likely to be suburban schools in small school systems, where traditional political control works tolerably well; they are likely to be the city schools that now serve the poor so badly.

Third, it is not true that only the "cream of the crop" would be well served by choice. All schools cannot compete successfully for the most academically able students. To survive, each school would have to carve out a market niche, some clientele of parents and students for whom it has special appeal. Some schools might specialize in educating the gifted; others might focus on youngsters with learning disabilities. Most would probably specialize by curriculum, some emphasizing math and science, some the performing arts, and so on.

Fourth, the benefits of a marketplace are not reserved for sophisticated consumers, and markets do not require all consumers to be sophisticated for them to work well. So long as a substantial proportion of consumers— there is no absolute requirement—are attentive to costs and benefits, all suppliers must be concerned that inferior or costly products will not be bought. As a consequence, even consumers who act without much thought—for example, supermarket shoppers who are too hasty to read labels or compare unit prices—enjoy the benefits of market competition. Uncompetitive products tend to be driven from the market by the careful shoppers, leaving even unwary consumers with mostly competitive choices. By the same logic, parents who know or care little about school quality and who would automatically enroll their children in the school nearest their home or their place of employment, would nonetheless choose schools that survived a competitive test.

We stress, finally, that we are not proposing a pure educational market but rather a governmentally structured one. All students are guaranteed adequate funding. Those with special needs receive supplementary support. Transportation is provided. Parents are assisted in making informed choices. Equity is not left to the market; government guarantees it.

Wouldn't a system of educational choice risk the promotion of undesirable values and jeopardize the transmission of common values such as democracy and racial tolerance?

Although there is little reason to believe that parents as a group hold very different educational values than society as a whole, there are some legitimate reasons for concern. One is that some parents may simply give little weight to academic quality in selecting schools. Parents might choose, for example, to send their children to a "football high school," where athletics are promoted at the expense of academics. We doubt, however, that academically unacceptable choices would be very common, even in a completely unregulated market. So long as most parents prefer schools that offer their children better rather than worse prospects of high-school graduation, gainful employment, college admission, and other outcomes that depend on academic achievement, schools will be encouraged to aim for quality. Such judgments, moreover, are not very difficult for parents to make, especially if they are provided with truthful information about educational outcomes. If parents make these simple judgments, schools that provide students with no future, or a relatively poor one, will usually find it hard to attract families, even if they field winning sports teams. Still, some government regulation may be necessary to curb excessive school specialization in nonacademic endeavors.

Another concern is that, without trading off academic performance, some parents might select schools that teach or support ideas that society as a whole would never agree should be taught—for example, explicit sex education or no sex education at all, creationism, particular religious principles, or racial separatism and bigotry. Of course, society could continue to limit or proscribe what is taught, but if it decided to go that route, it would risk perpetuating the bureaucratic ossification that market-oriented reform is supposed to counter. A compromise would be to limit regulation, as the regulation of private schools is now limited, to the most egregious abuses of the public trust—for example, the teaching of racial hatred—and leave the issue of other values in schools to be resolved by the market.

This compromise does not fully resolve the issue of values. It leaves open the possibility that as schools teach alternative values, even decent ones, such common American values as respect for democracy and tolerance of dissent will be jeopardized. However, we think this danger is small. First, some of the concerns about intolerance, social cleavage, and ignorance that were reasonable fears in the nineteenth century, when the "common school" was created, are not so plausible today. The United States is no longer a young and fragile nation trying to unify a population made up mostly of immigrants. Second, although schools today may have a certain amount of civics curriculum in common, they are not common schools in any meaningful sense. Students are segregated socioeconomically and racially—few schools are melting pots—and schools are scarcely able to address questions of values at all. Given this harsh reality, democracy might be better served by an education system that respects a diversity of schools, each arriving at its own conclusion about how difficult questions of values are best addressed.

Finally, we want to emphasize that the clearest evidence as to the values to be advanced in a system of educational choice comes from U.S. private schools. Despite limited government regulation, the private sector contains few schools that champion generally repugnant values or that support antidemocratic cults. Moreover, there is no evidence whatsoever that private-school students turn out to be worse citizens on average than students who learned their democratic lessons in public schools.

What about the one value that Americans historically have had greatest difficulty in supporting in education and elsewhere—the value of racial equality? Won't educational choice resegregate the schools?

Race has often figured in the decisions that parents have made about where to send their children to school. Sometimes this is because parents have used the racial composition of a school as a proxy, however imperfect, for school quality or safety. Sometimes parents are bigoted. The government has fought against such behavior with various policies aimed at discouraging school segregation and promoting equal educational opportunity; the government would certainly want to continue this effort in a system of educational choice. To do so, it should prohibit racial discrimination in admissions and hiring, subsidize the educationally disadvantaged—who are disproportionately minorities—and advise all students about educational opportunities in racially mixed schools.

The government might even want to impose racial admissions quotas or guidelines to guarantee that school populations satisfy desegregation objectives. It is far from clear, however, that such restrictions are necessary. Choice has been used successfully in many cities to promote desegregation. Using racially mixed "magnet" schools that are safe and excellent, urban school systems have encouraged children from different racial groups to sit in classrooms together. Although magnet schools have not worked everywhere, they have had a better record of promoting desegregation than compulsory busing. It is also worth noting that private schools, although not models of racial integration, are less segregated than public schools. Choice is hardly the enemy of racial equality it is sometimes claimed to be. Properly shaped by government authority, choice may be equality's strongest ally.

If educational choice is fully implemented—with transportation provided, choice offices created, and private schools admitted—won't this new system be terribly expensive?

In the short run, a thoroughgoing choice system may well cost more tax dollars than the current system of public education. More students would want to ride the bus to distant schools, and some share of this transportation—say, to the next district line—would need to be paid by the government. The admissions process and the distribution of funds would require new or expanded government offices. Students already attending private schools—and not costing taxpayers anything—would become eligible for public support if their private schools joined the public system. These new and real activities could add as much as 10 percent to the per pupil cost of public education.

In the medium to long run, however, certainly within ten years, these costs should be offset by substantial savings. If the choice system encourages the stock of schools to improve in quality and diversity, more students will find attractive schools near their homes and will not need transportation. Families generally favor schools close to home, and this preference should strongly influence the development of new schools and the transformation of old ones. If schools diminish in size—which better schools may well do—and if smaller schools share facilities—becoming "schools within a school"—the options close to home will increase further and the need for transportation will diminish with them.

A market system will also encourage the dismantling of district and state education bureaucracies. As the market concentrates decision-making at the school level, closest to parents and students, much of the administrative apparatus outside the schools will become unnecessary. It is impossible to estimate the savings that decentralization will produce, but the potential is great. About 15 percent of local education employment is explicitly administrative. Teacher salaries represent less than half of all education costs in most states. Private-school systems are known to operate much leaner bureaucracies than public-school systems. In New York City, for example, the central office of the public schools employs roughly 5000 people, while the central office of the archdiocesan schools employs 30 people.

Finally, a system of schools driven by market forces will operate more efficiently than one driven by political forces. With educational choice, resources will be allocated based on results, as judged by parents. Currently, resources are allocated to schools without direct regard for results. Ultimately, the greater efficiency of the market system would make it less costly than the existing alternative. How generously the government would choose to fund an efficient system of educational choice is impossible to say. But ironically, support for public educational spending might well increase if, through educational choice, the performance of public schools rose and families in private schools joined the public sector.

Choice as a Public System

This proposal calls for fundamental changes in the structure of American public education. Stereotypes aside, however, these changes have nothing to do with "privatizing" the nation's schools. The choice system we outline is a truly public system—and a democratic one.

We are proposing that the state put its democratic authority to use in creating a new institutional framework. The design and legitimation of this framework would be a democratic act of the most basic sort. It would be a societal decision, made through the usual processes of democratic governance, by which the people and their representatives specify the structure of a new system of public education.

This framework, as we set it out, is quite flexible and admits of substantial variation on important issues, all of them matters of public policy to be decided by representative government. Public officials and their constituents would be free to devise their own approaches to taxation, equalization, supplementary funding for the disadvantaged, treatment of religious schools, and other controversial issues, thus designing choice systems to reflect the unique conditions, preferences, and political forces of their own states.

Once this structural framework is democratically determined, moreover, governments would continue to play important roles within it. State officials and agencies would remain pivotal to the success of public education and to its ongoing operation. They would provide funding, approve applications for new schools, orchestrate and oversee the choice process, elicit full information about schools, provide transportation to students, monitor schools for adherence to the law, and (if they wish) design and administer tests of student performance. Meantime, school districts would continue as local taxing jurisdictions and would have the option of continuing to operate their own system of schools.

The crucial difference is that direct democratic control of the schools—the very capacity for control, not simply its exercise—would essentially be eliminated. Nothing in the concept of democracy requires that schools be subject to management by school boards, superintendents, central offices, departments of education, and other arms of government. Nor does anything in the concept of public education require that schools be governed in this way. There are many paths to democracy and public education. The path America has been treading for the past half century is exacting a heavy price—one the nation and its children can ill afford to bear, and need not. It is time, we think, to get to the root of the problem.

Reference

CHUBB, JOHN E. and MOE, TERRY M. 1990. *Politics, Markets, and America's Schools.* Washington, D.C.: The Brookings Institution.

4

Restructuring the Chicago Public Schools

G. Alfred Hess, Jr.[1]

On December 2, 1988, the Illinois State Legislature voted to pass the Chicago School Reform Act (P.A. 85-1418). This act fundamentally changed the structure of public education by creating almost 600 local school councils, each consisting of 2 teachers, 6 parents, 2 community representatives, a principal, and—in high schools—a nonvoting student. Based on the business theory of participatory decision-making, the councils are the primary vehicles through which the goals of Chicago school reform are to be achieved.

This reform has been called the most radical experiment in the history of public education. Its success or failure will have a major impact on how American children are educated. This chapter traces the evolution of Chicago's particular type of school reform, from the actual restructuring of the school system to mobilizing support for school reform from citizen activists, parents, business executives, state and national sources, and the media. It also examines the reasons that led the general assembly to act in this way and suggests some ways in which the Chicago experiment is and is not applicable to school reform efforts in other states.

The Chicago Public Schools: In Need of Reform

The Chicago School Reform Act builds upon the unique history of that city's public-school system. In 1985 the Chicago schools enrolled some 435,000 students, down from 585,000 in 1968 (Chicago Board of Education 1985). The school system was still recovering from a fiscal crisis in 1979–80, when it failed to meet its payroll and required a financial bailout

---

[1]Research assistance provided by Hilary Addington.

by the state. This left many of its financial decisions subject to review and approval by an oversight board, the Chicago School Finance Authority. Under the terms of the bailout, the system was forced to cut more than 8,000 positions from its budget (Hallett and Hess 1982).

The school system also operated under a desegregation consent decree that virtually eliminated all predominantly white schools. However, in a school system that had only about 15 percent white enrollment, that meant the vast majority of minority students continued to attend completely segregated schools and did not benefit significantly from desegregation (Hess and Warden 1987).

The system had involved parents in advisory roles for a number of years. Local advisory councils had been established at virtually all schools. Chapter I parent advisory councils were maintained in Chicago schools even after the federal government allowed their discontinuance. Bilingual advisory councils functioned in most schools, serving large numbers of Limited English Proficient students (Chicago provided special instruction to students who spoke more than eighty different languages). Local school advisory councils or PTAs had been involved in the selection of principals for nearly fifteen years, interviewing candidates and recommending three candidates, one of whom was almost always chosen by the general superintendent.

Yet, the system was not very successful in educating its students. In January 1985, Designs for Change, a local education research and advocacy group, released a study which showed that only one out of three graduating seniors was capable of reading at the national norm and that the proportion was much lower than that in inner-city schools (Designs for Change 1985). Two months later, the Chicago Panel on Public School Policy and Finance released a complementary study which showed that 43 percent of entering freshmen dropped out before graduation, with dropout rates in inner-city schools reaching 67 percent (Hess and Lauber 1985). When combined with the panel's earlier study, which showed that the 8,000 positions cut during the financial crisis were disproportionately teachers and other student contact staff (Hallett and Hess 1982), a picture emerged of a school system that ill-served its students and was more interested in protecting bureaucratic jobs than improving the schools. It was from this base that the school reform movement was launched.

The Ineffectiveness of Previous State Reform Efforts

In 1985 Illinois, like several other states, enacted statewide school reform legislation in response to the report *A Nation at Risk* (National Commission on Excellence in Education 1983). The 1985 act (P.A. 84-126) was long on accountability but short on serious efforts to improve the state's schools (Nelson et al. 1985). It did not seriously address the shortcomings of the Chicago schools, although reports of high dropout rates and low reading scores appeared as the bill was being debated. In a special section devoted to Chicago, the act created local school improvement councils at every school. These new bodies were encouraged to engage in school improvement planning and were given the right to review discretionary spending by the principal.

The accountability provisions of the act were probably more important in the long run, however, because they helped spotlight how poorly the schools were performing. In 1987 the new state report card showed that 33 of 64 Chicago high schools scored in the lowest 1 percent of all U.S. high schools on the American College Testing program (ACT) tests. In fact, Chicago schools dominated that lowest percentile, which included only 54 schools nationwide. Just 7 Chicago high schools scored higher than the tenth percentile. In the elementary grades, 60–70 percent of all students were reading below the national norms on the Iowa Test of Basic Skills.

It is not surprising that state school reform efforts had little effect on Chicago. Chicago is not very different from other large urban systems. Dropout rates in Boston, for instance, when calculated as we did in Chicago, are 53 percent, and that does not include the 35 percent that the Massachusetts Advocacy Center reports never make it to high school (1988). Using similar statistics, the Dade County Public Schools, which include both the city of Miami and its suburbs, report a 28-percent dropout rate (Stephenson 1985). New York reports a 33-percent rate, although knowledgeable critics point out that figure would be much higher if New York counted the youngsters who transfer into night school and then drop out (*New York Times*, September 24, 1988).

Meanwhile, suburban schools graduate upward of 95 percent of their students. In fact, in Illinois, according to the state report card, some suburban districts graduate up to 105 percent of their students! (Because the state report card is based on comparison of the size of the graduating class with the ninth-grade class four years previously, schools with large numbers of transfers in, primarily those in fast growing suburbs, graduate more students from twelfth grade than they earlier enrolled in ninth grade. The urban dropout rates reported above are based on longitudinal tracking of individuals, called cohort studies, rather than aggregate enrollment.)

That urban schools are not like suburban schools is understood by most people. Rural schools are often different from either urban or suburban ones. But state policymakers too frequently ignore such differences, except to complain about their costs to the state. Urban districts are frequently described as "black holes," and the color reference is usually not unintentional. Rural districts are small and inefficient. Both cost the state too much yet perform poorly. Suburban districts cost the state little but perform well. Even without much state aid, they spend much more on each pupil than the rest of the state.

If we all know these differences exist, why do states continue to search for a single uniform solution? Why do we try to enact one set of policies to fix all these schools? In reality, the problems faced by urban schools are quite different from those faced by suburban schools, and the solutions must also be different. The Council of Great City Schools (1987) reports that one-quarter of all youth live in central cities. Students who attend urban schools are predominantly from disadvantaged homes, and these students dominate inner-city schools. In Chicago more than one-half the entering freshmen at Austin High School come from low-income homes, and 82 percent of them are reading at least two grades below the "norm". These are not just a few problem kids on the margin of the school population; these disadvantaged youngsters dominate the school enrollment. Yet, from a policy perspective, we treat Austin like any other high school in the state!

In addition, urban school districts are organized differently. Outside Chicago, the average Illinois school district has 1,385 students attending about 4 schools of 300–350 students each. Chicago, however, enrolls 410,000 students in 542 regular attendance centers and 55 specialty sites. There are 36 high schools and 10 elementary schools so large that each enrolls more students than does the average Illinois district! In the suburbs, few districts have more than 10 administrators. In Chicago in 1988, 4,380 persons worked in the central and subdistrict offices. Another 38,000 employees worked in the system's schools. In urban systems such as this, central office staff are apt to be large, rigid bureaucracies, far removed from their schools, not successfully educating kids and not saving money.

The Chicago School Reform Act is a bold attempt to create a solution geared to the urban school problem. It would not necessarily be appropriate for suburban or rural schools, except perhaps in those states where large county districts have their own bureaucracies. Aspects of the Chicago restructuring plan may suit other settings, but the effort as a whole is aimed at the urban education problem. Other states with large urban centers may find elements of the Chicago experiment that would address their own situations.

The Chicago Restructuring Plan

The Chicago School Reform Act has three major components: a set of goals, a requirement to reallocate the resources of the system towards the school level, and a system of school-based management centered upon the establishment of a local school council at every school.

School Reform Goals

The 123-page statute sets forth ten goals to serve as the measures of school improvement over a five-year period. In essence, these require that Chicago students perform at national levels in achievement, attendance, and graduation rates and that the school system provide an adequate and rounded education for each enrolled student.

The specific goals are as follows:

- assuring that students achieve proficiency in reading, writing, mathematics, and higher order thinking that equals or surpasses national norms;
- assuring that students attend school regularly and graduate from high school at rates that equal or surpass national norms;
- assuring that students are adequately prepared for further education and aiding them in making a successful transition to further education;
- assuring that students are adequately prepared for successful entry into employment and aiding them in making a successful transition to employment;
- assuring that students are provided with a common learning experience of academic quality that reflects high expectations for all students' capacities to learn;
- assuring that students are better prepared to compete in the international market place by having foreign language proficiency and stronger international studies;
- assuring that students are encouraged in exploring potential interests in fields such as journalism, drama, art and music;
- assuring that individual teachers are granted the professional authority to make decisions about instruction and the method of teaching;
- assuring that students are provided the means to express themselves creatively and to respond to the artistic expression of others through the visual arts, music, drama and dance; and
- assuring that students are provided adequate athletic programs that encourage pride and positive identification with the school and that reduce the number of dropouts and teenage delinquents (P.A. 85-1418, Sec. 34-1.01.A).

Although these goals are wide-ranging, most reform advocates and monitoring agencies agree that the primary goals are the first two: raising student achievement to national norms and raising attendance and graduation rates to national norms. To hit these targets system-wide is a tremendous challenge and, at least in terms of graduation rates, is probably unreasonable, given what is known about the elementary school effects on student graduation rates (Hess et al. 1989). Yet, the act states that these goals must be met *at each school in the district!*

The Reallocation of Resources

One of the primary criticisms of the Chicago public schools during the 1980s was the continual growth of its central bureaucracy even as local schools were starved for adequate numbers of teachers, texts, supplies, and other resources. These criticisms were built on annual budget analyses presented by the Chicago Panel, analyses that had their origin in the panel's research into budget cuts surrounding the fiscal crisis of 1979–80 (Hallett and Hess 1982). The most telling analysis came in 1987, in testimony on the general superintendent's proposed budget after the nineteen-day school strike (Chicago Panel 1987). The panel's testimony showed the growth of the administrative bureaucracy each year since 1981, as the total student enrollment was dropping. These trends are shown in Figure 4-1 and Table 4-1.

As can be seen from Table 4-1, the percentage of staff budgeted to the system's administrative units increased each year from 1981 through 1988 (with the exception of 1983) from 9.0 percent to 11.0 percent. Since total

FIGURE 4-1. Bureaucrats per 1000 Students in Chicago Public Schools

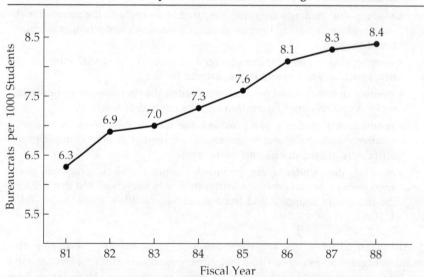

SOURCE: Hess 1987. Drawn from published annual budgets of Chicago Public Schools.

TABLE 4-1. Bureaucratic Growth in Chicago Public Schools (operating funds only)

Location	1981	1982	1983	1984	1985	1986	1987	1988
Enrollment	458,497	442,889	435,843	434,042	431,226	430,908	431,298	430,000
School Staff	29,339	27,822	28,855	29,185	29,418	29,462	29,919	29,964
Administrative Units	2,884	3,036	3,043	3,156	3,295	3,470	3,598	3,708
Total Staff	32,223	30,858	31,898	32,341	32,713	232,932	33,518	33,672
% Administrative	9.0%	9.8%	9.5%	9.8%	10.1%	10.5%	10.7%	11.0%
Administrative/1,000	6.3	6.9	7.0	7.3	7.6	8.1	8.3	8.6

SOURCE: Hess, 1987. Drawn from published annual budgets of Chicago Public Schools.

59

enrollment decreased during this period by nearly 30,000 pupils, the number of administrators per 1,000 students increased dramatically from 6.3 to 8.6 per 1,000 students. As the system recovered from the financial crisis of 1979–80, when it had cut more teachers than administrators, it added 1,449 staff; 824 of those new staff (56.9 percent) were in the administrative units. These units increased by 28.6 percent, while staff in schools increased by only 2.1 percent. Proportionately, the system concentrated more of its added resources on administrative units rather than on serving students at schools.

The panel also identified an illegal diversion of state compensatory aid funds from serving disadvantaged students into supporting the central bureaucracy (Chicago Panel on Public Policy and Finance 1988). Illinois, unlike most other states, bases its school aid formula partly upon the proportion of low-income students. Districts receive an additional weighting for low-income students in calculating their student counts. The weighting increases as the concentration of low-income students in a district increases. In 1987–88 the Chicago public schools received $238 million in compensatory aid as part of total state aid of $832 million. Under 1978 legislation, Chicago was to distribute 60 percent of this state compensatory aid (known as State Chapter I aid) to schools on the basis of their free lunch counts, while 40 percent was to be distributed on the basis of total enrollment. In fact, however, the board of education diverted nearly one-quarter ($42 million) of the funds targeted for disadvantaged students to underwrite central administrative costs under the pseudonym of "Program Support." Moreover, the board used state compensatory funds to provide basic services, such as kindergarten, guidance counseling, and librarians, in schools with heavy concentrations of disadvantaged students while providing the same levels of the same services at other schools with regular education fund resources. The result, of course, was no extra services for the neediest youngsters.

The Chicago School Reform Act included two provisions meant to alter this situation. Administrative costs were capped. The intent of the reformers was to limit the proportion of the system's budget that could be spent in the central office and subdistrict offices. But what was "disproportionate"? As initially drafted, the bill required not exceeding the proportion of administrative expenditures in the 1985 budget. One legislator wanted to use 1981 as the base. Then the associate superintendent for finance of the state board of education proposed an alternative that seemed less capricious. His suggestion, which was adopted, was to limit the proportion of noninstructional costs in the system to the average proportion of all other school districts in the state for the preceding year. The advantage of this recommendation was the obvious fairness of the criterion. The disadvantage, in practice, is that the state's definition of noninstructional expenditures includes a number of items at the school level, such as teacher retraining, that the Chicago reformers explicitly intended that additional resources should support. But the associate state superintendent predicted that his recommendation would free about $40 million, funds that would be available for redistribution to local schools, through downsizing the central administration.

The Chicago Panel, along with two of its member organizations—the Chicago Urban League and the United Neighborhood Organization (a coalition of four constituent groups in primarily Hispanic communities)—had been pressing the board of education for several years to change the basis for its allocation of State Chapter I funds (Hess and Warden 1987). Although Chicago's general superintendent acknowledged the propriety of the panel's recommendation, he claimed that such a resource shift would be too disruptive—a response that came even as he was increasing central office staff while proposing to cut teachers at the school level.

The reform groups were able to incorporate into the Chicago School Reform Act a provision to change the allocation of State Chapter I aid. No longer could these funds be used for any purposes outside local schools, except for 5 percent that had been used for desegregation purposes during the 1980s. (The reform act, in numerous places, seeks to avoid impeding the system's desegregation efforts.) This reallocation provision required that about $30 million of previously deducted "Program Support" funds now be distributed directly to the schools, starting in 1989. Another provision shifted the proportion of poverty-targeted funding from 60 to 100 percent over four years. Finally, the act required that Chapter I funds no longer be used to support basic programs present in all schools. The resulting freed funds would be available for discretionary use at the school level. The act also stipulated that the newly targeted aid be considered discretionary. This "supplemental/discretionary" provision required that an additional $10 million be shifted to the school level. The net effects of these various provisions was to channel to the average elementary school about $90,000 in new discretionary resources for the first year of school reform implementation. That figure should increase to about $450,000 in the fifth year.

School-Based Management Provisions

The primary vehicle for achieving the goals of the act and utilizing the reallocated resources was the new local school councils (LSCs) at each school site. These councils were to be the cornerstone of school management and decision-making. They were given three major responsibilities: to adopt a school improvement plan, to adopt a budget to implement that plan based upon a lump sum allocation, and to decide whether to terminate the incumbent principal and select a new one or to retain the incumbent, in either case signing the selected principal to a four-year performance-based contract.

Keyed to the establishment of the LSCs, a number of other provisions shifted responsibilities and authority of other aspects of the school system: teachers, principals, subdistrict superintendents, the general superintendent, and the board of education itself.

Local School Councils

Local school councils were mandated for each school site. Each is composed of six parents, two community representatives, two teachers, and the principal. In high schools they also include one nonvoting student. The parent representatives were originally elected by a vote of the parents with children attending the school; parents who were also employees of the system were not eligible to vote for parent representatives or to serve on LSCs as parent representatives. The community representatives were elected by residents living within the geographical boundaries of the school enrollment area who were neither parents of enrolled students nor employees of the school system; employees may not serve as community representatives. The Illinois Supreme Court declared this provision of the act an unconstitutional infringement of the one-person-one-vote principle on November 30, 1990. A temporary corrective (P.A. 86-1477) was adopted by the general assembly on January 8, 1991. (See page 114 for a fuller description of these events.) Two teachers are elected by all employees assigned to each school, exclusive of the principal. The principal serves on the basis of his or her assignment to the school (P.A. 85-1418, Sec. 34-2.1).

This particular configuration of LSC membership was designed during the Mayor's Education Summit, originally convened by former mayor Harold Washington. It was designed to give parents a major voice in the educational decisions affecting their children; it was also designed to avoid the problems encountered in New York City, where school employees for several decades were able to dominate elections to the thirty-two community boards of education that govern elementary schools. In Chicago system employees gained representation on each LSC but only in the teacher and principal positions. The composition of the LSCs was not overturned by the Supreme Court's decision.

Subdistrict Councils

Councils were also established for each administrative district in the city (P.A. 85-1418, Sec. 34-2.5). These councils were authorized to retain, terminate, or select their own subdistrict superintendent. The occupant of that position, in turn, was changed from a line officer with authority over principals and school employees to a monitor and facilitator of school improvement. The district superintendent (DS) is supposed to facilitate the provision of training for LSC members, to mediate disputes at the local school, to settle election disputes, and to monitor the establishment and implementation of a school improvement plan at each school in his or her district. If the DS judges that a school is not progressing satisfactorily, he can recommend to the district council that it be put on a remediation plan. If the school continues not to improve under the remediation plan, the district council can place it on probation, whereupon a board of education improvement plan is established to correct deficiencies. If no improvement is noted after one year, the board may order new LSC elections, remove and replace the principal, replace the faculty, or close the school.

The subdistrict council also plays a coordinating function for schools in geographical proximity to one another (except for the subdistrict consisting of all the city's high schools). It is composed of one parent or community representative from each school in the district. Each subdistrict council elects representatives to the system-wide board nominating commission.

The Board Nominating Commission

The nominating commission is charged with proposing 3 nominations to the mayor for each appointment to the newly composed board of education. During the initial year of implementation, an interim 7-member board of education was appointed by the mayor. The new permanent board, which replaced the interim board in October of 1990, contains 15 members with staggered 4-year terms. Thus, the initial nominating commission was responsible for proposing 45 candidates to the mayor by mid-April 1990. From the 15 slates of 3 nominees, the mayor was to select 1 appointee for each slot. If he finds a slate to not contain any satisfactory candidates, he can reject the entire slate and request that a new one be recommended to him (P.A. 85-1418, Sec. 34-3.1).

The Interim Board of Education

The interim board of education was appointed in May 1989. In addition to providing temporary governance to the district, it was charged with five major responsibilities: to institute a nationwide search for a general superintendent, to adopt system-wide reform goals and objectives, to reduce administrative expenditures to meet the cap on noninstructional costs, to adopt a budget that reallocated resources in line with provisions of the reform act, and to negotiate a contract with the system's teacher and other employee groups (P.A. 85-1418, Sec. 34-3).

The Permanent Board of Education

The new permanent board of education took over most of the powers of the previous board, with the exception of those granted to local school councils. To recognize the existence of these new, semiautonomous LSCs, the basic descriptive term was changed from "management of" to "jurisdiction over the public education and the public school system of the city" (P.A. 85-1418, Sec. 34-18). Specific new responsibilities included ensuring the proper reallocation of State Chapter I funds, establishing an open enrollment (or "choice") plan by 1991–92, establishing and approving "system-wide curriculum objectives and standards which reflect the multi-cultural diversity in the city," ensuring the civil rights of special education and bilingual pupils, reducing overcrowding, ensuring that Chicago students meet the state's new university entrance requirements, encouraging new teacher recruitment efforts, providing training for personnel for their new responsibilities, and establishing a fund to meet special priorities the board might establish while distributing funds to attendance centers in an equitable manner. The powers-and-duties section (P.A. 85-1418, Sec. 34-18.1-28) concludes with the notation "Nothing in this paragraph shall be construed to require any additional appropriations of State funds for this purpose."

Teacher Empowerment

Although other school-based management efforts across the country have focused on giving teachers new roles in decision-making, the Chicago plan gives more votes to parents and community representatives than to the professional staff. However, in most other school districts experimenting with school-based decision-making, few new powers have been captured by school improvement planning teams. Typically, the new powers are restricted to requesting individual case waivers from the board of education or the relevant employee union. In the Chicago plan, by contrast, extensive programmatic, budgetary, and personnel authority is granted to the LSCs. Since the intent of the reform act was to establish a new level of staff accountability for student achievement, it was deemed critical to ensure that the school councils were dominated by parents and community representatives.

Still, the idea of participatory decision-making was recognized in the relationships mandated between the councils and the professional staff. Primary responsibility for school improvement planning was vested in the principal, to be advised in this matter by the schools' Professional Personnel Advisory Committee (PPAC). The PPAC is composed of "certified classroom teachers and other certificated personnel who are employed at the attendance center." Its size and operation are determined by the certificated personnel at each school (P.A. 85-1418, Sec. 34-2.4a). The PPAC is established "for the purpose of advising the principal and the local school council on matters of educational program, including but not limited to curriculum and school improvement plan development and implementation."

The Principal

Although it is never stated explicitly in the Chicago School Reform Act's description of the principal's powers and duties, the act rests upon the assumption that the principal is the chief instructional leader in each school. The principal is given new powers and duties to strengthen his or her performance in that role. But principals were also made directly accountable to local school councils for their effectiveness. At the time of contract renewal, principals who are judged ineffective may be terminated, with no tenure rights other than those they hold as teachers.

Principals acquired the right to select teachers, aides, counselors, clerks, hall guards, or any other instructional program staff for vacant or newly created positions "based upon merit and ability to perform in that position without regard to seniority or length of service . . ." (P.A. 85-1418, Sec. 34-8.1). For the first time, the Engineer in Charge (building custodian) and Lunchroom Manager were also made accountable to the principal, although they were still not fully under the principal's control.

Principals also gained responsibility, in consultation with the LSC and the PPAC, for initiating a needs assessment for the school, for designing and recommending a school improvement plan for consideration by the LSC, and for drafting a school budget for submission to the LSC. Thus, the principal is to function as the school's instructional leader and is charged to propose ways to improve the school that will win the approval of the parents, community, and teachers who make up the school community. The principal won additional powers in staff selection, planning, and budget management and additional resources with which to work. In exchange, the principal's continued employment now depends upon the ability to convince the local school council that he or she is effectively exercising that leadership.

The Chicago School Finance Authority

Primary responsibility for monitoring the implementation of the act was vested in an existing oversight body, the Chicago School Finance Authority (CSFA). The CSFA was established in 1980 to oversee the finances of the Chicago Public Schools, but as the system returned to fiscal stability the Authority's role changed to annual reviews of the board's budgets to ensure that they were balanced (the CSFA could prevent the opening of schools if the budget were not balanced) and to paying off the large bonded indebtedness incurred to bail out the system from 1980 through 1982. The Chicago School Reform Act requires the board of education to gain the CSFA's approval of an annual plan for reforming the school system. The CSFA, in turn, is charged with ensuring that the major elements of the reform act are appropriately carried out by the board of education (P.A. 85-1418, Sec. 34A). But the sanctions available to the CSFA are largely limited to reporting inappropriate actions to the state General Assembly and other public officials, meaning that its oversight of reform is not nearly so potent a tool as its charge to ensure the financial stability of the system.

The Philosophical Basis of Chicago School Reform

The major components of the Chicago School Reform Act were not selected randomly or as the haphazard result of political compromises, although some compromises were required on lesser issues. The primary theoretical bases for the reform act can be found in the effective schools research literature and in participatory management theories that find their educational manifestation in school-based management.

Effective Schools

The effective schools literature traces its roots to the efforts of Ronald Edmonds (1979), a professor at Harvard University and later a high-level administrator in the New York Public Schools, where he tried to implement the findings from his research. Edmonds and his colleagues (for example, Brookman and Lezotte) sought out successful inner-city schools in which disadvantaged students were learning at or above national norms. He then contrasted those schools with comparable schools that were less successful. He and his colleagues and successors were able to identify a series of characteristics of what he called "effective schools." Chief among these was the conviction, among the faculty, that all students can learn successfully.

Although such an assertion seems self-evident, inner-city educators had long been excusing the poor performance of students in their systems, drawing on the 1966 Coleman Report. Sociologist James S. Coleman, principal investigator of a major study of urban schools for the U.S. Office of Education, had found that the only traditional variable that consistently correlated with low student achievement was the social and economic status of the student's family. Washington utilized that research to justify federal aid to disadvantaged students, now popularly known as the Federal Chapter I program. But in colleges of education across the land, future school administrators were taught to hold lower expectations for students from poor neighborhoods. Edmonds set out to show that these diminished expectations became self-fulfilling prophecies. He was able to demonstrate that, when faculties held high expectations for the abilities of their students, the youngsters were more likely to achieve at the national norms.

Edmonds also showed that the principal's leadership is a key characteristic of an effective school. Although no one particular style of leadership was associated with this effectiveness, it was related to the ability of the principal to establish a philosophical consensus about the educational program in effective schools. In addition, effective schools systematically utilized student assessment (testing) for diagnostic purposes, designing programs that were specifically geared to meet the educational needs of their students. These schools also maintained discipline within an orderly educational climate.

The Chicago School Reform Act was designed to foster the development of these characteristics in every city school. For years the leadership of the school system had used the poverty level of its students as an excuse for low performance. In a *Chicago Tribune* interview on January 18, 1987, former superintendent Manford Byrd cited the poverty level of the city's students as the reason dropout rates were so high and test scores so low. He explicitly rejected the findings of a Chicago Panel study (Hess et al. 1986) that suggested the system was shortchanging the city's high-school students by scheduling them in nonexistent study halls and using other scheduling mechanisms that reduced daily instruction to less than four hours (despite state law requiring at least five hours of instruction). He denied that this lack of comparable instructional time contributed to lower achievement and called the report a "trashing" of the public schools.

It was obvious to activists in the Chicago school reform movement that few school faculties would operate on the conviction that all students could successfully learn so long as they and their principals were responsible to administrative leadership more concerned to eliminate threats to bureaucratic stasis than to ensure the high achievement of the system's students. This conviction was supported by research conducted several years earlier.

Van Cleve Morris and Robert Crowson (Morris et al. 1984), two professors at the University of Illinois, had studied a number of principals in the Chicago school system. They coined the term "creative insubordinates" to describe those principals whom they found to be peculiarly successful. These were the principals who were willing to break the rules "creatively" to ensure that their schools performed effectively for their students. It was evident to the reformers, that the multitude of sanctions, both explicit and tacit, that were part of the Chicago Public Schools bureaucratic chain of command had a chilling effect on principal creativity and leadership at the school level. While the creative insubordinates went ahead despite the potential for sanction by their superiors, most principals lacked the intestinal fortitude to ignore the threats of their immediate superiors (the district superintendents, as formerly constituted) and other central administration bureaucrats.

The Chicago School Reform Act broke the heavy yoke of the bureaucracy and shifted the locus of principals' accountability from administrative superiors to parent-dominated local school councils. It was assumed that the primary concern of parents and community representatives would be student achievement. The reformers believed that principals would be empowered to exercise the instructional leadership necessary for effective schooling by removing the potential for bureaucratic sanctions, by granting principals the authority to shape the composition of the faculty of their schools, and by providing the flexibility and resources for school improvement planning.

Participatory Decision-Making

A second tenet of the reform act is the principle of participatory management, which has been sweeping across the U.S. business community. The trend in business toward decentralization and site-based management is rooted in the conviction that employees are more productive when they participate in the decisions that affect their effort. In public education that theory is embedded in the notion of school-based management or school-based decision-making. Activists in Chicago's school reform effort had examined several examples of school-based management.

Karl Marburger (1985), of the National Center for Citizens in Education, was consulted several times about his experiences with school-based management in communities across the country, including St. Louis, Salt Lake City, and New York. In Marburger's experimental sites, school improvement councils were half parents, half staff. But they enjoyed no additional powers at the school level, different from those previously experienced by the school staff. Their power at the school site depended on the extent to which principals wished to share the power they exercised. Marburger emphasized that school-based decision-making was a voluntary sharing of power by the general superintendent and by principals at local schools. Given the intransigence of the Chicago superintendent and the perceived number of ineffective principals, however, the Marburger approach was rejected.

The approach taken by several local affiliates of the American Federation of Teachers (AFT), parent of the Chicago Teachers Union, looked more promising. Hammond (Indiana) and Dade County (Florida) were experimenting with school improvement councils at participating local schools. These councils were authorized to develop school improvement plans that might even violate board of education regulations or provisions of the union contract. By agreement between the board of education and the union, waivers could be granted for potential violations of those regulations or provisions.

Elements of the AFT approach were incorporated into the Chicago School Reform Act. Although the local school councils were not to be dominated by teachers and professional staff members, as in Hammond and Dade County, teachers do have a role on the LSCs. However, the major parallel with the AFT approach is vested in the PPAC, the Professional Personnel Advisory Committee, which is meant to work collaboratively with the school principal on designing a school improvement plan, on matters of curriculum, and on other instructional matters. The reform act explicitly calls for the provision of waivers from both board of education policies and employee collective-bargaining agreements (P.A. 85-1418, Sec. 34-2.3). Since the Chicago Teachers Union had initiated the discussion of contract waivers, it is not surprising that waiver language was added to the contract negotiated during summer 1990 to reflect provisions of the reform act.

Educational Bankruptcy

One other important provision was included in the reform act on the basis of experiments in school reform elsewhere in the nation. In New Jersey and several other states, so-called "school bankruptcy" laws had been enacted, under which the state could declare a school district educationally bankrupt and move to take control of the district from local officials. In response to concerns that LSCs would become unaccountable for improvement at their schools, a similar provision was incorporated into

Chicago's school reform act. Reformers placed primary reliance, however, upon the accountability dictated by biennial elections for members of the local school councils. As in most other jurisdictions in this country, the primary responsibility for effective LSCs lies with the electorate.

The Necessity of a Legislative Approach

Why was legislation necessary? In other locales, less radical school-based management approaches have been undertaken voluntarily. In St. Louis and in several community elementary districts in New York City, for example, school-based plans were implemented with the consultation of Marburger and his associates. In Salt Lake City, under former superintendent Donald Thomas, school councils operated for a dozen years, although their effectiveness was questioned by outside researchers (Malen and Ogawa 1988). In Hammond, Dade County, and several other cities with AFT locals, school-based management was incorporated into the union contract.

In each of these situations, the key ingredient was the willingness of the superintendent of schools to engage in some form of power-sharing. Similarly, at the local school level, a necessary element was the willingness of the principal to enter into a power-sharing arrangement. Only in Hammond, after years of implementation, was there any requirement that principals be willing to engage in power-sharing or face removal.

In Chicago these conditions simply did not exist. As has already been demonstrated, the general superintendent was focused on power accumulation rather than power-sharing. His budget proposals progressively drained resources from the schools while expanding his bureaucratic empire. He accused those who questioned his priorities of "trashing" the public schools and, referring to their support by private foundations, of "pimping off the miseries of low income students." In sharp contrast to his counterparts in Dade County, Hammond, Rochester, San Diego, and Cincinnati, his approach to the teachers' union and other employee groups was confrontational rather than collaborative. The prickly relationships between administration and union culminated in the nineteen-day teachers' strike in fall 1987. The school reform effort gained significant momentum as a result of that strike.

In the absence of any inclination toward voluntary agreements that might lead to improvement of the Chicago public schools, an effort was mounted through the mayor's office to coerce the school system and its employees into a set of agreements patterned after the Boston Compact

(Schwartz and Hargroves 1986; Cippolone 1986). In October 1986, Mayor Harold Washington convened an education summit focused on what he called the "learn-earn connection." Facing a reelection campaign the next spring, Washington perceived potential vulnerability in the city's high minority-youth unemployment rate and in the high dropout rates and weak qualifications of public-school graduates. He called together some forty representatives of the business community, the school system, the teachers' union, area universities, and civic groups to address these issues.

The first year of the Education Summit was built upon the false premise that the school system would willingly take steps to reform itself if offered jobs for qualified graduates. The assumption was that promises of expanded employment opportunities for graduates would induce the administration to take steps to expand the number of its students who both graduated and showed higher achievement levels. The fallacy in the assumption was that Chicago school administrators cared what happened to their students after they leave high school. For school systems receive no inducements for the success of their students after they leave the system. So long as pupils are enrolled, the system receives state aid tied to a student-based formula. But even this aid is no great inducement to retain students, for the aid formula in Illinois provides less than one-half of the per-pupil costs of education, while property tax revenue is not affected by enrollment declines (for example, declines resulting from high dropout rates—cf. Hess and Lauber 1985). The fallacy was in assuming that school administrators would be willing to undergo the pain of restructuring and resource reallocation—that is, firing or reassigning their friends and colleagues—to secure a benefit for graduating students. In this event, summit-sponsored negotiations between the business community and the school system failed during summer 1987. They foundered on the superintendent's demand for $83 million in additional support before the system would agree to any significant effort to improve its schools.

In the second year of the mayor's Education Summit, after the disastrous 1987 school strike, the fears and desires of system administrators and union representatives were largely ignored. Under immense political pressure after the strike, neither administrators nor union leaders could refuse to participate in agreements that were dominated by the desires of parent and business representatives. Still, it was obvious to most participants that administrators and board members had little intent to implement significant aspects of the summit agreements. Meanwhile, Mayor Washington died during the second year of the summit and was replaced by a weak "acting mayor" who showed little inclination to pressure the school administration to adopt significant reform.

In addition to the contextual issues that made legislation appropriate, there were certain requirements to change existing law. The compromise enacted in 1978 about the use of State Chapter I funds had been flagrantly violated by the board of education. Correcting that situation meant sharply reducing the board's range of discretion. Similarly, the creation of LSCs with real power meant replacing the local school improvement council provisions of the 1985 reform act. The effort to change the relationships between school site employees, so that custodians and lunchroom managers would be responsive to principals, also required changing the school code's previous provisions. New governance and certification provisions had to be inserted in place of existing provisions of the school code. Thus, legislation was needed to correct previous statutory mandates.

New legislation was also required to alter certain behavior patterns. The Chicago Panel had demonstrated the insatiable growth of the central bureaucracy, eating up the newly acquired resources of the school system. If school reform were to work and new discretionary funds were to become available at the school level, this propensity for top-heavy growth had to be constrained. Thus, a cap on the size of the administration was written into the statutes, along with monitoring authority for the state board of education.

Reform Implementation

Once the Chicago School Reform Act was signed in 1988, attention shifted back to Chicago. The general superintendent created a reform task force, with eighteen subordinate task forces, to examine changes required by the legislation. Still, resistance to the mandates of the act was high among administrators and members of the board that was to be replaced by an interim board on July 1, 1989. The primary election for a permanent mayor to serve out the balance of Mayor Washington's term was scheduled for March 1989. Richard M. Daley, son of Chicago's former mayor, became the leading candidate. He made education reform the centerpiece of his campaign. Several education reform activists took active roles in his campaign and in shaping his school reform platform. Once again, school reform was caught up in mayoral, and thereby racial, politics. With Daley's victories in the primary and general elections, school reform gained an active booster in city hall.

He was able to forge an alliance with the speaker of the state House of Representatives to achieve two significant victories in the spring 1989 legislative session: the date of implementation of school reform was pushed forward to May 1, 1989, and an increase in the income tax was passed to provide new revenues for the city and the Board of Education.

On May 26, Daley appointed a new interim board of education, dominated by persons with ties to the school reform movement.

During late spring and summer 1989, the interim board accomplished four of five major tasks assigned to it under the reform act (Chicago Panel on Public School Policy and Finance, 1989). It cut 544 jobs out of the central administration and reallocated the resulting resources to local school budgets as discretionary funds for the forthcoming local school councils. It negotiated a contract extension with its employee groups to ensure the smooth opening of schools in the fall. It also negotiated the dismissal of the general superintendent and hired his replacement. And the interim board successfully conducted elections for the local school councils. Some 313,000 persons went to the polls, there to choose among more than 17,000 candidates the 5,400 parents, community representatives, and teachers who would sit on the new LSCs. The interim board failed only in its mandate to submit a system-wide reform plan to the overseeing Chicago School Finance Authority before the opening of the school year. (A draft was submitted to satisfy the legal requirement; it was then returned to the board to be amended and resubmitted by late January.)

With the election of the 540 local school councils, reform moved to the school level. In the first year, LSCs were to design and adopt their local school improvement plans, to adopt a school budget for the ensuing school year, and in half the system's schools to determine whether to terminate the incumbent principal and select a new one or to offer the incumbent a new contract. The remaining schools were scheduled to make a similar determination about their principals during 1990–91. With few exceptions, the LSCs carried out all of these responsibilities.

Citywide training and organizing efforts continued during the first year of implementation, with reform groups offering extensive training to local school council candidates in the months prior to the October 12 and 13 elections. These groups also mobilized to get out the vote. After the elections, they provided up to thirty hours of training for individual school councils that requested this outside assistance. The reform groups also mobilized widespread support for school reform by involving more than one hundred organizations in a Citywide Reform Coalition to address continuing problems in improving the quality of education in Chicago schools. Finally, the reform groups, through their own coalition, the Alliance for Better Chicago Schools (ABCs), continued to pressure the interim board and the new general superintendent for timely and appropriate support from the central administration for school-based decision-making.

On November 30, 1990, the momentum related to the implementation of the Chicago School Reform Act was interrupted by the announcement of an opinion by the Illinois Supreme Court that the act was unconstitutional. The ruling was in regard to *Fumarolo et al.* vs. *Chicago Board of Education,* a suit brought by members of the Chicago Principals Association. The principals claimed the law unconstitutionally deprived them of their tenure rights and put their jobs in jeopardy by subjecting them to the evaluation of local school councils, which were unconstitutionally elected.

The Illinois Supreme Court agreed with the principals that the LSCs were elected using an unconstitutional voting mechanism that diluted the vote of community residents (who could elect only two members while parents could elect six). The court ruled the LSCs were important units of government and therefore should be subjected to strict scrutiny under the equal protection clauses of the federal and state constitutions, even though they could not levy taxes. The court was silent about the election of teachers. It gave no indication that the weighted constitution of the LSCs (6 parents, 2 community representatives, 2 teachers, and the principal) need be changed. Thus, a voting mechanism that allows parents and community residents alike to vote for the 6 parents and 2 community residents would probably be acceptable.

The court found that the principals' claims about their tenure rights were invalid. It ruled that their tenure had been established in law, had not been incorporated in separate contracts with the Chicago board of education, and therefore could be discontinued in law as long as due process was followed in the legislative procedures. The court stayed the effect of its opinion until motions for a rehearing could be filed, and it invited the city or the legislature to fix the offending parts of the act before its ruling became final.

On January 8, 1991, the Illinois General Assembly enacted P.A. 86-1477 to maintain the reform effort in Chicago. The new act validated all past actions of the Chicago board of education and local school councils. It provided that the mayor of Chicago appoint all members of LSCs and the board of education to their posts until new elections could be held in October 1991. The mayor had already agreed to reappoint all present members of both bodies. These members cannot be dismissed by the mayor. The ammendatory act required that a new election mechanism be adopted by the legislature prior to July 1, 1991. Otherwise, most of the provisions of the amendatory act were simply restatements of the provisions of P.A. 85-1418.

In July 1991, the Illinois General Assembly enacted a new voting mechanism which gave parents and community residents the right to vote for both parent and community representatives on the Local School Councils. Legislation was also passed strengthening the principal's supervision over the custodial and lunchroom staff and providing a mechanism to remove non-performing LSC members.

Thus, Chicago school reform is back on track.

Conclusion

The Chicago School Reform Act inaugurated a historic experiment in decentralizing authority in a major urban school system. The act was designed to create the conditions for the development of "effective schools" throughout the city. During its first year of the reform plan's implementation, its basic elements were successfully put in place. Local school councils were established at every school. In half the schools, a principal selection process was undertaken; the result was a turnover of at least one-third of the affected principals. School improvement plans have been designed, and lump sum budgets fashioned. It is too early to see any significant impact on student achievement as a result of the initial year. This is the challenge now facing the Chicago school reform effort: to implement changes in schools at the classroom level that create better environments for learning. To do that, local school leaders need many more ideas than they currently have about how to proceed in their schools. To foster the discussion of viable school improvement options is the task before us now.

References

Brookover, William B., and Lezotte, Lawrence B. 1979. *Changes in School Characteristics Coincident with Changes in Student Achievement.* East Lansing: Michigan State University.

"Byrd Defends School Anti-Dropout Role." 1987. *Chicago Tribune,* January 18.

"Chancellor Seeks Dropout Program In New York's Elementary Schools." 1988. *New York Times,* September 24.

Chicago Board of Education. 1985. *Racial/Ethnic Survey—Students, as of October 31.* Chicago: The Board.

Chicago Panel on Public School Policy and Finance. 1987. "Testimony Before the Chicago Board of Education." Distributed by Chicago Panel on Public School Policy and Finance, Chicago, October 14.

Chicago Panel on Public School Policy and Finance. 1988. "Illegal Use of State Chapter I Funds." Paper distributed by Chicago Panel on Public School Policy and Finance, Chicago.

Chicago Panel on Public School Policy and Finance. 1989. "Interim Board Accomplishes Four of Five Miracles." *Panel Update.* Chicago: Chicago Panel on Public School Policy and Finance, October.

Cippolone, Anthony. 1986. "Boston Compact in the Schools: Does It Make a Difference?" Unpublished paper presented at the American Educational Research Association, San Francisco.

COLEMAN, JAMES S. 1966. *Report of Commission on Equal Educational Opportunity.* Washington, D.C.: U.S. Printing Office.

COUNCIL OF GREAT CITY SCHOOLS. 1987. *Challenges to Urban Education: Results in the Making.* Washington, D.C.: The Council.

DESIGNS FOR CHANGE. 1985. *The Bottom Line: Chicago's Failing Schools and How to Save Them.* Chicago: Designs for Change.

EDMONDS, RONALD. 1979. "Effective Schools for the Urban Poor." *Educational Leadership* 37 (October 15–18): 15–24.

HALLETT, ANNE CARLSON, and HESS, G. ALFRED, JR. 1982. *Budget Cuts at the Board of Education.* Chicago: Chicago Panel on Public School Finances.

HESS, G. ALFRED, JR., and LAUBER, DIANA. 1985. *Dropouts from the Chicago Public Schools.* Chicago: Chicago Panel on Public School Policy and Finance.

HESS, G. ALFRED, JR.; LYONS, ARTHUR; and CORSINO, LOU. 1989. *Against the Odds: The Early Identification of Dropouts.* Chicago: Chicago Panel on Public School Policy and Finance.

HESS, G. ALFRED, JR., and WARDEN, CHRISTINA A. 1987. *Who Benefits from Desegregation?* Chicago: Chicago Panel on Public School Policy and Finance.

HESS, G. ALFRED, JR.; WELLS, EMILY; PRINDLE, CAROL; KAPLAN, BEATRICE; and LIFFMAN, PAUL. 1986. *Where Is Room 185? How Schools Can Reduce Their Dropout Problem.* Chicago: Chicago Panel on Public School Policy and Finance.

MALEN, BETTY, and OGAWA, RODNEY T. 1988. "Professional-Patron Influence on Site Based Governance Councils: A Confounding Case Study." *Educational Evaluation and Policy Analysis* 10 (4): 251–70.

MARBURGER, KARL. 1985. *One School at a Time.* Columbia, Md.: National Committee for Citizens in Education.

MASSACHUSETTS ADVOCACY CENTER. 1988. *The Way Out: Student Exclusion Practices in Middle Schools.* Boston: The Center.

MORRIS, VAN CLEVE; CROWSON, ROBERT; PORTER-GEHRIE, CYNTHIA; and HURWITZ, EMMANUAL. 1984. *Principals in Action: The Reality of Managing Schools.* Columbus, Ohio: Merill.

NATIONAL COMMISSION ON EXCELLENCE IN EDUCATION. 1983. *A Nation at Risk.* Washington, DC: U.S. Government Printing Office.

NELSON, F. HOWARD; HESS, G. ALFRED JR.; and YONG, RICHARD. 1985. *Implementing Educational Reform in Illinois.* Chicago: Chicago Panel on Public School Finances.

SCHWARTZ, ROBERT, and JEANETTE HARGROVES. 1986. "The Boston Compact." *Metropolitan Education* 3: 14–24.

STEPHENSON, ROBERT S. 1985. *A Study of the Longitudinal Dropout Rate: 1980 Eighth-grade Cohort Followed from June 1980 Through February 1985.* Miami: Dade County Public Schools.

5

An Urban Superintendent's Perspective on Education Reform

Thomas W. Payzant

There has never been any doubt about America's commitment to progress. Our relatively brief national history is full of social, economic, and political examples that have caught the attention and won the admiration of observers from around the world. Scholars may argue about myth and reality, but the spirit of discovery, advancement, and accomplishment permeates America's experience as it has become the strongest democracy in the world and a formidable economic and political power. Despite a record that shows more than two hundred years of often dramatic change, however, some observers warn as we enter the last decade of the twentieth century that our minds are closed (Bloom 1987), decline has begun (Kennedy 1987), and progress has stalled.

Over the years many observers have tried to capture the essence of America. Few have done it better than Alexis de Tocqueville, whose observations made more than one hundred and fifty years ago have stood the test of time better than those of more recent commentators. Tocqueville (1969, p. 12) was clear with his criticisms, but he admired much of what he found in the young American democracy and he was sanguine about its future.

> The first duty imposed on those who now direct society is to educate democracy; to put, if possible, new life into its beliefs; to purify its mores; to control its actions; gradually to substitute understanding of statecraft for present inexperience and knowledge of its true interests for blind instincts; to adapt government to the needs of time and place; and to modify it as men and circumstances require. . . .

77

> Hence, we have our democracy without those elements which might have integrated its vices and brought out its natural good points. While we can already see the ills it entails, we are as yet unaware of the benefits it might bring.

Public education and schools have their important place in America's history and Tocqueville (1969, p. 45) recognized this, too, when he wrote that

> It is the provision for public education which, from the very first, throws into clearest relief the originality of American civilization.

Were Tocqueville visiting America today, he might be surprised to find that the structure and organization of schools, the roles of people in them and the teaching methods used are more similar to than different from those used a century ago. He probably would have predicted the tension that exists between those who want to preserve tradition and those who call for radical changes in the schools, and he would be delighted that his earlier observations about the press, the public, and the experts are still timely, as educators wrestle with the attention focused on their enterprise and the public pressure for its reform, not knowing whether to resent the meddling or embrace the interest.

Certainly Tocqueville would have been intrigued by one dramatic change: our pursuit of the goal of universal public education. The difficulty is that completion of high school in 1991 does not guarantee the access to economic, social, and personal success and fulfillment that completion of an eighth-grade education provided as recently as the 1940s. Expectations for what students must know and be able to do are higher, and we are anxious about the widening gap between what they should learn and what they demonstrate they have learned.

When data on student achievement, high-school completion rates, courses taken, matriculation at postsecondary institutions, and college graduation are disaggregated the message is even more distressing. By these and other measures, African Americans and Hispanic Americans are significantly behind their white and Asian American counterparts. International comparisons of achievement of students living in industrialized nations also place Americans near the bottom in most subjects. Demographers have heightened our awareness and anxiety as they describe an increasingly racially and ethnically diverse American population, with growing numbers of "haves" and "have-nots" and a shrinking middle class.

The case for change is strong. It cannot be business as usual in our schools if we expect to carry out the traditional purposes of American education—development of the mind, economic self-sufficiency, citizenship, character formation, and personal fulfillment—and do it in a new context in which educators both talk and act on the belief that all children can learn and deserve to be taught. More of the same is not good enough.

In this chapter I make a case for how educators and policymakers should proceed to renew and change America's public schools and how policies and practices that deal with issues of restructuring, parent enabling, choice, assessment, and accountability are critical components of a workable strategy for change. While I will cite examples from my experience in San Diego, the sixth largest city in America, my larger purpose is to convince educators and policymakers that many of the challenges facing public education in America are not unique to urban, suburban, or rural areas and that the responses to those challenges will require us to open our minds to new ways of working together to solve the problems that ultimately are the responsibility of everyone.

School Restructuring

Restructuring is a term borrowed from business. There it is associated with strategic planning that results in moving more decision-making responsibility and accountability down the organization chart to people closest to the customer and to the service or product provided. Corporate support functions are streamlined, layers eliminated, bureaucracies trimmed. The resulting organizational change is systemic. It typically includes fundamental questioning of traditional assumptions, leading in turn to dramatic redefinitions of roles and responsibilities for people throughout the organization. Properly managed, restructuring can result in radical changes in organizational culture and revitalize companies that are stagnating and in danger of failing.

While there is much to be learned from the private sector's experience with restructuring, many public policymakers, educators, and others associated with education have been apprehensive about replicating the experience of business in America's public schools. They cite differences between the public and private sectors, the controls placed on government institutions, and the special nature of a people-intensive enterprise as reasons for caution in responding to suggestions that schools should be run like businesses. Nonetheless, it is clear that restructuring is becoming one of the cornerstones of educational reform for the 1990s, even though no consensus has emerged on what it is and how policymakers should deal with it.

Richard Elmore and Associates (1990) suggest three approaches to the debate on restructuring schools. First, schools can be improved by taking what we already know from research about learning and teaching and applying it in practice. This will necessitate fundamental changes in the way schools operate. Second, schools can be improved by professionalizing teaching and giving educators more control over the conditions of their work. The roles and responsibilities of the adults working in schools and in district offices would be quite different from what they traditionally have been. Third, schools can be improved by encouraging parents and students to hold them accountable for learning outcomes. New forms of parent involvement, choice among schools, and educating parents to improve their parenting skills are among the issues to be considered.

Another possible dimension of restructuring involves interagency collaboration among the many institutions that provide services for youth and families. Such collaboration can result in agencies finding new ways to improve the quality of the services each provides. It has the potential to steer discussion away from the protection of institutional turf and denial of responsibility for outcomes and toward collaborative strategies that lead to better use of limited resources and deliver higher quality services.

There are some barriers to restructuring. In a nationwide survey for the Southwest Educational Development Laboratory, Duttweiler and Mutchler (1990) found the following: 51 percent of respondents resisted changing roles and responsibilities; 38 percent feared losing power; 38 percent saw a lack of definition and clarity; 38 percent believed that resources are inadequate or inappropriate; 30 percent acknowledged a lack of skills; 27 percent bemoaned the dearth of hierarchical support; and 19 percent feared taking risks. All the expected factors that cause resistance to change will be present, particularly when the goal is fundamental and dramatic systemic change rather than peripheral tinkering with the status quo.

What policy directions are necessary to encourage restructuring of our schools and school districts? I will use San Diego's experience with restructuring to introduce the discussion of key questions and to suggest some implications for policymakers as they explore ways to initiate and support reforms to enhance learning for all students.

The San Diego Experience

With 122,000 students, the San Diego city school district is diverse and growing. By the year 2000, the enrollment will reach 140,000 students. Today, the school population is 27 percent Hispanic, 19 percent Asian, 16 percent African American, and 38 percent white. The two largest Asian American groups are Filipino and Indochinese. Students speak more than 60 different native languages. More than 26,000 students have limited English proficiency. Almost 13,000 students are enrolled in special education programs.

Although student achievement in reading, language arts, and mathematics improved at most grade levels and for most racial and ethnic groups during the 1980s, a significant achievement gap still exists between Hispanics and African Americans on one hand and Asians and whites on the other. The average four-year dropout rate in 1989 was 26.9 percent, which means that of every 1,000 students who began the ninth grade, 269 will not graduate with their peers four years later. For African Americans and Hispanics the rates were higher, 28.6 percent and 39 percent respectively.

San Diego faces many challenges that will not be met unless dramatic changes occur. Both equity and excellence are goals to be reached. Restructuring in San Diego is a process for renewal and change. It is not a project or a program that leads to a specific product or outcome. The catalyst for our current restructuring efforts was the findings of a seventeen-member group of community leaders appointed by the superintendent in May 1986 to study the impact of changing technology, demographic and economic shifts, and cultural pluralism on the needs of San Diego's children in the twenty-first century. This group, the Schools of the Future Commission, presented its report in June 1987. The report, *Which Way to the Future? San Diego and Its Schools at a Crossroads* stated that profound discrepancies exist between what schools provide children today and what they must provide in the years just ahead.

The commission argued that, in the future, children must be able to reeducate themselves throughout life. They must be able to communicate in other languages, to make difficult decisions about the effects of new technologies on our environment, and to find employment in an increasingly competitive skilled job market. The commission urged the district to explore school restructuring whereby teachers, other educators, and parents would be empowered to make decisions about classroom and school organization, curriculum, budget, staffing, and accountability to enhance teaching and learning for all students. The board of education accepted the commission's report and recommendations in June 1987, and the superintendent appointed a leadership team, the Innovation and Change Leadership Group (ICLG), which included equal representation of teachers and administrators and also contained parent and community representatives. The ICLG was responsible for developing a plan to implement the Schools of the Future recommendations, and is now coordinating restructuring efforts throughout the district.

The ICLG's first task was to broaden the district employees' knowledge and the public's awareness of reform issues. From November 1987 to March 1988 the ICLG worked with several local universities, the San Diego County Office of Education, and the Association of California School Administrators to sponsor seminars featuring participants involved with the Carnegie Task Force on Teaching as a Profession, Pittsburgh's

Schenley High School, Jefferson County (Kentucky) Schools, and Dade County (Florida) Schools.

The ICLG then wrote a "Purpose and Belief Statement" and set forth the criteria and process for enlisting schools in the restructuring effort. The group's core beliefs defined the purpose and parameters of restructuring. It said restructuring

- is a commitment to a long-term strategic planning process
- can be accomplished with existing district resources and within district policies and contracts
- requires an environment of trust, flexibility, and risk-taking
- requires a balance between greater autonomy and more responsibility for schools
- can be successful in San Diego and result in a valuable model for other communities. (San Diego Board of Education 1988)

To launch the restructuring process and to heighten awareness and interest in the initiative, the ICLG sponsored "Super Saturday: A School Restructuring Work Session" in April 1988. Teams of five—the principal, two teachers, a staff member, and a parent—from 38 schools voluntarily convened for a day-long planning session to learn about the restructuring process. The event was co-sponsored by the Panasonic Foundation, which formed a partnership with San Diego City Schools for long-term support of the district's restructuring efforts.

After opening comments and an overview of the general concepts of restructuring, Super Saturday participants divided into smaller working groups to review a draft of the ICLG's purpose and belief statement and to discuss the process for enlisting schools in the restructuring movement. This required meeting with faculty, staff, parents, and students.

According to the guidelines, if two-thirds of its faculty and staff voted to support the belief statements and if parents and students generally indicated their support of restructuring, a school could express its written intent to participate. After its enlistment, each school would then elect a steering committee responsible for coordinating the planning process. By late spring 1988, twenty-five San Diego schools had committed to participate in restructuring.

At the end of June 1988, teams from 15 elementary, 6 middle or junior high, and 4 senior high schools met for "Super Planning Week," a four-day strategic-planning workshop to develop the skills needed to lead a school staff through the planning process. Each team participated in a model-planning and team-building exercise, which included how to develop a vision-and-goal statement, how to generate options for achieving that vision, how to write an implementation plan, and how to design ongoing evaluation and assessment procedures. In the weeks after, the district initiated several activities to support restructuring efforts in the schools. Support groups were formed at all school levels to facilitate communication and collaboration among restructuring schools.

At the same time, top district administrators began to meet with their staffs to discuss how the central office could best support restructuring schools. Their discussions focused on the effects of greater school autonomy on the relationship between central office and individual schools and what new systems, procedures, and policies might need to be developed to promote successful restructuring. The superintendent delivered a progress report to the larger school community in his annual address to district leaders in August 1988. His message conveyed his support, enthusiasm, and hope that school restructuring would be a key theme for the 1988–89 school year. Carrying that theme forward, beginning in October 1988 the district sponsored a series of workshops geared to the professional development of teachers. Topics included how to increase the number of minority students graduating from high school and entering four-year colleges and how to use Socratic teaching methods most effectively.

The school restructuring initiative was formally recognized by the board of education in a policy statement on November 8, 1988. This particular school-board meeting, which was held at a restructuring school, Linda Vista Elementary, featured comments from various restructuring schools and from members of the ICLG. The board's policy expressed its support for "school restructuring as a process to achieve a fundamental change in school organization and instruction that will prepare all students for the future" (San Diego Board of Education 1988). It set forth the board's beliefs about restructuring, established requirements for participating schools, and outlined the planning and implementation process.

The policy states that risk is manageable in a climate of change if those who participate in restructuring hold certain common beliefs and faith in the overall process. These include belief in the potential of all students to achieve success and become lifelong learners; belief that school should be the focus of change and should be given autonomy as well as responsibility to realize that change; belief that change will take time but can be accomplished effectively; and recognition that the process involves many people whose roles will change, but that new empowering, not limiting, relationships can emerge among them.

The policy formally established the planning and implementation process outlined by the ICLG and cited the need for a waiver process. Without the ability for schools to waive state and federal regulations, administrative procedures, board-adopted policy, or negotiated contracts, major organizational change would not be possible. In January 1989 the board approved a waiver process for school restructuring. The first waiver that enabled teachers and parents to participate in the selection of a principal was granted to a school in February.

The San Diego Teachers Association had been involved in the restructuring process since the fall of 1987. The president and past president of the union were charter members of the ICLG. It was not until fall 1988, however, that an opportunity occurred for dramatically different working relationships between the school district and all its employee bargaining units. In October the board and teachers' association reached a landmark collective-bargaining agreement. A new four-year contract based on collaboration, shared decision-making, and trust provided all involved with the challenges to leave behind ten years of adversarial collective bargaining. One new element in the agreement addressed restructuring and educational reform. The contract recognized that restructuring may call for changing roles and responsibilities, including more teacher involvement in decision-making at the school level, new systems of accountability, altered schedules, and encouragement for peer coaching, observation schedules, and team performance reviews. A system to review potential waiver requests to accommodate school reform experiments was written into the contract. After this agreement with the teachers, each of the other employee unions negotiated four-year contracts with the district that expire in 1992 and contain similar language on restructuring.

Restructuring does not simply give school staff members and parents license to do whatever they want. Successful organizations in both the public and private sectors that are committed to decentralization of decision-making and responsibility for outcomes also have a vision for the organization, a mission statement, and expectation for action. During 1989 the superintendent and board of education worked with the ICLG and others in the district and community to develop a vision, mission statement, and expectations for action, all of them centered on the enhancement of teaching and learning. The district's vision has three parts—change, excellence, and empowerment.

The board and superintendent also reviewed the purposes of education for San Diego students and restated their belief that everything the district does to enhance teaching and learning in schools should be influenced by a sense of purpose.

By the spring of 1990, 49 of San Diego's 155 schools were involved in the district's restructuring initiative. Thirty are elementary schools, 11 are middle or junior-high schools, 6 are high schools, and 2 are atypical schools. A majority have conducted serious planning efforts leading to innovative organizational and instructional change. About one-fifth have slowed or stalled in their planning.

Some schools that have not taken an official staff vote to restructure have actually moved more boldly to examine and change some of their instructional practices than the official restructuring schools. A small number, perhaps a dozen schools, have begun to implement plans that require fundamental systemic changes in teaching and learning. What follows are four mini–case studies that provide examples of restructuring in San Diego.

Linda Vista Elementary School: Restructuring Around Language

Linda Vista is a pre-kindergarten-through-grade-6 elementary school located in an area of San Diego traditionally known as a "newcomer" community. As immigrant groups establish themselves in the city, many settle first in the Linda Vista area because of the availability of low-cost housing. The school's population of 923 students is 52 percent Indochinese, 25 percent Hispanic, 11 percent white, and 7 percent African American. More than 15 primary languages are spoken by the students.

Linda Vista was one of the first schools in the district to engage in restructuring. Beginning in 1987, staff members, parents, and central office personnel held a series of meetings to discuss new ways to organize the instructional program at the school. They developed a plan that divided the day into two parts. Mornings are reserved for language skills and social studies. For the morning classes, the students are grouped not by age but by proficiency in English. In the afternoon, students are grouped heterogeneously for a program in which two subjects are taught for three weeks, after which two others follow. For example, after three weeks of computer writing and library research, a student might spend the next three weeks investigating art and music.

Innovative staffing arrangements include use of part-time personnel to reduce class size in the morning program and to allow for teacher specialization in the afternoon classes.

Grades have been eliminated. The staff is developing plans for the use of student portfolios and other performance-based assessment techniques. Without the pressure of grades, students are progressing more quickly in English, and attendance has improved. Also, in 1989–90, for the first time, the school placed 27 children in gifted classes.

Correia Junior High School: Restructuring into Interdisciplinary Teams

Correia Junior High School enrolls nearly 1,000 students. White students make up about 52 percent of the enrollment, and Hispanic and African American students constitute 34 and 9 percent, respectively. The rest are Indochinese and Filipino.

Correia offers a balanced curriculum to its diverse student population, emphasizing an interdisciplinary approach to teaching and learning. During the 1988–89 and 1989–90 school years the staff engaged in a planning process to restructure its academic program by forming interdisciplinary teams of teachers. Many teachers participated in summer curriculum development institutes. Several teams presented innovative programs addressing such areas as bilingual studies, extended academic core curriculum, and gifted education.

One team provided instruction in English, social science, and mathematics to about 120 eighth-grade students. Although these 4 teachers used interdisciplinary teaching techniques to some extent, their restructuring efforts in 1989–90 focused primarily on organization. Their 120 students were divided into clusters of 12 students each. These clusters then grouped to form different-sized classes for instruction. When large-group instruction took place, 1 teacher might lecture to a class of 60 students. This meant that 3 other teachers were free to work with the 60 other students in small-group settings.

Because the same 120 students were shared by 4 teachers, the team was free to design a schedule that met the changing needs of students, teachers, and subject matter. Teachers treated the four-period block as shared instructional time rather than separate periods and did not follow the school's fifty-five-minute class time and five-minute passing time bell schedule.

The principal reported that only 6 of the 120 youngsters in the core classes were referred to the school counselor during 1989–90. In a group of that size, at least 30 students would typically have been referred for disciplinary reasons. Parents of students in the classes also had more frequent contact with the school than other parents in the school. They tended to make phone calls to the school, visit classes, and attend parent conferences and open houses more regularly.

Students in the interdisciplinary classes had better attendance records than the other students. The greater number of collaborative activities and assignments in the interdisciplinary classroom seemed to improve attendance because students depended on one another for completion of group projects. Finally, when the California Test of Basic Skills scores of these students were compared with those of other students in the school, they were significantly higher in eight of ten areas tested.

San Diego High School: Restructuring into Houses and Magnet Programs

San Diego High School is a large inner-city school located in downtown San Diego. Although most of its 1,600 students come from neighborhoods that surround downtown, approximately 250 come from other areas of the city for the International Baccalaureate (IB) and Writing Academy magnet programs offered at the school. Over 50 percent of the population is Hispanic, 30 percent is white, and African Americans and Indochinese each constitute about 10 percent of the total.

In 1985, San Diego High reorganized to offer its two new magnet programs. The academically challenging IB program helped to encourage many highly motivated students to stay and brought in youngsters from other areas. The Writing Academy focused on the improvement of students' communication skills by training teachers in writing-across-the-curriculum techniques and by offering specialized student services and programs.

During spring 1989 the staff began to explore the idea of restructuring. The team, which expanded to include parents and students, chose to focus on improving the education for at-risk students. After several meetings the staff made a decision to plan for school-wide advisories to help students feel more "at home" at school. A subgroup also made plans to reorganize their instructional methods and curriculum. They visited restructuring schools and programs in other districts across the country.

In September 1989 several initiatives began at San Diego High School, including team teaching, flexible scheduling, and computer-assisted learning for students with few entering credits. In a noncurriculum area, the school staff selected a budget committee to oversee the curriculum budget and parts of the principal's discretionary fund.

Although restructuring efforts are still in the formative stage, there are some clear early indications of improved student performance. Test scores of twelfth-grade students on the statewide district writing assessment in December 1989 improved significantly from the previous year, surpassing district and state averages. Attendance improved slightly, and the percentage of college preparatory courses taken rose from 51.6 percent in 1986–87 to 56.2 percent in 1988–89.

O'Farrell Community School for Advanced Studies: Restructuring a New School

O'Farrell Community School opened in fall 1990 with a seventh-grade class of approximately 350 students. The school features a new governance model and curriculum and instruction that respond to the academic, social, and emotional needs of early teens. In September 1991 the school expanded to a full 6-7-8 middle school with an enrollment of approximately 1,200 students.

For eighteen months before the school opened, educators and community members were actively involved in designing it. The central vision of the planning team was that all children can learn and should have access to the same high-level curriculum. The staff is committed to the goal that any child who spends three years at O'Farrell will be ready for the advanced academic program of any San Diego high school. They are also committed to meeting the social and emotional needs of all students and developing a sense of commitment to community and community service.

All students at O'Farrell are offered an interdisciplinary curriculum combining language arts, mathematics, social studies, and science. The school is divided into three educational "families," each with a student-to-teacher ratio of 22:1. Community service, art, music, industrial arts, and physical education are offered during a half-hour block each day. All students have a teacher/advocate and meet in an advocacy group daily. All teachers have one-and-a-half hours of common preparation time daily to meet with their colleagues, design school curricula, and make educational family and school decisions.

The school and the county department of social services have formed a partnership that includes on-site access to social service agencies and direct assistance in addressing the social and emotional needs of middle-grade children. A coordinator of these services, co-funded by the school and the Department of Social Services, is a regular member of the O'Farrell staff.

Central Office Restructuring

Through the first two-and-a-half years of restructuring in San Diego, the superintendent said that schools could volunteer to participate but that the central office had no choice. In December 1989 and January 1990 the superintendent met with teams from each school to present the district's new vision and its expectations for action. He stated that more of the same would not be good enough because the twin goals of equity and excellence had not been reached, the dropout rate was too high, and an achievement gap still existed, and many students from a growing and increasingly diverse student body were not succeeding in school or prepared for postsecondary education and the world of work. Schools might choose not to restructure, but no school could rest on its laurels as long as some children in the school are not succeeding.

In a similar presentation to teams of people from all central office departments the superintendent stated that as long as even one school in the district was restructuring, central office staff members would have to change their ways. The central office role would have to become one of motivating, enabling, facilitating, helping, and supporting rather than telling, directing, controlling, judging, and deciding.

By late spring 1990 the board had approved a reduced number of goals and objectives for 1990–92. These goals anticipate that all schools will become involved in restructuring, a process for renewal and change, although there will still be latitude for school staff and parents to determine how they will work to meet district goals and objectives in ways that respond to the unique needs of children in their schools.

Policy Implications of School Restructuring

What are the implications for state, school district, and local school action? Should state policymakers simply frame the discussion about educational change or should they prescribe the reforms? How do policymakers move their deliberations from a focus on compliance to a new focus on outcomes? What strategies will be necessary to design a comprehensive reform package and keep it from being dismembered as various interest groups object to specific parts of it? If restructuring involves change in traditional power relationships, what will be the incentives to realign the power? How will tensions between "top down" and "bottom up" policymaking be managed?

Dennis Gray (1990, p. 4) wrote in a recent issue of *Basic Education* that "this large cast of characters has now declared restructuring to be essential. Maybe that's right. We'll never know unless the policymakers and the teachers who have to make reform into something more than rhetoric just have the chance to become the kind of thoughtful people we all want the schools to produce after the reforming is done." It is the responsibility of policymakers at all levels to begin the thoughtful deliberations about restructuring that must inform future discussions with teachers, other educators, parents, and community members and give shape to wise public policy.

Governance

There is no one best way to reform public education. Clearly the states have major responsibility for schooling. Governors and legislators understand the limited role of the federal government. It is proper for them to take leadership in establishing a vision for public education in their states and to develop resource allocation plans that enable local school districts to meet the states' general expectations for action.

The major policy challenge facing state (and federal) policymakers in the 1990s is to restructure their own thinking and perhaps even their decision-making structures to change the policy focus from a narrow one dealing only with education and schools to a broader one that encompasses the wide-ranging needs of children, youth, and families and sees the connections among them. Policies addressing pregnancy prevention, preschool care, infant and child nutrition, parenting instruction, child care, welfare and work support programs, preschool education, health, and prevention and treatment of drug abuse all have implications for K–12 education. Painting a big policy picture in which all the elements are addressed and the whole becomes greater than the sum of its parts is the challenge. Policymakers must find new ways to deflect the special interests that today control so much policymaking by particularizing every decision and judging it against the limited criteria they prescribe. The cost of achieving this new kind of public policy will be the alienation of some special interests. It will require creativity in forming new coalitions to provide political bases for integrated decision-making.

Policymakers cannot rely on others to make the case for educational reform. One way all human beings resist change is to project the need for change onto someone else. It is easy to say that what I am doing is fine and what you are doing must change, but the test of leadership is to say that change begins with us. Since all of us are limited by our own experiences, leaders must often begin by exposing decision-makers to new ideas and examples of what others are doing. Governors and state legislators can model behavior for local policymakers and educators by demonstrating their openness to new ways of thinking, deciding, and acting.

This is not to say that the traditional forms of direction provided by executive and legislative branches of the states are inappropriate. For example, the state curriculum frameworks developed in California provide excellent guidelines and standards for school districts in each major curriculum area. They also are an important reference for the adoption of instructional materials and the development of performance-based assessment instruments that are used to determine what students know and can do. As state policymakers develop financial and other incentives for schools to change, they must resist the temptation to seek a single best way to entice or, worse yet, force schools to restructure. For example, it would be counterproductive to replace the traditional private sector industrial labor relations model of collective bargaining, which is used in the public sector in many states, with a single model of collaborative shared decision-making imposed on local schools.

Policy makers must avoid several minefields as they address education governance issues. There is a great temptation to mandate the involvement of people in shared decision-making as a basic component of a restructuring process, but mandatory participation and "bottom up" change via "top down" central policy direction can confuse those affected by the policy and result in policymakers having limited credibility. Policymakers committed to restructuring as a process for change properly make policies that answer the "what" questions and leave prescriptions and answers to the "how" questions to educators and parents who are closest to children and classrooms.

The second minefield to avoid is the one characterized by the knee-jerk reaction to crisis management. If policymakers respond immediately to a crisis by intervening with dogmatic, prescriptive policies that undermine their very efforts to push decision-making away from central sources of power to the grass roots, then there will never be the acceptance of responsibility for outcomes by those closest to the problems and their solution. Change takes time, and quick results cannot be expected when the organizational culture of schools and districts must change.

Professionalization of Teaching

Everything policymakers and educators do to restructure schools will be unimportant unless it results in better teaching and learning. The roles that teachers play and how their workplace is defined are critical. Our experience and common sense suggest that students will learn with good teachers, and teachers have a better chance to excel at teaching when the schools are organized to facilitate it. If good teachers view their workplaces in a negative way or find them inadequate, they will generally leave the school and perhaps even leave teaching. Even those who continue in the classroom often find their efforts to succeed thwarted by inadequate working conditions.

Changes in the workplace must be more than cosmetic for teachers to function as professionals, and the thrust of those changes must be to improve instruction for students. If teachers are to function as professionals, policymakers must include them in their deliberations and provide the status and recognition given to other professionals. Policies must encourage teachers to develop their own talents, to play different roles, and to accept different responsibilities without being forced to leave the classroom for economic gain. The work year and days of teachers must be changed to ensure them time for professional growth, involvement in decision-making in schools, planning, and interaction with colleagues and other adults. The teacher's isolation in the classroom in the traditionally structured school is one of the greatest barriers to professionalization.

Finding incentives for teachers to break out of the isolated classroom to work with their colleagues in teams, to engage in interdisciplinary teaching, to build time schedules that accommodate various teaching and learning strategies, and to group students in ways that encourage different rates and styles of learning are noble policy goals. Adequate facilities, decent equipment, and sufficient materials certainly are reasonable expectations for any professional to have about the workplace.

It is difficult to build political consensus around compensation policies for teachers. Years of tradition and the strong views of some teacher organizations discourage many policymakers from acting on alternatives to the single-salary schedule for teachers. Equally challenging is the development of approaches to performance appraisal that involve teachers in setting performance standards for their colleagues and taking responsibility for judging professional effectiveness as members of other professions do.

Policymakers must also encourage colleges and universities to change. Few teacher-training programs view the teacher as a professional functioning in a workplace quite different from what is typically found in schools today. The Holmes Group (1990, p. 38) urges teacher-educators to work with practicing teachers to help novice teachers "see and try a range of activities that teach from learners' strengths" and help children become active rather than passive learners. Although teacher-educators continue to advocate knowledge of subject matter and pedagogy, the Holmes Group argues persuasively that "teachers need to become students of their students—their cultural metaphors, languages and linguistic understandings, leaning styles, to recognize them as resources for learning."

Policymakers must also understand the challenges that face teacher's unions. They exist to serve the needs of their members. To the extent that they can do this by helping their members to be treated as professionals and to function as professionals, the education reform objectives of policymakers can be well served also. Finding the right balance between the interests of school employees and the students they help educate, then striking this balance in ways that enhance the workplace for employees and the learning outcomes for students, are critical to the success of restructuring.

Learning and Student Outcomes

Restructuring invites policymakers to focus on learning outcomes for students. It is appropriate to establish policies that give general direction to the schools about what students should know and be able to do. Research has revealed a great deal about how people learn, but teaching practice has been slow to reflect that knowledge. The Holmes Group (1990, p. 13) summarizes what we have learned from cognitive scientists:

> First, that people are inveterate constructors of meaning: they're going to make sense of it in some way. Second, people make sense of the environment differently in learning different content. Third, context causes people to make different sense of things from what they do in school. And fourth, within all of that, different cultures will value these things in different ways.

What policymakers must do is test the likely impact of proposed initiatives against the knowledge we have of learning to project whether implementation of the policy will have the intended outcome for learners. Once policies are underway, analysts must judge their impact against that same standard.

If people are motivated in different ways, learn at varying rates and respond to different activities, why are practically all schools organized routinely with space arranged in nine-hundred-square-foot units called classrooms, schedules made for standard periods or time blocks regardless of the learning activities planned, students arranged in groups of thirty for most of the school day, and student potential gauged with limited diagnostic instruments that treat intelligence as one-dimensional?

There is nothing wrong with policies that determine that some things are more important than others for students to learn. In San Diego the board of education has established a common core curriculum for middle and junior-high schools and senior-high schools. All students have access to an academic program that will enable those who complete it to exercise a full range of options after graduation, including postsecondary education or immediate entry into the work force. However, the board did not pass the policy without providing schools with a year to plan for its implementation and with resources for staff training and the development of tutoring and other support for students who need extra help to succeed in the common core curriculum.

Interagency Collaboration

The delivery of services for children should be better coordinated. Greater interagency collaboration can result in improved services to children and families and more efficient use of limited resources. Recognizing this, several years ago representatives from government agencies that serve San

Diego families living in poverty began meeting informally to consider ways to better coordinate their activities.

These discussions resulted in New Beginnings, a collaborative effort involving the San Diego city and county governments with the Community College District and San Diego City Schools. The group's first step was to undertake a feasibility study of a one-stop coordinated services center, located at a school site and designed to cut through bureaucratic barriers and provide more easily accessible support for children and families.

The study was conducted at Hamilton Elementary School, located in an area dominated by low-income apartment blocks and public housing projects. The school, which was built in 1978 to accommodate 750 students, now serves 1,300 students from kindergarten through fifth grade. The main buildings are augmented by 26 portable classrooms.

The final report was released in July 1990. It detailed many findings and concluded that

- There is a need for basic, fundamental reform in the way schools and government agencies deliver services to families.
- The school setting is a primary, sustained contact point for working with families. However, a school-governed integrated services program is not advisable.
- What appears to be one single system to families is really a fragmented set of services.
- Expanding staff roles and job descriptions which can release the energy and creativity of frontline workers who are presently stifled by their systems.
- Eligibility procedures which are complex and agency-specific create barriers for families.
- Present funding mechanisms require agency specialization so that problems are being addressed instead of people.
- Lack of data sharing among agencies, workers, and families prevents optimal services.
- The present system treats families with less respect than they desire and need.
- Family mobility is a serious barrier to receiving services. (*New Beginnings—A Feasibility Study of Integrated Services for Children and Families*, 1990, pp. v–viii)

The report recommended that New Beginnings next conduct a three-year pilot program at Hamilton to provide basic medical care and social services to poor children and families in the area. Those recommendations were adopted by the governing bodies of the four cooperating agencies.

The three-year program began March 1991, supported by an $85,000 grant from The Stuart Foundations. The remaining costs of about

$100,000 are being paid by the four agencies involved. Eight employees from the agencies have been reassigned to work only in the Hamilton area.

It is already clear that a great deal about improving interagency collaboration will be learned from the Hamilton project, and what is learned will help expand the concept to other schools in the district. All the participants recognize that many challenges lie ahead, as law and regulations are revised and attitudes change. There is a long way to go, but New Beginnings could dramatically change the way public services are provided to those who need them.

Policymakers at all levels should analyze existing policies and revise them to encourage interagency cooperation that goes beyond isolated projects and yields systemic change. Incentives creatively packaged can lead to improvements in the quality of services provided to families and children and youth. Cost effectiveness can increase, and the schools will be able to focus on their academic mission.

Parent Enabling and Choice

It is difficult to think about fundamental change in American education without considering the role of parents. Common sense buttressed by compelling research acknowledges the connection between parental support for education and student success in school. Thus, there is little disagreement about the importance of getting parents involved in the education of their children. The controversy is associated with how to do it. Changes in the family and its functions now make some traditional techniques impractical. Parenting is difficult under the best of circumstances, but few parents think about learning how to do it.

A handbook published in 1990 by San Diego City Schools summarizes important research on parent involvement:

- Schools, through their policies and actions, can reach out to parents to help them be involved in the education of their children.
- Involving parents in the education of their children has a positive effect on student achievement.
- Parent involvement is most beneficial when it is well planned, systematic, long lasting, and when parents play many roles.
- While all forms of parent involvement are desirable, home-based parent involvement (home-learning and enrichment activities coordinated with children's classwork) appears to be the most valuable in regard to student achievement.

- Teachers' initiative and willingness to reach out to parents are key factors for effective parent involvement.
- Parents whose involvement is actively sought by teachers have more positive attitudes about their children's schools and teachers.
- Parent involvement is an underutilized resource for the enhancement of student achievement.
- Socioeconomic status and lack of education have no effect on the willingness of parents to help their own children. (*Partners for Student Success Home and School: A Handbook for Principals and Staff*, p. 12)

Policymakers must avoid concluding from this research that only the traditional family of working father, homemaker mother, and two children holds hope for strengthening the connection between home and school. Policymakers cannot ignore demographics. Families are increasingly single-parent families, two-working-parent families, or extended families. The context has changed.

Despite disturbing statistics about the number of children living below the poverty line and the greater incidence of child abuse, one value has not changed: Most parents do care a great deal about their children and want them to succeed. What we cannot assume is that good parenting results from instinct. Those who were lucky enough to have had good role models as parents may have a head start; those not so fortunate may repeat the mistakes their parents made. Thus, one prerequisite for effective parent involvement may be parenting education.

Missouri's Parents as Teachers program has shown promising results. Trained specialists visit the homes of mothers with infants and teach them to understand the stages of development of young children and to work positively with their youngsters to develop their full potential. Forming habits of mind and patterns of behavior that enhance parents' ability to provide support for their children are the goals. In San Diego the department of social services includes in its training programs for welfare mothers classes in parenting, which include role-playing a parent-teacher conference at their child's school. The board of education has adopted a policy designed to engage parents in their children's education. The board has also included $100,000 in its annual budget for incentive grants for which schools compete to assist them in parent-enabling activities. The board requires every eighth-grade student to have a conference with the parent and school counselor to plan the high-school course of study. The State of California provides some money for local school districts to offset part of the additional cost of the eighth-grade and tenth-grade follow-up conferences.

The work of Yale's James Comer has provided a model for a social development curriculum that engages parents in the life of the school and development of an education support system for their children. Selected schools in a number of districts, including San Diego, are replicating the Comer model.

Community-based organizations in San Diego are working with schools by offering parent institutes that help parents develop skills in assisting their children, dealing with the schools, and advocating change in schools. Private foundations provide challenge grants to encourage such joint ventures between schools and community-based organizations.

Involvement of parents in school governance is another way of empowering them. School-based decision-making can bring parents into deliberations about substantive matters of curriculum, staffing, resource allocation, and evaluation. The governance structure that includes parents rests on the assumption that those involved in making decisions will accept ownership of them and responsibility for making them work.

Choice among schools is the most controversial of the ideas associated with parent enabling. The special place that choice occupies in America's hierarchy of values positions it well to capture the attention of those who want a simple answer to the multiple problems facing American education. Certainly, no discussion of parent enabling in education is complete without consideration by policymakers of how children are assigned to schools. In the United States one's school attendance is usually determined by residence. Policymakers have found this arrangement easy to justify. It is usually most convenient for parents to have their children attend school in their own neighborhood. Typically it is easier to make enrollment projections and plan school facilities when boundaries are stable and clear. This practice, for the most part, confines the ability to choose a school to those who have the financial means to select a private school. About 10 percent of the nation's school-age children have parents who have exercised this option; the other 90 percent attend public schools.

During the last two decades, choice options within the public sector have increased as the result of state and local policy direction and because of court orders in desegregation cases. Generally these policies place some limitations on choice, most often space availability, impact on schools' racial balance, and transportation regulations. Although those attempting to get federal policies to provide tuition tax credits or vouchers have failed to gain sufficient support to bring about these changes, several states have enacted legislation designed to increase the options for parents. In Wisconsin legislators approved a controversial voucher plan that enables up to one thousand Milwaukee public-school children to attend private nonsectarian schools, with a $2,500 per student allotment transferred by the state from the public school district to the school of the parents' choice.

Chubb and Moe (1990) have intensified the debate about choice by arguing that professionalism, autonomy, improved learning, and parent participation cannot exist in the present system of public schools. As they summarize their analysis in Chapter 3 of this book, the key factor in determining a school's effectiveness is its degree of freedom from central control. They see bureaucracy as the antithesis of professionalism, and they have no confidence that existing systems of accountability provide for autonomy. They characterize decentralization as unstable because whenever a problem emerges, politicians and policymakers respond with a centralized solution that generates more regulations and bureaucracy.

These and other analysts favor competition and choice. Their solution for bringing about dramatic improvements in public schools is to create a market model. Few will disagree with the statement that "Educational reform, if it is done right, is essentially an exercise in harnessing the causes of effective performance." However, many will not agree that we must sacrifice all elements of direct democratic governance and bureaucracy and embrace a selective market model. Concern about excesses of government control are legitimate, but the common good must be balanced against the rights of the individual. In suggesting that public authority must be put to use in creating a system that is almost entirely beyond the reach of public authority, Chubb and Moe tilt the balance to favor the latter at the expense of the former.

There is a middle ground for policymakers. It is controlled choice within the public sector. Fundamental value issues cloud the debate about the use of public tax dollars for private schools. Most exist because of their desire to be free from the controls of public policy. The price of their independence is not to rely on public tax dollars to finance their schools. Public educators are willing to compete with independent schools when policy constraints apply evenly to each.

What kind of controls are reasonable to consider in public-school choice plans? Space availability is one. Conversations about the costs of education tend to focus on operating costs and ignore the staggering amounts needed to provide facilities and other essential infrastructure. Another consideration is racial balance. Poor academic education in an integrated setting is no more acceptable than good academic education in a segregated setting. This should be a public policy goal that acknowledges the fundamental principles of this country, its increasing diversity, and its commitment to both the "unum" and the "pluribus." A third control is transportation. Without a way of getting a child to a school outside the neighborhood, a parent has no meaningful choice. Unless schools of choice are to be available only to the affluent, policymakers must consider transportation as they formulate policy on school choice.

The San Diego city school district has a controlled choice plan. Forty-six magnet programs are open to students throughout the city. There are no academic entrance requirements. A student's priority for enrollment is determined solely by space availability and racial balance criteria. Transportation for students who attend magnet schools outside their school attendance area is provided. Magnet schools now enroll 32,607 students,

9,000 of whom live outside the neighborhoods in which the schools are located. The district also has a Voluntary Ethnic Enrollment Program, which allows students to attend schools outside their neighborhoods to improve racial balances in both sending and receiving schools. Transportation is provided for the 7,268 students who presently choose to participate. Special attendance permits are also issued annually to over 2,500 students who petition to attend a school outside of their neighborhoods for such reasons as child care, desire for special courses of study, or proximity to a parent's place of employment.

Many of the factors that Chubb and Moe praise are also present in controlled choice plans. San Diego's magnet schools compete with each other and with non–magnet schools. They are constantly looking for ways to heighten their appeal to students and parents. If they fail to attract students, they jeopardize their magnet status and funding. State integration funds and federal assistance grants provide the venture capital, and a court order adds to the incentive to create quality programs in integrated settings that will attract students. Controlled choice schools must be dynamic, just as schools in a market model must be in order to maintain their competitive edge.

Policymakers should not look to ensure a single choice model. There are enough examples now to show that schools can do a better job of empowering parents and providing choice as they restructure to enhance teaching and learning and at the same time reconcile the inherent conflicts between public interest and private good. Moreover, policies that truly enable parents to help their children should not be confined to the academic aspect of schools. As argued throughout this chapter, policymakers must view school reform in the larger context of establishing policy that meets the broader needs of children, youth, and families and makes the connections among them.

Accountability and Assessment

No discussion of education reform is complete without consideration of the most troublesome topics on the reform agenda: the difficult issues of assessment and accountability. Policymakers are held responsible for the outcomes of their decisions by the people who elect or appoint them. Policymakers join parents and other citizens in expecting educators and students to be accountable, too. This seems logical and uncomplicated until the terms of accountability are addressed and the means for assessing results are considered.

Accountability in public education is not a new concept, but the debate about its terms is changing. In the past, accountability has been driven by compliance. Those who heeded the prescriptions and regulations of policymakers were deemed responsible. When accountability was not evident, policymakers responded with more rules and regulations to follow. There was little discussion of outcomes. That is now changing as pressure builds from parents, citizens, and some educators to assess the outcomes of learning and hold those involved in teaching and learning responsible for the results—what students know and can do.

Linda Darling-Hammond (1988) provides a useful framework for policymakers to understand various models of accountability. Political accountability is familiar to those who must stand for reelection and be judged by their constituents. Legal accountability is provided by the courts as they make determinations about violations of the law. Bureaucratic accountability, the kind that has dominated education for several decades, is fundamental to government agencies whose role is to determine whether rules and procedures are being followed. Theirs is an enforcement role. With market accountability, clients determine what goods and services they need and the consumer ultimately determines whether the producer is accountable. Finally, in the professional model of accountability, members of the profession establish its standards of performance, the training required for entry to it, and evaluate its members.

Political and legal accountability will certainly continue. The question is whether the education reform movement of the 1990s will move more toward market and professional models of accountability and away from the bureaucratic model. As Darling-Hammond points out, there is often a tension between public and individual client accountability or between government goals for public schools and the individual goals that parents have for their children. "Ironically, these prescriptive policies, created in the name of public accountability," she writes, "have begun to reduce schools' responsiveness to the needs of students and the desires of parents" (Darling-Hammond 1988, p. 12). Accountability is what parents and the public expect, but the frequent use of the word and its popularity in the abstract obscures the problem of defining what it means. Further, as the debate about various approaches to assessment yields more specific suggestions about how to deal with accountability, acceptance of any one strategy is more difficult to achieve.

In the past educators oversold the public and policymakers on the worth of norm-referenced standardized achievement tests as instruments to assess student achievement. As long as the major goal of the schools was basic literacy, a curriculum focusing on basic skills made sense and such tests could provide serviceable indicators of progress. But the curriculum reflects what is tested, and students accordingly get heavier doses of basic skills instruction when their schools' reputations are determined by scores on standardized tests.

Today we understand that basic literacy is not a sufficient goal for schools. Expectations are higher because students have to make decisions, solve problems, and adapt to change. In short, they must be able to think to make a living. The traditional multiple choice tests do not assess these skills, and it is unfair to assess students with instruments that do not allow them to show what they know and can do. Thus, it is encouraging to see widening interest in alternative forms of assessment that are performance based. The California Assessment Program (discussed in detail in Chapter 7) is an exemplary example of a statewide assessment program designed to measure what groups of students know and can do, based in this case on the thoughtfully developed California statewide curriculum frameworks.

Other data besides test results also can be useful. Attendance, dropout rates, types of courses taken, grade point averages, matriculation at postsecondary institutions, and employment are examples of outcome measures that can be used to assess how schools are doing. Portfolios containing student work and student exhibitions, demonstrations, and performances are among the other approaches to assessment that focus on learning outcomes.

In California and several other states, schools provide parents with annual report cards using some of these outcome data. Properly used, such report cards can be a valuable tool for involving parents and staff members in candid assessment of a school's strengths and weaknesses and in facilitating the strategic planning process at the school. Improperly used, the report cards can become glitzy public relations documents that obscure rather than highlight a school's deficiencies and achievements.

Policymakers must push for the development of and experimentation with alternative forms of assessment that focus on learning outcomes. They must insist that data be disaggregated by gender and ethnicity. Averages can be misleading if they suggest that all is well in a school when in a fact a subgroup of students is performing poorly. Unless information is available by subgroups, problems will not be acknowledged as the first step in finding solutions to them.

San Diego's data clearly show an achievement gap between African Americans and Hispanics on one hand and between Asian Americans and whites on the other. The response has been to establish a specific gap-closing objective for the entire school district to work on. Policymakers prescribe the objective but do not say how to meet it. Educators are responsible for determining how to close the achievement gap—and for demonstrating results.

One other aspect of accountability and assessment is a candidate for controversy. How can conflicting views of human nature and individual motivation be dealt with as policymakers consider incentive rewards and sanctions? What happens to those who are held accountable when more or less progress toward objectives occurs? What difference does it make if parents, educators, and students succeed or fail? For students, the stakes are obviously high and the consequences clear. Success in school opens doors; failure closes off opportunity. But not much changes for parents or educators. It is easy to espouse the idea of sanctions and to make cynical comments about how educators steer clear of them, but in fact policymakers have not tried many noble experiments that create tangible rewards for educators who demonstrate extraordinary results. Educators have responded more favorably than most professionals would to kind words and pretty plaques. It is not surprising that they have been skeptical about sanctions that jeopardize job security or reduce economic benefits.

The weight of tradition, doubt that fairness will be the standard followed, and anxiety about change do not provide much encouragement for dramatic breakthroughs in the domain of rewards and sanctions. Yet, it is wrong to suppose that the private sector is far ahead of the public sector in finding creative ways to tie rewards and sanctions to accountability. Few institutions in the private sector have tenure rights for employees, but they have almost as much difficulty generating the will to make difficult personnel decisions as do public employers.

A more promising policy direction is to look at incentives as a means of changing behavior and to focus on teams of people rather than individuals. Joint responsibility for outcomes, one accepted by a team of people, can result in members using the dynamics of the group in a positive way to deal with individuals who are not doing their share. Policymakers should also consider some of the innovative approaches being used in the private sector to improve productivity and increase the quality of the products and services produced.

Conclusion

The 1990s will be a watershed for education in America. For public education to survive, it cannot be business as usual. Fundamental renewal and change must occur. Reform must be systemic to meet the needs of all students. America needs workers who are able to think for a living if we are to remain internationally competitive. The pressures and fears associated with dramatic demographic changes will threaten our commitment to universal public education if we forget that it resists the development of an elite class and the emergence of a large underclass. We must have an enlightened citizenry to maintain our democratic government and free economy.

Past efforts to reform public education have often failed because of fragmentation, unrealistic expectations for quick results, lack of comprehensiveness, and inadequate funding. History will surely repeat itself if educators and policymakers fail to make connections among the various elements of the reform agenda—restructuring, parent enabling, accountability and assessment. The whole is greater than the sum of the parts, and a project-by-project approach will not be successful at effecting education reform this time around.

The challenge to educators and policymakers is to work together to develop a comprehensive plan for dealing with the needs of children, youth, and families. This requires incentives for new forms of creative collaboration among those who have learned through experience not to cooperate with others who are competing for limited resources. It requires policymakers to take courageous stands and exercise their political will against the special interests that now dominate decision-making at all levels. It requires new forms of leadership to communicate the complexity of issues to skeptical constituencies who must increase their understanding of the crisis that faces our children, their education, and the future of us all. It must bring together reluctant constituencies to support comprehensive strategies for change that transcend the conflicting expectations of strong special interest groups.

The reform movement of the 1990s will fail if responsibility for leading it rests with those interests that have been traditional opponents of change. Strong, effective public schools are in all of our best interests. We all have a responsibility to help keep children's issues and public education high on the political agenda at all levels of government. Although responsibility for outcomes must be shared by many, accountability must be targeted for change to occur. Experience has proven that when everyone is responsible, often no one is truly accountable.

Americans favor simple answers to complex questions. We like quick results and love to quantify them. Superficial change responds to these expectations; lasting systemic change does not. We must eschew the former and embrace the latter. Perseverance, tenacity, and patience are required. Although it is plainly too soon to evaluate current reform efforts, we should be encouraged by many things that are taking place across the country and optimistic that the rhetoric of commitment to high-quality education will become reality and result in a public education system in the 1990s where all children will learn.

References

AMERICAN ASSOCIATION OF SCHOOL ADMINISTRATORS. 1990. *A New Look at Empowerment*. Arlington, Va.: The Association.

ANDERSON, SUSAN. 1989. "Drawn off Course." *California Tomorrow* 3(Fall): 6–13.

ASSOCIATION FOR SUPERVISION AND CURRICULUM DEVELOPMENT. 1990. *Public Schools of Choice.* Alexandria, Va.: The Association.

BLOOM, ALLAN. 1987. *The Closing of the American Mind.* New York: Simon and Schuster.

CENTER FOR POLICY RESEARCH IN EDUCATION. Decentralization and Policy Design. 1990. *CPRE Policy Briefs.* Brunswick, N.J.: Eagleton Institute of Policies, Rutgers University.

CHUBB, JOHN, and MOE, TERRY. 1990. *Politics, Markets and America's Schools.* Washington, D.C.: Brookings Institution.

DARLING-HAMMOND, LINDA . 1988. "Accountability and Teacher Professionalism." *American Educator* 12 (Winter): 8–12, 38–43.

————. 1989. "Accountability for Professional Practice." *Teachers College Record* 91 (Fall): 59–80.

DUTTWEILER, PAT, and MUTCHLER, SUE. 1990. *Barriers to School Restructuring.* Austin, Tex.: Southwest Educational Development Laboratory.

ELLIOTT, EMERSON J. 1989. Accountability in the Post-Charlottesville Era. *CRESST Evaluation Comment.* Los Angeles: University of California, Graduate School of Education.

ELMORE, RICHARD F., and ASSOCIATES. 1990. *Restructuring Schools: The Next Generation of Educational Reform.* Center for Policy Research in Education. San Francisco: Jossey-Bass.

FOWLER, R. SCOTT. 1990. *The Business Role in State Education Reform.* New York: Business Roundtable.

GARDNER, HOWARD. 1990. "The Difficulties of School: Probable Causes, Possible Cures." *Daedalus* 119 (Spring): 85–113.

GRAY, DENNIS. 1990. "Restructuring, Co-Opted." *Basic Education* 34 (January): 2–4.

HOLMES GROUP. 1990. *Tomorrow's Schools: Principles for the Design of Professional Development Schools.* East Lansing, Mich.: The Group.

JOHNSON, SUSAN MOORE. 1990. *Teachers at Work Achieving Success in Our Schools.* New York: Basic Books.

KAUBE, AMY. 1989. *Restructuring the Schools.* (Number EA 37.) Eugene: University of Oregon, College of Education (ERIC Digest Series).

KENNEDY, PAUL. 1987. *The Rise and Fall of the Great Powers.* New York: Random House.

LIEBERMAN, ANN, and MILLER, LYNN. 1990. "Restructuring Schools: What Matters and What Works." *Phi Delta Kappan* 71 (June): 759–64.

McDONNELL, LORRAINE M. 1989. "Restructuring American Schools: The Promise and the Pitfalls." *ERIC Clearinghouse on Urban Education Digest* 57. New York: Columbia University Teachers College.

NATIONAL GOVERNORS' ASSOCIATION. 1990. *Educating America: State Strategies for Achieving the National Education Goals.* Washington, D.C.: The Association.

New Beginnings—A Feasibility Study of Integrated Services for Children and Families. 1990. San Diego: San Diego Community College District.

Participation Guide: A Primer for Business on Education. 1990. New York: Business Roundtable, National Alliance of Business.

Partners for Student Success Home and School: A Handbook for Principals and Staff. 1990. San Diego: San Diego City Schools.

PAYZANT, THOMAS W. 1989. "To Restructure Schools, We've Changed the Way the Bureaucracy Works." *The American School Board Journal* 176 (October): 19–20.

Policy Guide: A State Policymaker's Guide to Public School Choice. 1989. Education Commission of the State.

SAN DIEGO BOARD OF EDUCATION. 1988. Minutes of the Board of Education of the San Diego Unified School District, November 8. San Diego City Schools.

SCHLECHTY, PHILLIP C. 1990. *Schools for the 21st Century.* San Francisco: Jossey-Bass, 1990.

SCHOOLS OF THE FUTURE COMMISSION. 1987. "Which Way to the Future? San Diego Schools at a Crossroad." San Diego: The Commission, 1987.

TOCQUEVILLE, ALEXIS DE. 1969. *Democracy in America.* Edited by J. P. Mayes. Garden City, N.J.: Anchor.

ACCOUNTABILITY FOR RESULTS

6

Designing Accountability to Help Reform

Terry K. Peterson

Accountability and School Reform

In the 1990s most states and communities in the United States will face twin challenges in education: dramatically improving the educational results of all students and operating in a tight fiscal environment.

In these times, education accountability and education improvement need to stick together. More and more, legislators, government officials, and educators will demand greater efficiency and effectiveness from the tax dollars appropriated for education. Unfortunately, this is easier said than done.

Sometimes laws and regulations intended to make the education system more accountable actually make it less efficient and, in the long term, less effective. At first blush, tight requirements at the state level concerning how certain local education programs will be carried out may seem reasonable. When these regulations are implemented in the schools and classrooms, however, they may actually hamper progress and boost costs.

Many school systems are attempting to restructure their decision-making processes and service delivery to be more efficient. When successful, these endeavors typically included four steps:

1. working with individual schools to set output targets compatible with the goals of the entire enterprise
2. developing participatory leadership and decision-making processes to solve local problems and to run day-to-day operations to reach targeted outcomes

3. removing state district rules and regulations that unnecessarily restrict these new local operations

4. assisting "school teams" with information, training, technical assistance, and support.

These strategies call for numerous changes in policy, structure, use of time, parent and business involvement, training, funding, and personnel practices, as well as relationships among educators and other providers of children's services. Redesigned assessment and accountability mechanisms are needed in this new approach, too, because outcomes and results are the central measure of success in today's education and economic climates. Two regional workshops sponsored by the Education Commission of the States in 1990 identified thirteen steps for policymakers to take in restructuring schools. These workshops affirmed the primary importance of outcomes in education by stating that they "develop a vision of desired student outcomes and a vision of a restructured education system" (Armstrong 1990).

This chapter focuses on assessment and accountability, but we should be mindful of the many other changes simultaneously needed in other aspects of education. New forms of assessment and accountability are an important part of any restructured educational system for the 1990s, but they constitute just one element of a fairly complex equation for success. A well-functioning system of assessment and accountability needs to answer, at minimum, the following questions:

1. Which goals or outcomes are critical to focus on?

2. What measurements, indicators, or data will tell us if we are making progress toward those goals, taking into account the limitations of multiple choice tests and minimizing disruptions to the learning process in collecting data from classrooms?

3. How do we know if we are successful, mindful that circumstances differ among schools, districts, and states?

4. How can information from the assessments be used by policy makers to improve decision-making in general, reward success, and intervene in situations of poor performance?

Such questions need to be answered for each level of the educational enterprise—school, district, and state. In addition, the answers to these questions for each level need to be compatible with one another while at the same time adjusting for the real-life dynamics of classrooms and schools. After all, the ultimate purpose is to improve teaching and learning among all students, not merely to design an elegant accountability system.

Although the complexity of this endeavor can appear overwhelming, in fact it reflects the reality of educational governance and decision-making in the democratic system of the United States and in today's global environment. By taking into account these multilevels of educational decision-making and their interplay, major conflicts may be avoided prior to implementation.

These four central questions will be discussed in this chapter from two perspectives: in a general way and also through a review of South Carolina's eight-year experience in trying to grapple with educational reform and redesigning its assessment and accountability system.

On What Goals Should We Focus?

There is growing evidence that what gets measured is what gets acted upon. The results on which a state or other unit of education focuses will influence the allocation of time and energy toward those items. Work by the Southern Regional Education Board (SREB) to improve education in the South in the 1990s depends on the principle that the "citizens of any state are not likely to achieve more in education than they and their leaders expect and aim for" (1990, p.1). Accordingly, substantial thought should be given to identifying the areas of student performance and other outcomes essential to the future of a state, school district, and school in a rapidly changing environment.

In the late 1980's and early 1990's a number of groups have devoted considerable energy to analyzing educational goals. A reasonable starting point for policymakers would be to review these recommended goals. From such lists, policymakers could select or adapt goals important to the future of their own state and community. Important areas of concern that are not included on these lists could be added.

Two sets of goals are particularly good starting points: the goals set for the year 2000 by the nation's governors and President George Bush and the goals recommended by the SREB for the year 2000 for the fifteen southeastern states. Table 6-1 summarizes these goals, showing similarities and differences between the two sets.

A number of states and groups concerned about education reform and student performance have recommended other goals on which education should focus. Although many are similar to the goals recommended by the governors or the SREB, other areas also merit policymakers' attention. For

TABLE 6-1. Two Sets of Goals for the Year 2000

	National Goals of Governors and President	Southern Regional Education Board Goals
Similarities:		
1.	All children will start school ready.	All children will be ready for the first grade.
2.	The school dropout rate will be reduced by one-half.	Attain a High-school graduation rate of 90 percent.
3.	Leave grades 4, 8, and 12 with competency in challenging subject matter, including English, mathematics, science, history, and geography.	Student achievement for elementary and secondary students will equal national levels or higher.
4.	Every adult literate.	Ninety percent of adults will have a high-school diploma or equivalency.
Differences:		
1.	Rank first in the world in science and mathematics.	Four of 5 students entering college will be ready to begin college-level work.
2.	Make schools free of drugs and violence, and disciplined school environment conducive to learning.	Significant gains will be achieved in the mathematics, science, and communications competencies of vocational education students.
3.		The percentage of adults who have attended college or earned two-year, four-year, and graduate degrees will achieve the national average or better.
4.		The quality and effectiveness of all colleges and universities will be regularly assessed, with particular emphasis on the performance of undergraduate students.
5.		All institutions that prepare teachers will have effective teacher-education programs that place primary emphasis on the knowledge and performance of graduates.

(continued)

TABLE 6-1.   (continued)

National Goals of Governors and President	Southern Regional Education Board Goals
Differences:	
6.	All states and localities will have schools with improved performance and productivity demonstrated by results.
7.	Salaries for teachers and faculty will be competitive in the marketplace, will reach important benchmarks, and will be linked to performance measures and standards.
8.	States will maintain or increase the proportion of tax dollars for schools and colleges while emphasizing funding aimed at raising quality and productivity.

example, a Michigan group studying work force readiness for the future included teamwork skills as one of three main areas of importance. (See Table 6-2.)

The Maryland Governor's Commission on School Performance recommended goals in a broad array of academic areas, including most areas recommended by the governors and the SREB, as well as a section on

TABLE 6-2.   Teamwork Skills for the Year 2000 in Michigan

Employers want a person who can:
• identify with the goals, norms, values, customs, and culture of the group
• communicate with all members of a group
• show sensitivity to the thoughts and opinions of others in a group
• use a team approach to identify problems and devise solutions to get a job done
• exercise "give and take" to achieve group results
• function in changing work settings and in changing groups
• determine when to be a leader or a follower, depending upon what is necessary to get a job done
• show sensitivity to the needs of women and ethnic and racial minorities
• be loyal to the group

student personal growth. This particular section covered self-discipline, curiosity, study skills, personal decisions, responsibilities to others, motivation/persistence, positive self-concept, and maintenance of health and physical fitness (1989).

A committee of the Southern Arts Federation recommended that goals and assessment in education include creative thinking and the arts. For instance, they urge all students to develop an indepth understanding of one artform. Some suggest that the arts may be more important in the future than in the past in dealing with different learning styles of students, the fast pace of change, cultural diversity, and the need for adaptability. Fostering the arts and creative thinking also has an international economic dimension, the arts being one of the few areas in which the United States has a favorable foreign trade balance.

The Process of Setting Goals

As important as the selection of goals is their ownership by the community and the educators affected by them. Hence, the process of setting goals should involve leaders from many sectors and include mechanisms for large numbers of local educators, parents, and citizens to discuss and participate in the decision-making sequence. Regional forums and seminars could be helpful in accumulating advice from local citizens. Toll-free phone lines, polls, surveys, and publicity campaigns can also help engage the public in considering the goals and coming to accept the need for educational improvement.

Because of the changing features of society and the economy, goals set for one period will likely need revision at some later point. On the other hand, it is important to set goals and a course of action and stick with them long enough to allow the process to work. Too many education analysts and policymakers have developed a school reform strategy akin to that of an impatient gardener who digs up plants daily to see whether they are growing. Such a short-term view ensures that neither plants nor reforms ever take root.

Measurements and Indicators

In education, there seems to be a fascination with finding out "once and for all" where a state, school district, or school ranks. Some people search for a simple number that would explain everything about public education in a locality or state. This approach is doomed to failure because public education, by its very nature, has multiple goals, and no measure can adequately describe the condition of even a single goal or individual student.

It is generally prudent to gather and analyze several types of information that have some logical relationship to the goals or areas of importance—a multiple indicator approach. In the economic area it is common to hear reports such as "among 14 economic indicators, 7 were up, 2 unchanged, and 5 were down." A similar approach makes sense in education.

Identifying and tracking multiple indicators reflective of each goal gives a more comprehensive and realistic view of educational outcomes. For example, relying on a single multiple choice test to assess the extent to which students are reaching the goal of improved basic skills would likely deny policymakers or educators a full understanding of basic skills performance.

If a system relies on only one test to assess basic skills achievement, educators could focus directly on specific basic skills test items in their instruction rather than teaching to broad and generalizable basic skills objectives. Moreover, writing is often included as a basic skill. Writing implies the capacity to compose and edit paragraphs and groups of paragraphs. A single multiple choice test by itself cannot adequately measure writing or other complex skills.

Furthermore, an outcome as measured may be as important as the content being appraised. For example, if we want students to learn to write thoughtful compositions, conduct science experiments, and solve complex problems, we need new assessment procedures that ask students to perform these tasks. Lauren Resnick and others call it "designing assessments for the thinking curriculum" (1989, p. 5). Some call this type of assessment process a "performance" or "authentic" assessment.

Designing a system of multiple indicators for each broad goal or area, although not overly cumbersome or time-consuming, takes time and a thoughtful review of existing information sources as well as efforts to develop improved techniques. A recent national panel, the OERI State Accountability Study Group—named by the U.S. Department of Education—identified a number of indicators that states, districts, and schools may want to include. (See Table 6-3.)

If information for an indicator or a set of indicators is not currently available but is felt to be essential in monitoring goal attainment, steps should be taken to develop such assessment strategies, allowing for field testing and minimizing additional paperwork. If concrete steps are not taken at the beginning of a goal-setting or "report card" development process, it is unlikely that more complex, but perhaps more meaningful, indicators will be put in place expediently.

In addition to developing appropriate multiple measurements of essen-

TABLE 6-3.   Examples of Multiple Indicators of Student Performance and the Context of Schooling Recommended by the OERI State Accountability Study Group

- student course-taking and, for elementary students, the amount of time spent on different subjects
- attendance
- promotion and dropout rates
- proportion of vocational education students meeting academic requirements
- proportion of students meeting university entrance requirements
- student participation in the arts and extracurricular activities
- student attitudes and social behavior (for example, vandalism)
- student achievement, broadly defined to include writing skills, higher-order skills, and subject matter competence

To provide a comprehensive picture of the schooling context, states should also consider collecting data on

- teacher quality
- fiscal resources and their allocation
- administrative leadership
- curricula
- local assessment, evaluation, and planning systems
- community support

tial goals, it is also important to address the interrelationships among accountability mechanisms at the different levels of education (that is, school, district, and state), as well as the connections among outcomes and educational policies and practices. After studying four states involved in major efforts to redesign their accountability systems, Stephen Kaagan and Richard Coley (1989, p. 22) pinpoint four concerns they believe every state would profit from addressing:

- An understandable but often premature drive to report results so as to hold school officials accountable;
- Reluctance at the state level to assume responsibility for the quality of the indicators system;
- Tentativeness with regard to the exploration of critical relationships among school processes; system outcomes such as student performance, and background or contextual variables; and
- Slow and uneven formation of the necessary building blocks to support and indicator system.

When designing the indicators and measurements related tot he goals, we should keep in mind the initial effect of increasing or decreasing participation on outcome data. For instance, excluding at-risk and handicapped students from a basic skills test will boost the average score on that test compared with a time in which they were all included. On the other hand, dramatically increasing the number of students participating in assessments will likely lower the average score compared to the previous year. Unless an accountability system monitors both participation and performance, results may be meaningless or—worse—misrepresented.

For example, the rapid expansion of Advanced Placement (AP) courses taken in Florida and South Carolina in the mid- and late 1980s resulted in both states ranking in the top six in the nation in the participation level of their students in these tougher classes. Because of this substantial increase in participation, however, AP test scores dropped, at least initially, in both states.

Table 6-4 and 6-5 show this connection between participation and AP scores in South Carolina. After an initial drop in AP scores in between

TABLE 6-4. Number of Students Taking Advanced Placement Examinations and Number of Examinations Taken in South Carolina (1983–84 to 1988–89)

Subgroup	1983–84	1984–85	1988–89
Number of students taking examinations	2,400	4,678	6,125
Number of examinations*	3,046	6,262	8,521
Advanced placement candidates as a percentage of graduates			
South Carolina	6%		18%
Nation	5%		11%

SOURCE: *What Is the Penny Buying for South Carolina,* 1989.
*Differs from the number of students taking exams, since students can take more than one exam.

TABLE 6-5. Percentage of Advanced Placement Examinations Qualifying Students for College Credit

Subgroup	1983–84	1984–85	1988–89
South Carolina public schools	55%	39%	56%
Nation	70%	67%	65%

SOURCE: *What Is the Penny Buying for South Carolina,* 1989.
*Although participation almost tripled in South Carolina, the most recent scores were highest in recent history and closed the gap compared to the nation.

1983–84 and 1984–85 while participation almost doubled, student scores began to recover. Over the five-year period, participation nearly tripled. Scores are now at their highest level. In my opinion, these indicators show meaningful progress, at least for students on the upper end of the achievement scales. Yet, if scores alone were monitored, the overall improvement would not have been noticed.

Multiple indicators allow the monitoring of both participation and performance. Ideally, progress will include improvements in both. But it could be indicated only by a dramatic increase in participation and no reduction in scores, or vice versa.

On many traditional measures of performance, the average scores of low-income and minority students are not as high as those from middle income environments. Although every effort should be made to eradicate any bias in measurements that might contribute to these results, this dynamic needs to be considered in developing assessment and accountability systems in ways that do not reduce the expectation that all children must succeed in school. Therefore, in addition to assessing overall performance of students using multiple indicators, it is important to analyze the performance of students from various income and ethnic groups. It is insufficient to have the average student performance improve if some students fail to progress or the performance gap between poor and rich fails to close. On the other hand, average performance may fail to improve even while all major ethnic groups improve because groups historically scoring lower are increasing their participation rate in schools in most states.

Benchmarks

Annual benchmarks offer clues to the extent to which progress is being made toward the long-term goals. For instance, if a goal is to improve readiness by the year 2000 as the governors and President Bush suggest, we might assume that by 1991 we should make progress toward closing the gap in readiness by 10 percent. That would mean some 150,000 more first-graders ready in America than in 1990. Strategies to reach this goal include providing more at-risk 3- and 4-year-olds with quality child development and family services. Serving nationwide in the first year an additional 150,000 3- and 4-year-olds with quality child development programs and an equal number of parents of preschoolers with better information to prepare these children for first grade would help to reach the 10-percent goal.

Yet, even if these early childhood strategies are enacted and funded, we could not reasonably expect to reach this 10-percent benchmark by 1991 because the 3- and 4-year-olds in 1990–91 would not even be in first grade in fall 1991. Four-year-olds in 1990–91 would not enter first grade until 1992–93, and then they would have only one year of the new child development and parent support help behind them. So the goals, benchmarks, and rate of implementation of school reforms and other initiatives must be synchronized with each other; otherwise, educators, policymakers, and the public will be frustrated and confused.

How Do We Know If We Are Successful?

It generally makes sense to focus an accountability system on determining whether schools, school districts, and states are making satisfactory progress on multiple indicators that reflect important educational goals. However, schools, districts, and states are commonly compared by ranking their performance on one indicator at one point in time. Although such information may be useful to determine relative standings at a particular time, I believe that focusing primarily on such rankings may work against school improvement and restructuring efforts.

A community's overall education system will improve only if most or all the schools in that community improve. A state's education system will improve only if all or most of its school districts do. America can make strides in education only if all or most states' educational performance improves. Merely ranking or rating schools, districts, or states on the results of one measurement taken in a given year does not provide any information on whether the results are getting better or worse.

It is possible for high performers in one-point-in-time rankings to have recorded an actual loss in their performance compared to earlier years, and it is also possible for low performers to have made gains. In such circumstances, those losing ground but still with a high ranking will likely be praised while those with the lower relative ranking will likely be criticized, even though they are making progress. In this setting the teachers, students, and principals affiliated with the high-ranking but worsening institutions will be reinforced for their behaviors. On the other hand, those affiliated with low-ranking but improving institutions will likely be chastised. This scenario obviously could work against further improvement efforts at both extremes while schools, districts, or states ranking in the middle remain largely untouched by one-time rankings.

Focusing on improvement implies that every student, classroom, school, district, or state is important, and each entity is accountable for better results. Although it would be nice to dream of becoming a world-class marathon runner and wake one morning with the necessary endurance and stamina to reach that goal, in the real world it takes gradual conditioning and persistence. A person interested in running marathons has to start his or her training regime wherever they start. Similarly, schools, districts, and states have no choice where to start in student performance. They should therefore be judged on what they do with what they have in relation to where they began.

Making Fair Comparisons

It seems that everyone wants to know where his or her child or grandchild, school, city, state, or nation ranks in education. As discussed earlier, point-in-time comparisons or rankings are not terribly useful in long-term school improvement and restructuring efforts.

Yet, it is fair to want to know where schools, districts, states, and nations stand in relation to one another. How can fair comparisons be made? Normally by monitoring results of the same school, district, or state on multiple indicators of important goals over time. If improvements are made on most indicators, that is good news; if most indicators move in a negative direction, that is bad news. Such a longitudinal comparison against oneself is normally the fairest because it takes into account both where one starts and the context of one's situation. However, rapid changes in the demography of schools and communities could make even this type of comparison unfair.

Nor is a longitudinal comparison itself sufficient to tell you whether your gain or loss is something to be excited or concerned about. One way to develop a better yardstick is to look at the rate of gain or loss on similar indicators in similar schools, districts, or states and compare yourself to those progressing the fastest against meaningful benchmarks or goals. California and South Carolina construct comparison bands of similar schools to assess the degree of progress made.

How Is Assessment Data Used?

It is important to visualize the purposes of an assessment system before finalizing the details of the system. Having information may be interesting, but the value of the system of assessment and accountability should be its usefulness in informing parents, educators, and policymakers of the state of education; rewarding improvement; and identifying needs of problems.

Although much of the current discussion about accountability revolves around using assessments for rewards and sanctions, the "over-arching purpose of an educator indicator system," Margaret Goertz astutely notes, "is to permit refined and balanced judgments about the quality of education and to the extent possible, a better understanding of the relationships between actions by policymakers and change in that quality" (1989, p. 3).

A report by itself may or may not generate action. In my estimation, it is important to build in a number of key components to ensure that the goal-setting and the accountability system actually improve decision-making and provide the focus sought through this process.

A useful accountability system for improving education probably includes the establishment of a broad-based committee to help interpret the assessment data and recommend actions to revise strategies, recognize gains, and avoid problems. This approach can be utilized at the school, district, and state levels.

For the state, legislative oversight of education or other reform legislation is not a new concept. One study (Wohlsetter 1989) suggests that although legislative oversight of educational reforms has helped maintain and improve reform schemes, it may not be sufficient in the future if it relies heavily on anecdotal information and constituent complaints. Major education reforms and school restructuring may demand the involvement of more stakeholders and a longer time frame than has typically been found in the operation of legislative oversight committees.

One way to encourage a longer-term view of school reform is to create a broad-based oversight body involving leaders from business, education, and state government (that is, the governor and legislators). A blue ribbon committee of stakeholders could be organized to monitor the implementation of the proposed reforms, review statewide assessment information, propose modifications, and develop new strategies.

To maintain strong state government involvement, such a blue ribbon committee could report to a legislative oversight committee, the governor, and the general public. A reliable, objective source of data at the state level needs to be established to supply information to oversight committees. Options include creating a special division of accountability in the state department of education, under the state board of education, or in a consortium of colleges and universities.

Priscilla Wohlsetter provides an insightful discussion of four alternative models of state accountability mechanisms and evaluates them in terms of the guidance, support, warning, and enlightenment that they bring to education reform. She also rates these four models based on their capability to get something done after findings are made. (See Table 6-6.)

At the school level, a building council can be created to analyze assessment results. The council, together with the principal, parent leaders and leading teachers, could then use the results to develop a plan to address any shortcomings and build on the successes of their school. For such councils to be effective, many will require continuous technical

TABLE 6-6. Ratings for Accountability Mechanisms on Critical Components

Models & Variations	Be Empowered by State Government	Have Monitoring or Oversight as a Primary Mission	Be Independent from Implementors	Have Strong Relationships with Other Policy Actors and with Leaders Outside Government	Communicate Findings to Multiple Constituencies
Legislative Oversight Committee Model					
Education-Finance Committee (Tennessee)	Moderate	High	Moderate	Moderate	Low
Legislative Leader Committee (Texas)	Moderate	High	Moderate	Moderate	Low
Evaluation-Audit Committee (Virginia's Joint Legislative Audit & Review Commission)	High	High	High	Low	Moderate

Executive Branch Model				
State Board of Education (Connecticut)	Moderate	High	Low	Moderate
Partnership Model				
Education-Business Partnership (South Carolina)	High	High	Moderate	High
State-Local Partnership (New York)	Moderate	Moderate	Low	Moderate
Third-Party Model				
University Consortium (Policy Analysis for California Education)	Low	High	High	High
Performance Auditors	High	Low	High	Moderate

assistance, training, and support on such topics as team building, goal-setting, assessment, and communications. Many principals will also need assistance with the elements of participatory leadership.

At the district level, policies and staffing need to be put in place to assist schools in developing and implementing strategic plans based on their assessment results and needs. The district administration and school board could form task forces or teams to assist with analyses of specific weaknesses that may be surfaced by the assessment and accountability results.

Furthermore, reports on progress or the lack of it should be publicized, as should recommendations for future actions. The media will initially cover this information without prompting; later, however, they probably will not. Education associations, chambers of commerce, and other interested groups can be asked to cover assessment reports. Specially designed handouts and transparencies can be made available at speeches and meetings. Mailings to superintendents, principals, teachers, parent organizations, and schools can be used to laud them when exceptional progress is made and to request their help in addressing problems and shortcomings.

Rewarding Improvement

Usually, scant recognition comes to educators, students, and parents involved in broad improvement in student performance in an entire school, district, and state. Recognition is most often given to individual students or teams that excel. These individuals, teams and their coaches, teachers, and supporters rarely constitute a major portion of a school's population. In addition, their success, especially if achieved on the playing field, may not directly relate to goals for educational excellence. Yet general improvement in student performance across an entire school, in many schools in a state, and in many states has to be an essential objective.

As a result, we find growing interest in providing school-wide rewards and recognition for those involved in schools and districts that make significant progress. Such recognition can take the form of financial incentives (additional aid to schools for nonsalary or salary enhancements) as well as symbolic rewards (for example, flags or certificates). A newsletter sent home to parents from Dreher High School in South Carolina demonstrates the potential positive aspect of school-wide incentive awards. The front page contains three main features—one headline recognizes eighteen students and a picture with seven students, but the main headline recognizes the entire school for winning an incentive award.

To maintain and encourage improving performance, I favor rewarding

TABLE 6-7. Criteria to Identify High-Performing Schools Recommended by the OERI State Accountability Study Group

---

Any identification of high-performing or significantly improving schools should be objective and based on multiple indicators, not on a single test score. Indicators of special relevance for high performing schools might include

- measures of higher order skills and writing ability
- course enrollments, including the proportion enrolled in advanced placement classes
- the proportion of students meeting university entrance requirements
- the proportion of vocational students meeting academic standards
- the distribution of performance among varying student groups

As with all indicators of school performance, the state should take into consideration how different types of students are achieving on each of these indicators. The study group also recommends that states consider using additional verification from other sources, such as site visits.

- If state recognition of performance rests upon an application process, the state (or another agency) should offer technical assistance to districts or schools that require help in applying. Such assistance may be particularly important in states with locally defined goals and might be provided by intermediate service units, universities, or other organizations close to the local level.

---

performance based on the amount of gain compared to similar schools and/or in terms of meaningful gains toward the school's own goals. Also worth considering is a bonus for meeting locally determined goals or solving local problems that differ from state goals. Dade County, Florida, has experience in using a bonus reward for meeting local school goals.

The OERI State Accountability Study Group made a number of important recommendations for using accountability data to recognize and reward school improvement. (See Table 6-7).

Intervening in "Bankrupt" Schools

In "high-stakes" accountability situations, where substantial consequences follow from the results, great care should be taken to ensure that comparisons are fair and that suitable indicators of essential goals are employed. Nowhere is such care more important than where assessment systems are used to identify poorly performing schools and districts.

In general, it makes sense to identify poorly performing—some call them "bankrupt"—schools and districts based on both extremely low absolute performance and failure to improve. The State Accountability Study Group recommended that state intervention in poor performing schools or districts go through stages as follows:

1. Inform local districts and schools of problems that have been identified, so that administrators and boards of education can take action.
2. Inform citizens so that they can take action.
3. Target additional resources and assistance on the troubled school or district.
4. Mandate improvement activities; for example, require the district to develop a remediation plan and then monitor its progress; withhold state funds; or require increased local fiscal effort.
5. Begin state intervention in district management, including removal of local administrators.

With increasing interest in the individual school site, states may want to consider a similar continuum of actions for poorly performing schools. In Kentucky's new reform package, the first stage of such a continuum involves the assignment of one or more "Kentucky Distinguished Educators" with the authority to make extensive changes in the operation of the unsuccessful school. The last stages of the continuum include declaring a school to be "in crisis" for failure to improve after the third biennial assessment. Once a school is declared in crisis, a number of actions follow.

When education measures and indicators are both used for high-stakes purposes such as this, it is important that they track the goals and match the level of responsibility of the unit or group being assessed. For example, it is important to know the student dropout rate at the state, district, and high school levels. But such information is not terribly useful for elementary schools or middle schools. Similarly, participation rates in early childhood education will not be of much relevance to secondary schools.

The South Carolina Experience

As part of its large-scale education improvement efforts, South Carolina employs an unusually comprehensive approach to assessment and accountability. Before describing these measures, it is useful to review the origins and main components of the reform effort.

In early 1983 leaders in South Carolina, under the counsel of the Governor Richard Riley, initiated a massive grass-roots process to determine the state's education needs and potential ways to meeting them. The reform package emerging from this effort ultimately consisted of sixty-one initiatives funded by a one-cent sales tax intended for a separate Education Improvement Act (EIA) Fund.

The broad goals of the state's reforms included raising student performance by increasing academic standards; strengthening the teaching and testing of the basic skills; elevating the teaching profession by strengthening training, evaluating, and compensation; improving leadership, management, and fiscal efficiency of schools; implementing quality controls and rewarding productivity; and creating more effective partnerships among schools, parents, community, and business.

The sixty-one state initiatives included higher standards for students, teachers, and administrators, as well as schools and districts; extra help to those failing to meet the standards; improved training of teachers and school administrators; new education programs for above-average, average, and at-risk students in all grades; incentives to reward outstanding schools, teachers, and principals; various actions to foster involvement of parents, business, and citizens in the schools; targeted resources in numerous areas; and contained new accountability measures (Peterson 1988). Because of the size and scope of the EIA, certain provisions were phased-in over six or seven years.

In 1989 the EIA was followed by another reform package, "Target 2000: School Reform for the Next Decade." This more recent measure builds upon the EIA and launches a number of new initiatives. The goals of Target 2000 are to provide the best chance for success of each child's early educational experience; make gains in reading, writing, mathematics, and science basic skills; cut the high-school dropout rate in half by 2000; emphasize thinking skills and creativity in a variety of subjects beyond basic skills; encourage and reward schools initiating new and innovative ideas; continue to enhance the stature of the teachers; strengthen accountability at all levels; and develop programs to encourage parent involvement.

Early evidence indicates that this package of reforms, the new investments undergirding them, and the statewide grass-roots efforts are paying off. In fact, the results are as good or better than most reformers had hoped. In the latest assessment report by a state oversight committee (South Carolina Business-Education Subcommittee 1989) progress was observed in moving toward all the state targets and goals adopted in 1983.

The aforementioned background information is necessary for the reader to see how assessment and accountability fit into the specific reform efforts in South Carolina.

Goal Setting and Consensus Building

The Education Improvement Act established eight specific targets, as well as six general goals, to be reached by 1989 or 1990. These targets and goals were necessary not only to give South Carolinians a clear indication of the intended result of the expenditure of more hard-earned tax dollars for education but also to focus the comprehensive reform efforts on outcomes. Thousands of people were involved in this process through local forums, toll-free phone lines, an orchestrated school visitation program of state leaders, and an active speaker's bureau. All this input and advice was synthesized by two blue-ribbon committees and then refined and adopted by the general assembly.

As discussed earlier, South Carolina's newest reform package, Target 2000, which was passed in 1989, also contains long-term goals in eight areas.

A number of state leaders in South Carolina created ongoing oversight bodies—one composed primarily of business and educational leaders, the other composed mostly of legislative leaders. These oversight bodies are provided with substantial information from special studies and for the first seven years from a specially created division of public accountability in the state department of education. These groups report annually to the legislature, governor, and general public about the extent to which the reform goals are being achieved.

In addition to statewide monitoring, South Carolina pays a great deal of attention to each individual school to ensure that it addresses its own needs and problems and to make certain that improvement is stressed. To accomplish this, the state has launched four accountability measures for individual schools and is considering a fifth.

First, every school must have an improvement council composed of teachers elected by teachers, parents elected by parents, the principal, and appointees of the principal. The council develops the school improvement plan with the principal and the plan is updated yearly. Over 10,000 people serve on South Carolina's school improvement councils. As might be expected, not all 1,100 councils work well, but many do. A 1988 survey (South Carolina State Board of Education 1988) found that most parents and teachers who knew of the council felt it had a strong impact; however, although 84 percent of teachers knew of the council, only 28 percent of the parents were familiar with it. As a result of these findings, the oversight committees have urged a number of improvements in the role of councils in school reforms. A project at the University of South Carolina also provides ongoing technical assistance and training for councils, and in 1990 it inaugurated a publicity campaign to explain the councils to parents and the general public.

Second, to heighten each school's motivation to improve, South Carolina annually appropriates approximately $5 million to be distributed among approximately 250 schools that make the largest achievement gains compared to similar schools. Bonuses for high-school student and teacher attendance are included. If a school meets all these outcome standards, it receives roughly $35 per student to reinvest in its school improvement plan. Thus, a winning school of 1,000 students receives about $35,000. A followup study (South Carolina State Board of Education 1988) of the School Incentive Reward Program (SIRP) found that the majority of teachers and principals feel that the incentive program underscored the concept of rewarding schools for achievement gains and that winning a SIRP award was an important school goal; it provided added motivation in the schools and promotes teamwork and common purpose among teachers.

Concerns for achieving the additional goals of the Target 2000 reform package, and interest in expanding the array of measurements used, have resulted in the addition to the incentive program of two new criteria—reducing the dropout rate and improving problem-solving/higher-order-thinking skills. Legislation passed in 1991 will allow and encourage 12 schools to explore the use of alternative and performance assessment strategies.

Third, to give teachers, principals, parents, and the public a yardstick to judge their schools, each school receives a report card that shows how it did against itself compared to the previous year, as well as how it compared to similar schools, the state average, and, where available, national averages on such gauges as reading and mathematics achievement, student and teacher attendance, and dropout rates.

Fourth, to encourage school site innovation and restructuring, a provision in the Target 2000 legislation allows consistently improving schools a great deal of freedom from state regulations and accreditation standards. The first group of schools meeting the deregulation standards was notified in spring 1990. Almost 12 percent of all schools in the state qualified for the first round of deregulation.

Fifth, sanctions for consistently low performance and failure to improve may be added to the school-level accountability system in the future. The state department of education contemplated the inclusion of such measures as part of a possible new school accreditation system in 1988. Although this was dropped at the same time, a similar approach was discussed by the South Carolina delegation at the "Better Education Through Informed Legislation" conference in Nashville on July 28, 1990.

South Carolina's reforms also contain measures to hold school districts more accountable. Local school boards are required to respond to each school improvement plan. Although all boards do not yet do a thorough job of this, some do. This approach keeps the pressure on for improvement at the school and district levels.

Districts with low performance levels on achievement tests, poor attendance by teachers or students, and/or high dropout rates fall into a impaired district status. These are visited by a team of top-notch principals, superintendents, and teachers from other districts who observe classrooms and schools and interview parents, educators, and community leaders. Based on these findings, the team issues recommendations, and, upon approval of the state board of education, the district must implement them within a specified time limit.

If a district fails to comply with the recommendations without good cause, it faces withholding of funds or removal of its superintendent. So far, 10 percent of South Carolina districts have been through this process, and in the course of six years there has been only one repeater. No district has reached the stage of removing the superintendent or withholding funds.

Districts deemed to be impaired are given some added funding and technical assistance for one year. A follow-up study of the program (South Carolina State Board of Education 1988) recommended that this extra support continue for at least two years and that the intervention process be done in more stages to allow for more local actions prior to drastic state involvement.

Finally, it should be noted that schools are financially rewarded for improvement, as are districts with 75 percent or more of their schools winning awards in the school incentive program.

In addition to accountability measures at the district levels, South Carolina has new accountability provisions at the state level. The provisions are as follows:

- From 1984–1991, annually the division of public accountability in the state department of education on behalf of the State Board of Education prepared and issued an annual assessment report on the entire Education Improvement Act. The report focused on outcomes such as test scores, college going rates, attendance, truancy, public confidence, and teacher satisfaction. It provides a comprehensive view of education trends and summarizes 5–15 special studies conducted during the year on various initiatives in the reform package. The Division's legal authorization expired in 1991 and its role will be replaced by the use of contracts for special studies under the auspice of the Select Committee, State Board of Education, State Superintendent, Governor, and Business-Education Subcommittee.

- To ensure that the original intent of the South Carolina Education Improvement Act is carried out, a joint subcommittee of the two blue-ribbon committees that originally formulated the reform package remains in force, meeting periodically to monitor implementation of the EIA (Peterson 1989). This panel also issues an annual report to the legislature, the governor, and the public on the status of school reform and suggests improvements and solutions to problems. A summary report is distributed to persons interested in education reform throughout the state.

The success of the business-education-state government partnership during the 1980s led the general assembly to reconstitute the original blue-ribbon committees in Target 2000 into one large committee appointed by the state superintendent, the governor, and legislative leaders. The joint subcommittee was retained as a monitoring arm of the new group.

- To make certain that the legislature keeps itself informed about the progress and problems of the EIA and Target 2000, a select committee composed primarily of legislators was also created. It provides regular oversight and a systematic way to resolve policy problems and conflicts. A number of key leaders in the legislature continue to serve as active members in the select committee seven years after passage of the EIA.

South Carolina is attempting to address school, district, and statewide education accountability in a comprehensive way through its reform packages. It is my impression that these accountability measures are working fairly well, although fine-tuning and revisions will continue to be necessary. The legislative select committee, the business-education subcommittee, and the broad-based blue-ribbon committee provide not only state level accountability on an ongoing basis but also a mechanism to modify the reforms, alter regulations and implementation strategies, and propose new reforms as necessary.

References

ARMSTRONG, JANE. 1990. "A Road Map for Restructuring Schools." *Education Week* 9 (March 28):p. 24.

CALIFORNIA STATE DEPARTMENT OF EDUCATION. 1984. *Performance Report for California Schools.* Sacramento: The Department.

CENTER FOR POLICY STUDIES IN EDUCATION, FLORIDA STATE UNIVERSITY. 1990. *Conditions of Education in Florida 1989–90.* Tallahassee, FL: The Center, 1990.

CREECH, JOSEPH D. 1990. "Educational Benchmarks." Report presented to Southern Regional Education Board, Atlanta, Ga.

DIVISION OF PUBLIC ACCOUNTABILITY. 1985–89. South Carolina State Board of Education. *What Is the Penny Buying for South Carolina?* Columbia, S.C.: The Division.

FOSTER, JACK D. 1990. *The Kentucky Education Reform Act.* Frankfort, Ky.: Kentucky Governor's Office.

GOERTZ, MARGARET E., and KING, BENJAMIN. 1989. "Developing a State Education Indicator System in Missouri." Paper presented at the Annual

Meeting of the American Education Research Association in San Francisco, March 29.

KAAGAN, STEPHEN S., and COLEY, RICHARD J. 1989. *State Education Indicators: Measured Strides, Missing Steps.* Rutgers University, Center for Policy Research in Education.

MARYLAND GOVERNOR'S COMMISSION ON SCHOOL PERFORMANCE. 1989. The Report of the Governor's Commission on School Performance. Annapolis, Md.: The Commission.

NATIONAL GOVERNORS' ASSOCIATION. 1990. "Educating America: State Strategies for Achieving the National Education Goals." Report of the Task Forces on Education to the National Governors' Association. Washington, D.C.: The Association.

OERI STATE ACCOUNTABILITY STUDY GROUP. 1988. "Creating Responsible and Responsive Accountability Systems." Report of the OERI State Accountability Study Group to the U.S. Department of Education. Washington, D.C.: The Group.

PETERSON, TERRY K. 1988. "Building, Passing, Implementing and Assessing Educational Reform in South Carolina." Paper presented at the Annual Meeting of the American Education Research Association in New Orleans, Louisiana.

PETERSON, TERRY K. 1989. "Making Sense (Cents) out of the Statewide Accountability Measures in Education Reform in South Carolina." Paper presented at the Annual Meeting of the American Education Finance Association, San Antonio, Texas, March.

RESNICK, LAUREN B. 1989. "Tests Are Standards of Achievement in Schools." Essay prepared for the Educational Testing Service Conference on the Uses of Standardized Tests in American Education, New York, October.

SOUTH CAROLINA BUSINESS-EDUCATION SUBCOMMITTEE. 1985–1989. Annual report on the South Carolina Education Improvement Act. Columbia, S.C.

SOUTHERN REGIONAL EDUCATION BOARD. 1990. *Educational Benchmarks.* Atlanta, Ga.: The Board.

SOUTHERN REGIONAL EDUCATION BOARD. 1988. *Goals for Education: Challenge 2000.* Atlanta, Ga.: The Board.

WOHLSETTER, PRISCILLA. 1989. "Accountability and State Education Reforms: Some Emerging Alternatives." Paper presented at the Annual Research Conference of the Association for Public Policy Analysis and Management in Arlington, Virginia, November 7–8.

7

Accountability and Assessment California Style

Francie Alexander

California has undertaken an ambitious reform of its curriculum in all subject areas. A comprehensive strategy is in place that addresses professional development, parent involvement, and instructional materials. One of the most significant features of the overall reform strategy is an advanced accountability system that includes state-of-the-art assessment techniques. This chapter describes California's accountability system and assessment program and examines implications for policymakers based on one state's experience with these issues.

Curriculum

Concern is widespread that the nation's schoolchildren are not being well prepared for life in the twenty-first century. Recent studies and test results show that American students lag behind their international counterparts in mathematics and science. Recognition of this dismal state of affairs has led to establishment by the President and governors of a national goal that calls for our students to be first in the world in mathematics and science by the year 2000. International comparisons aside, the findings of the National Assessment of Educational Progress in History, reported in *What Do Our 17-Year-Olds Know?* by Diane Ravitch and Chester E. Finn, Jr. (1987), show that one-third of the students tested do not know when or why the Declaration of Independence was written.

California's concern with these shortcomings has been translated into an unprecedented effort to revamp its curriculum in all subject areas. Providing all students with a richer core curriculum has been the

133

cornerstone of the education reform movement that started eight years ago. The report of the National Commission on Excellence in Education, *A Nation at Risk,* criticized the "cafeteria-style curriculum" that allowed high-school students to graduate with limited exposure to basic subjects. California's response has been to require that all students have access to a balanced educational diet that includes English-language arts, literature, mathematics, science, history-social science, the visual and performing arts, foreign languages, health, and physical education. The overall goals of the curriculum reform effort are to prepare students to compete economically, to participate in the political process, and to achieve personal fulfillment. The future productivity of the economy, the strength of our democratic institutions, and the quality of life in this country depend on successful achievement of such goals.

Accountability

Accountability systems provide useful information that can be used to focus attention and resources toward the attainment of goals. The accountability measures used in California are carefully joined to the overall curriculum reform effort. The state's accountability efforts, like the goals of its curriculum reform, are based on a consensus among parents, professional educators, policymakers, and the public. California's accountability program as described in the *Background Papers for the California Education Summit* (1990a) is based on the premise that the right indicators of performance be reported to the right audience at the right time. For example, to measure the success of the effort to see that students have access to a core curriculum, data are collected on courses completed at the high-school level and on the numbers of students who meet the state's college entrance requirements. California now has a reliable data base that also contains information on the number of students who complete advanced science courses at each school. Localities and states need this kind of information to track their progress toward the goal of improving this country's standing in mathematics and science education. The following is a brief summary of each of the components of California's accountability system and a proposal for synthesizing all indicators into a composite score or rating.

Since 1984, each public school in the state has received an annual report, *Performance Report for California Schools.* In addition to information on course enrollments and access to higher education, the report includes data on test scores, dropout rates, and attendance. The report compares the school's performance to that of other schools with similar student bodies and to the performance of all schools in the state. It also demonstrates what progress has been made toward statewide targets for improving educational opportunities.

The content in the reports is reviewed in ongoing discussions regarding new indicators that need to be incorporated into future reports. For example, the report will be modified as needed to reflect the findings of the high school task force which will be released in 1992. Table 7-1 shows indicators that might be included in a report. Table 7-2 is a sample showing a portion of a high-school performance report.

In addition to school reports produced by the state, California's accountability system includes report cards prepared by the schools to keep the local communities better informed. Proposition 98, an initiative approved by California voters in 1988, requires all elementary and secondary schools to prepare school accountability report cards each year. These cards include information on student achievement, use of substitute teachers, dropout rates, expenditures, class size, teacher placement, train-

TABLE 7-1.   Data on School Performance

Indicators of results
Graduation/dropout rates
Teacher, student attendance
Student writing samples
Achievement and competency test scores
Students' problem-solving skills
Participation in arts and extracurricular activities
SAT/ACT scores
National Assessment of Educational Progress scores
Student status after high school
Employer satisfaction
Progress toward State Board goals
Course enrollments (in advanced placement, foreign languages, sciences, arts)
Percent of students meeting State university entrance requirements

Indicators about policy
Amount and value of homework
Class size
Placement in academic tracks
Average teacher salary
Teacher qualifications
Per pupil spending
Implementation of state reforms

Indicators about context
Community support and wealth
Student characteristics of race, wealth, language, parents' education

---

SOURCE: California Department of Education 1990b.

TABLE 7-2. Performance Report for California Schools

Quality Indicators	1987–88 Base-Year Value	1988–89 Value
Course Enrollments		
3 or more years mathematics	78.8	87.0
Advanced mathematics	61.6	79.7
4 or more years English	57.1	79.6
3 or more years science	42.7	56.0
Chemistry	52.1	64.9
Physics	27.2	24.4
Advanced science	0.0	62.5
4 or more years history	23.4	34.2
4 or more years foreign language	34.2	40.1
1 year fine arts	49.4	49.1
Enrollments in A-F* courses	1.7	56.4
Graduates completing A-F* courses	49.9	56.6
Units required for graduation	22.0	22.0

SOURCE: California Department of Education, 1990. Other candidates for accountability measures are provided in a recent federal report—*Measuring Up: Questions and Answers About State Roles in Educational Accountability* (U.S. Department of Education, 1988).

*Note: A-F courses signify University of California entry requirements.

ing and evaluation, instructional materials, counseling, classroom discipline, and the quality of instruction.

A significant feature of the accountability system is that recognition of high-level achievement is built in through the California School Recognition Program. Results included in performance reports and documented by school visits have been used to identify the state's distinguished schools. As well as rewarding high-level performance, the accountability system makes it possible to identify schools that are not working. The state's accountability system is one that recognizes and rewards achievement and focuses attention on those areas in which improvement is needed.

The accountability system also includes program quality reviews and school accreditations. Both activities involve self-studies by schools and site visits by colleagues. All the information provided by the various components of the accountability program has an impact on the day-to-day operation of schools and on long-term planning at the local and state levels.

Taking all of the components of the current accountability into consideration, an index can be developed that synthesizes all information into a composite bottom line measure of performance. The purpose of such an index is to help schools measure progress over time and to make comparisons with other schools and the rest of the nation.

A proposal for including an over all measure of this kind in the performance reports on each school can be found in Appendix 7-1 at the end of this chapter.

Assessment

The most important component of the state accountability system is the California Assessment Program (CAP), which provides information on what students know and are able to do. The CAP program started in 1972 as one of many post-Sputnik education reform efforts. It has changed over the years, most significantly during the 1980s, and now boasts state-of-the-art tests that are used to measure the effectiveness of the curriculum reform movement. The 1989 report of the Governmental Accounting Standards Board used CAP data and the California school performance reports as outstanding examples of comprehensive performance monitoring.

The purpose of CAP is to provide essential information about the effectiveness of public schools in terms of how well students are prepared for work, citizenship, and personal fulfillment. Toward that end, a method called matrix sampling is used, which focuses the assessment on the effectiveness of educational programs and institutions rather than the progress of individual students. Currently, students are tested annually in grades 3, 6, 8, and 12 in the areas of reading, written expression, mathematics, science, and history. Approximately 300,000 students are tested at each grade level annually. Legislation enacted in 1991 calls for tests to be administered at grade 4 (language arts and mathematics), 5 (history–social science and science), 8 (all subjects), 10 (all subjects).

This approach allows for a broad range of items to be tested. For example, students in one classroom will receive different forms of a test so that perhaps three hundred items for a subject area can be tested even though an individual student completes a test of about thirty items. Thus, students can be tested for a brief period of time, each taking a small portion of the complete test, yet the scope of the assessment could be approximately ten times as broad as an individualized test and the results for a school at least twice as reliable. A matrix test has been compared to a pizza, with each student getting a slice.

The results of CAP are presented on a scale ranging approximately from 100 to 400. This scaling system enables school districts to measure their progress over time. CAP also provides a variety of ranks and percentiles so that the public can monitor the progress made by its schools. CAP provides information to the public and to policymakers and is designed to answer the questions (1) How well are these students doing relative to those of earlier years? (2) How well does this school compare with other schools in California? and (3) How well does this school compare to other schools with similar types of students?

Overall ranks are provided so that the performance of students in a particular school can be compared statewide. Schools are also provided with relative rankings so that comparisons can be made in terms of schools with similar populations. This is important for policy considerations, since factors such as language background are predictive of school success. Without such information, some schools that have made progress with students who have diverse language backgrounds would not receive the credit they deserve.

Schools also receive information that helps to identify the strengths and weaknesses of their instructional programs. For example, they can determine how well students are doing with problem-solving in mathematics and comprehension in reading.

Additions and improvements to CAP that have been made in support of the curriculum reform effort include development of a grade-8 test that accurately reflects the state's new curriculum guidelines; revision of the grade-12 test to achieve coherence with the curriculum; creation of content area tests in history and science; direct writing assessment for students in grades 8 and 12; development of high school end-of-course examinations; and revisions of all tests to emphasize the requirements of a thinking curriculum that demands more problem-solving and applications of learning to various situations.

The importance of CAP to the state's overall efforts should not be underestimated. As expectations have been raised concerning what school systems need to do to prepare students for the twenty-first century, more information is being reported with greater accuracy and reliability. Although all school systems espouse worthy goals, California puts great stock in the maxim "What you test is what you get." Critics of testing are becoming more vocal about the exclusive use of simple multiple choice tests, which result in curricula narrowing. Some critics, referring to this as the "30 percent problem," contend that scarcely 30 percent of what is needed to be a thinking, literate, numerate citizen or worker is tested. Such tests can be administered quickly and cheaply, but ignore the breadth and depth of a more rigorous curriculum. California has started to move from an overreliance on "bubble" tests, which ask students to choose the correct response from among alternatives, to "beyond the bubble" tests, on which students respond to performance items that require them to analyze, organize, interpret, explain, evaluate, and communicate.

The direct writing assessment is a vivid example of testing that positively influences teaching and learning. The CAP direct writing assessment was introduced in grade 8 in 1987 and in grade 12 in 1988. This teacher-developed assessment is designed so that the tasks performed by the students will mirror high-quality instruction. For each type of writing assessed, a set of writing tasks or prompts are provided, as is a scoring guide that identifies the thinking and writing requirements. The essays are then scored by hundreds of teachers at regional scoring centers, thus linking the assessment effort to the state's staff development program. Special handbooks for teachers also advance the staff development agenda.

California's direct writing program has been one of the outstanding successes of the educational reform as reported in *California: The State of Assessment* (1990c). A recent study by the Center for the Study of Writing at Berkeley found that most teachers surveyed (78 percent) indicated that they now assign more writing. Students also report an increase in the number of writing assignments completed. In reporting the latest results of statewide direct writing assessment, California students were compared to their counterparts in the rest of the nation in terms of the amount of writing accomplished. One finding was that California's twelfth-graders reported writing more for school than the nation's twelfth-graders. Twenty-seven percent of California's twelfth-graders reported writing two or fewer papers for school in the previous week (California Assessment Program, 1990), while 49 percent of the national sample of twelfth-graders reported writing two or fewer papers for school in the previous six weeks (U.S. Department of Education 1990a).

CAP is moving "beyond the bubble" in other subject areas as well. In grade-12 mathematics, for example, students have the opportunity to respond to open-ended questions. The questions are complex and involve more than choosing a single correct answer. The California Department of Education published *A Question of Thinking: A First Look at Student's Performance on Open-Ended Questions in Mathematics* (1989), which describes how students may use many ways of thinking to solve a problem as compared to multiple choice items, which may draw only on predetermined thought processes.

The state's new science assessment requires students to demonstrate knowledge of the concepts and processes of science and the ability to solve problems and to engage in hands-on performance tasks. Over 50,000 sixth-grade students had the opportunity to "do" science in a 1990 field test of performance tasks. For example, one of the tasks was to perform a chemical test on samples of lake water to determine why fish are dying.

CAP's history–social science assessments are consistent with the state's ground-breaking *History-Social Science Framework*, which lays out a new curriculum for this contentious, often fragmented and disorganized subject area which has been tagged "the patchwork curriculum." The framework aims at helping students develop historical, geographic, economic, and ethical literacy through in-depth study of historical periods, with heavy reliance on primary sources and literature. In addition to improved multiple choice items, the accompanying assessments ask students to write short and in-depth answers to demonstrate their content knowledge and critical thinking skills. Other areas being developed for the history assessments are oral presentations and group work. The State Superintendent often says that he wants high school students to be able to make a five-minute oral presentation on democracy.

Although performance-based, the CAP tests still use some high quality or enhanced multiple-choice items. No one test can provide all of the information needed to answer all questions about how students are doing. Just as California's accountability system uses multiple indicators, so does its assessment program encourage multiple methods of measuring student progress. With the move toward matrix testing in the early seventies, individual student assessment became the responsibility of local school systems, many of which use nationally normed standardized tests for that purpose. These tests have the limitations of bubble-based tests already described.

Because of such criticism, one of the new directions under development for CAP in the 1990s is to design a test that can be used to report individual scores as well as school performance data while maintaining the commitment to stimulate high quality instruction. The state is also looking at procedures for reviewing and recommending commercially developed tests in the same manner as textbooks. As a result of these efforts and prodded by national criticism, there seems to be some movement by test publishers to develop performance-based material.

Performance standards are being developed for each grade level that CAP assesses. These are derived from the curriculum standards that are expressed in the state's framework and will provide a clear picture of what students should know and be able to do at each grade level. The preparation of these performance standards will be the most important developmental work conducted by the California Department of Education in the 90s.

Additional end-of-course examinations are also being prepared for use in high schools. These should provide an excellent mechanism for improving the quality of courses offered and recognizing and rewarding outstanding student achievement. Currently, these Golden State examinations are being offered in algebra, geometry, economics, U.S. history, biology, and chemistry. Students who achieve at established levels are acknowledged with school recognition, honors, or high honors.

Portfolio assessment is also having an impact on CAP. Although the maintenance of student records and projects in a portfolio is largely a local issue, CAP is studying ways that such data can be collected from teachers and reported at the state level.

Another interesting area of test development is group assessment. In the business world, we look for people who work well with others and communicate effectively. In the classroom, however, demonstrating such qualities is sometimes called "cheating." To prepare students better for the workplace, group performance tasks in history–social science are being prepared.

To further enhance the relationship between schools and employers, efforts are underway to do a better job of communicating information about work habits and test results to business and industry. College-bound students know that their high-school transcripts will be scrutinized as part of the college application process, but students making the transition to work are not always held accountable for their high-school performance. Portfolio assessment and group performance are but two ways that would better inform the hiring process and provide incentives for work-bound students. A proposal for a Final Student Portfolio that provides multiple indicators of what was accomplished in high school can be found in Attachment 2 to Appendix 7-1 at the end of this chapter.

Although there has been significant investment in maintaining a state-of-the-art assessment program, CAP is still a cost-effective program. Its annual budget of $10.3 million represents only .055 of 1 percent of the $18 billion spent on K–12 education in California. The per student cost is only a little over $2.00. The California Education Summit held on December 12–13, 1989, and attended by representatives of business, education, and the legislature recommended that 3 percent of the state's annual education budget be set aside for accountability and assessment efforts.

The California Assessment Program reinforces and encourages state efforts to provide all students with a rich, thinking curriculum. It pursues and tries to realize what California hopes to accomplish in the assessment arena:

• What if students found assessment to be a lively, active, exciting experience?
• What if they could see clearly what was expected of them and believed that the assessment provided a fair opportunity to show what they had learned?
• What if they were challenged to construct responses that conveyed the best of what they had learned—to decide what to present and how to present it—whether through speech, writing, or performance?
• What if they were educated to assess themselves, to become accurate evaluators of the strengths and weaknesses of their own work, and to

prescribe for themselves the efforts they must make to improve it—ultimately, the most important form of assessment available to our students?

- What if the assessment allowed students to use their own backgrounds and indicated ways of building on their strengths for further learning?

- What if their learning were recognized by the school and the community when they had made outstanding progress—regardless of their initial level of achievement?

- What if teachers could look at the tests and say, Now we're talking about a fair assessment of my teaching

—one that focuses on the essence of the student outcomes that I am striving for—not one that focuses on the peripheral skills or the isolated facts which are easiest to measure;

—one that shows they can produce something of value to themselves and to others—an argument, a report, a plan, an answer or solution; a story, a poem, a drawing, a sculpture, or a performance; that they can conduct an experiment, deliver a persuasive oral presentation, participate cooperatively and productively in groups;

—one that is accessible to all my students, yet stretches the most capable students as well—not one that measures some mythical minimum competency level;

—one that matches the assessment that I use on a day-to-day basis to guide my teaching and that guides my students in their learning—not one that takes an artificial form and then naively expects students to give a natural response in an artificial situation;

—one that doesn't take valuable time from the teaching/learning process, but is an integral part of that process;

—one that doesn't treat me as a "Teller of Facts," providing and prescribing the concepts and the content that students are to study—but rather as a coach and a fellow learner, helping my students to become active learners who are prepared to discover what is important to them now and enthusiastic about learning in the future?

- What if the new assessments led parents, taxpayers, legislators, and the business community to exclaim:

—I can see that the schools are focusing on the important things—that students are achieving levels of academic excellence which truly prepare them for the future.

—I can see that students are learning what they need to fulfill themselves as individuals, to become concerned and involved citizens and workers who can adapt to the changing demands of our world—creative people who can think and take initiative, who care about what they do, and who can work with others to solve problems.

—I can see the results in the newspapers which give me the information I need in terms I can understand, which show me the progress our schools are making on assessments that really matter, and where they need my help and support? (California Department of Education 1990)

Implications for Policymakers

Several policy implications may be drawn from the California experience with accountability and assessment. First, accountability systems that include assessment components should be linked to comprehensive reform strategies. Before people and institutions can be held accountable, there needs to be a shared sense of goals and general direction. In California the curriculum improvement effort is the centerpiece of an overall reform strategy that includes staff development, use of upgraded textbooks and new technologies, involvement of parents and communities in the educational process, plans for supporting "at-risk" students, early childhood education, and comprehensive children's services. Curriculum improvement is the engine of the education reform effort; the accountability system is its steering mechanism.

Second, the California experience shows that accountability systems are compatible with system-wide restructuring. Increased efforts are underway to allow more autonomy at the local school level but are guided by agreed-upon goals and informed by data collected as part of an ongoing accountability effort. Being held to the same standard in no way limits the creative and innovative approaches that may be used at the local and school building levels to achieve a common goal.

Third, the accountability system in California was based on consensus. For example, California voters ensured the funding base for schools by passing Proposition 98. One provision of the initiative was to require all schools to provide report cards to local communities. The educational community also supported this initiative. Educators agreed with the public that schools should be funded at a certain level and held accountable for the results. The plan has been revised over time in response to changing conditions, most recently by the California Assessment Policy Committee which helps to maintain consensus.

Finally, the state's accountability system includes multiple reporting categories and an assessment program that utilizes up-to-date multiple measures of achievement. Multiple performance-based measures help to provide the right information to the right audience at the right time.

If we are going to prepare students successfully for the twenty-first century, it is important to monitor what they know and how well they are being prepared for the next level of education and for work and life experience after formal education. Further, it is imperative that we know what works and what does not.

As we work toward the achievement of national education goals, accountability and assessment models such as California's provide valuable information for informing and guiding the process. According to State Superintendent of Public Instruction Bill Honig, "One of the hallmarks of the effort to improve schools has been accountability. The CAP tests focus attention on where schools need improvement. Without it, you're flying blind."[1]

References[2]

CALIFORNIA DEPARTMENT OF EDUCATION. 1989. *A Question of Thinking: A First Look at Student's Performance on Open-ended Questions.* Sacramento, Calif.: The Department, 1989a.

CALIFORNIA DEPARTMENT OF EDUCATION. 1990a. *California Summit on Education* (Background Papers). Sacramento, Calif.: The Department.

CALIFORNIA DEPARTMENT OF EDUCATION. 1990b. *California Assessment Program.* Sacramento, Calif.: The Department.

CALIFORNIA DEPARTMENT OF EDUCATION. 1990c. *California: The State of Assessment.* Sacramento, Calif.: The Department.

FINN, JR., CHESTER E., AND RAVITCH, DIANE. 1987. *What Do Our 17-Year-Olds Know?* New York: Harper and Row.

U.S. DEPARTMENT OF EDUCATION. 1988. *Measuring up: Questions and Answers About State Roles in Educational Accountability.* Washington, D.C.: The Department.

U.S. DEPARTMENT OF EDUCATION. 1990a. *Learning to Write in Our Nation's Schools.* Washington, D.C.: The Department.

U.S. DEPARTMENT OF EDUCATION. 1990b. *National Goals for Education.* Washington, D.C.: The Department.

---

[1] Due to major new school legislation signed by governor Wilson (SB 662), the student assessment system is being redesigned. As previously indicated, grade levels tested will change and individual student tests will be administered to assess student progress in relation to new performance standards. The system will continue to incorporate improved methodologies and to foster good instruction in the manner of the state's poineering efforts in direct writing assessment. End-of-course testing (Golden State Exams) will be expanded to include additional classes and the middle school level. The California plan takes into account national standards and assessment efforts and will attempt to provide comparable results.

[2] All documents published by the California Department of Education may be obtained by writing to the Bureau of Publications, P.O. Box 944272, Sacramento, CA 94244-2720.

Appendix 7-1. New California Education Report: A Working Paper

GRADE 12, HIGH SCHOOL EDUCATION REPORT

PURPOSE OF THE NEW EDUCATION REPORT

School performance is difficult to assess because schools are highly complex, multifaceted institutions. In the area of academic excellence alone, the measures are vast and include: student achievement, course enrollments, dropouts, college-going rates, and many more. The grade 12 *Performance Report for California Schools* contains over 40 quality indicators of school performance. This wealth of information may be overwhelming and make it difficult to draw conclusions. In order to capture the broader perspective of school performance, we have developed an average performance value. As with other data in the Performance Report, the average performance value reports state and school progress and allows for comparisons among schools and over time.

The average performance value and supplementary data described below have several important properties: they are simple to calculate, are easy to explain, validly compare schools, and provide direction for investment of school resources to increase student performance. These data include: state average, state rank, relative rank, change from base value, change from previous-year value, change in the pool of students meeting performance levels (percent change), and values of individual quality indicators. There is a natural tendency to compare schools; however, perhaps more important is the change in a school's measures over time.

SOURCE: California Department of Education, Program Evaluation and Research Division, Educational Planning and Information Center, November, 1990.

MEASUREMENT CHOICE

The average performance value is based on real-world performance levels where a higher performance rating for each quality indicator reflects a higher percent of students scoring above a set criterion. This broad perspective provides a quick way to measure performance and a simple way to compare schools.

The school distribution of student performance on each quality indicator is measured by counting the number of students at or above a particular performance level and converting the count to a percent. Analyses have shown that this "percent above" measure is statistically robust in that it is not greatly affected by the shape of the distribution.

Having specified performance levels allows schools great flexibility in approaching ways to increase the number of students achieving the performance level. The message intended is that the needs of all students in the school should be met. This is accomplished by selecting quality indicators and performance levels which measure different levels of student performance.

QUALITY INDICATORS

The number of quality indicators included in the education report has been limited to reduce complexity. All Performance Report quality indicators were considered and a sample of the fifteen most important and best indicators measuring a broad range of student performance was chosen (see Attachment 1). These quality indicators were selected because they are representative of the Performance Report, measure different levels of student performance, and measure important student performance outcomes. During analysis and review of Performance Report quality indicators, a new indicator was added (geometry enrollment) and the methods used to calculate some indicators were changed (e.g., dropout rate, CAP performance levels).

The remaining quality indicators were excluded from the education report because they added no new information, duplicated information, did not help to distinguish among schools at different performance levels, or did not report data on the majority of schools in the state.

Additional quality indicators may be added to the education report as data become available. Some of these include: CAP history/social science, CAP science, grade 9 dropout rate, and vocational education quality indicators.

Logical and statistical analyses of the chosen quality indicators reveal that they form several groupings: CAP achievement, curriculum (geometry enrollment, 4 or more years of English, a-f course enrollment), dropout (three-year derived dropout rate), and college bound (a-f course completion, four-year college attendance rate, SAT, and advanced placement).

Many approaches were used in selecting these quality indicators. Suggestions from a Task Force (consisting of superintendents, evaluators, and education professors) and a Superintendents Review Committee were taken into consideration along with information from statistical analyses of each indicator, separately, and in combination with other indicators. These selected quality indicators are listed in Attachment 1 and discussed below.

CAP Achievement

This group of quality indicators consists of measures relating to student achievement at all levels. Two performance levels for each CAP test (reading, mathematics, and direct writing) are included to provide maximum incentives for schools. Improvements at the two ends of the distribution can be evaluated. The Adequate performance level (percent of students scoring at or above the 35th percentile in reading, the 30th percentile in mathematics, scoring 4 or better in direct writing) is necessary because it describes students performing at minimally acceptable levels. The Adept performance level (Commendable and Exceptional for direct writing) measures the high end of the CAP distribution (percent of students scoring at or above the 75th percentile in reading, the 70th percentile in mathematics, scoring 5 or better in direct writing). These measures add important information to the education report. Statistical analyses reveal that the Adept performance level is not duplicative of the performance of the same students measured by the SAT or other college-bound quality indicators.

Curriculum

This group of quality indicators measures the percent of students taking more rigorous courses and is included in the education report to encourage all students to enroll in these courses.

Geometry

Some educators argue that one of the best curriculum measures in mathematics is algebra completion. However, since this course is typically taken in 8th or 9th grade it is not a good quality indicator for high schools. Geometry completion was chosen as a high school measure of mathematics. This supports and encourages two years of rigorous mathematics for all students (geometry and its prerequisite, algebra).

Four or More Years of English

There is no structured course sequence for English (like mathematics). After exploring curriculum policy and statistically analyzing course enrollments, no course was found to represent a rigorous level of accomplishment (like geometry) which all students should complete before graduation. Therefore, the recommended graduation requirement of four years or more of English is included in the education report.

A-F Enrollments
In an attempt to increase the number of students (not just college-bound) taking a-f approved courses, the education report includes a-f course enrollments.

Dropout Complement
The education report includes a measure of the three-year derived dropout rate. The actual number used in the education report is the complement of the dropout rate (100 minus dropout rate). This is one of the most important measures of the education system since the students need to be enrolled before learning can take place, and for this reason, it is given a larger weight in calculations as explained below.

College Bound
This group of quality indicators consists of measures typically associated with achievement of students bound for college.

A-F Course Completions
The University of California requires students to complete a course of study for admission known as the a-f course. The percent of students completing the a-f course is a strong measure of student performance, as well as an indicator of who is college bound, or at least college eligible. This indicator measures the percent of students completing a-f requirements.

College Attendance
There are three types of college-going rate data available: UC, CSU, and community colleges (CC). Unfortunately, data for students attending private colleges or colleges out-of-state are not available. Community college data are seriously flawed. California Postsecondary Education Commission personnel, the source of community college data, are reluctant to release these data because the validity of the data is questionable. Districts have complained that these data can either vastly inflate or underreport the number of their graduates attending community colleges. Because of major flaws in data collection and reporting, the CC rate will be excluded from the education report and college-going rate will be based solely on UC and CSU data until more accurate CC data are available.

SAT Verbal and SAT Mathematics

The SAT "percent above" measures (scores of 450 or better on SAT verbal, scores of 500 or better on SAT mathematics) are calculated per 100 seniors. These measures do not penalize a school for encouraging all students to take the SAT. Even if many of these students receive low scores, the school's "percent above" scores would not be adversely affected.

Advanced Placement

These exams are offered in 24 areas and a score of 3 or better generally constitutes a passing grade and qualifies a student for college credit. The "percent above" measure represents the number of scores of 3 or better per 100 seniors, and like the SAT, does not penalize schools for encouraging more students to take AP exams even if many would receive low scores. Since students can take exams in more than one area, it is possible for a school to get "percent above" scores of more than 100%, but it is unlikely. Schools in districts which have not given permission for release of their SAT and AP scores will be given the base-year value at the 50th percentile of their comparison group for SAT and AP.

CALCULATION

Average Percent

The "average percent" is the average of "percent above" scores for all the reported quality indicators (dropout rate is weighted by a factor of four in this calculation). The theoretical range of values for the average percent is 0 to 100.

Weighting

There is an implicit and natural weighting based on the number of quality indicators measuring a particular facet. For example, six of the quality indicators are CAP and they account for about one third of the report. To add emphasis to the dropout rate, its value is given additional weight by multiplying it by four when calculating averages.

State Rank

Each high school will receive its state rank based on its average percent. This rank will enable schools to compare their performance with schools statewide. The state rank will be calculated in the same way ranks are calculated for quality indicators in the Performance Report.

Base Values and Calculation of Change Scores

School progress will be monitored over time. The base year "percent above" scores for all reported quality indicators will be averaged into a base percent. This is a new concept which allows the combining of quality indicators with different base years. It will be particularly useful when new quality indicators are added to the report. In the tradition of the Performance Report, change from a base will be reported. The base year of the education report is 1987–88, however, data are not available for all component quality indicators in that year. The first year of CAP direct writing is 1988–89. Therefore, the base average percent will include 1988–89 data for direct writing and 1987–88 data for all other quality indicators. Change will be calculated by subtracting the base average percent from the current average percent.

In addition, one-year growth will be reported. This is calculated by subtracting the previous year's average percent from the current average percent.

Relative Rank

The relative rank is the comparison group percentile rank of the current average percent. It is the rank a school's current average percent receives when compared to the distribution of base average percents of similar schools (defined by the student demographic factors of: parent education level; percent of students with limited-English proficiency; student mobility; and the percent of students receiving assistance under the Aid to Families with Dependent Children program). The relative rank will enable schools to compare their performance to similar schools.

New Quality Indicators and Calculation of Change Scores

In time, new quality indicators may be added to the report (e.g., CAP history/social science, CAP science, grade 9 dropout rate, vocational education quality indicator) and data collection for quality indicators may change (e.g., dropout rate, grades tested by CAP). The base average percent will include base year values for all quality indicators regardless of when they were first published in the education report. Then each year, the average current percent will be compared to the average base percent to calculate change.

New Schools

The report will be calculated for new schools after their second year, because it takes two years to accumulate the data for college-going rates.

New schools will not have base-year data for most quality indicators. The average base percent for these schools will be calculated using the first year of data available for the school. The year the school came into existence will be reported with the school's average base percent and change scores so appropriate comparisons can be made with average change state wide and change exhibited by other schools.

Targets

The performance and growth targets will be the same used for the individual quality indicators in the Performance Report. The performance target for the current average percent will be a relative rank greater than 75 (the 75th percentile of the comparison group in the base year). The growth target will be the average of the individual indicator growth targets. Exceptions will be made for new schools where growth targets will be adjusted to take into consideration the age of the school.

Because of the simplicity of report calculation, school personnel will be able to determine what improvement is necessary to reach targets.

SCHOOL REPORTS

The education report will be accompanied by explanatory material. Average percents with accompanying statistics (state rank, relative rank, growth) will not be reported for small schools (those testing less than 100 in grade 12). It will, however, be possible to calculate these from information provided.

DISTRICT EDUCATION REPORT

DISTRICT REPORTS

District education reports will be created for districts with at least 1,000 students enrolled. There will be three levels of district reporting: high school, middle school, and elementary school. The base "percent above" and current "percent above" values of all quality indicators included in the district report will be reported along with score change for these quality indicators. The current average percent will be accompanied by the state rank, relative rank, and change values. Districts will also receive explanatory information.

HIGH SCHOOL, GRADE 12

The high school district report will be based on the average of school report quality indicators (weighted by a grade 12 enrollment) except for the dropout rate quality indicator, which will be the actual district dropout rate.

MIDDLE SCHOOL, GRADE 8

School reports will not be created for middle schools. The middle school district education report will be created from the Performance Report quality indicators. Calculations and reporting will be the same as outlined above. School values for quality indicators will be weighted by grade 8 enrollment then averaged to calculate district values.

ELEMENTARY SCHOOL, GRADES 3 AND 6

School reports will not be created for elementary schools. The elementary school district education report will be created from the Performance Report quality indicators. Calculation and reporting will be the same as outlined above. School values for quality indicators will be weighted by CAP number tested then averaged to calculate district values.

California Department of Education   DRAFT   January 16, 1991
SCHOOL PERFORMANCE REPORT SUMMARY, 1989-90

School: *Sunny Valley High School*
District: *Sunny Valley Unified*
County: *Norcal*
CDS: 12-12345-1234567

Percent of students reaching the following performance levels	1989-90 Percent	Target Met	1-Year Growth[1] from 1988-89	Growth[1] from Base[2] 1987-88	1989-90 Relative Rank[3]
CAP Achievement					
Reading - Adept & above	37.1	*	0.0	−0.9	92
Reading - Adequate & above	80.2	*	3.1	4.1	93
Mathematics - Adept & above	32.5	*	1.1	2.1	53
Mathematics - Adequate & above	75.0	*	3.4	2.1	59
Direct Writing - Commendable & exceptional	32.1		1.0	1.8	91
Direct Writing - Adequate & better	75.2	*	0.0	1.2	98
Curriculum					
Geometry completion	70.1	*	1.2	2.6	82
Four or more years of English	95.4	*	4.6	5.3	85
A-f course enrollments	52.0		0.1	1.7	72
Dropout Complement (100 minus % dropping out) Three-year derived rate, weighted by four to calculate averages	89.3	*	1.4	2.3	70
College Bound					
A-f course completions	48.2	*	2.2	2.0	86
Four-year college attendance	30.1	*	1.6	0.8	91
SAT verbal - at least 450	17.3		−1.4	1.2	68
SAT mathematics - at least 500	25.1	*	0.7	1.7	81
Advanced placement - 3 or better	11.4		1.1	1.4	51
AVERAGES Divide sum by 18	57.7	*	1.4	2.0	n/a

	1990 Average Percent	Percent Change from 1988-89	Percent Change from Base	Relative Rank
School values	57.7*	2.5	3.6	76
District values	60.0*	2.0	2.5	78
State values	49.3	1.6	1.9	n/a

Percent change is the increase in the pool of students who met performance levels.

* Targets Met: Asterisks (*) indicate performance or growth targets were met for the quality indicators and the 1990 average percent value. Refer to the interpretive guide for details.

[1] Growth indicates the average change in the percent of students meeting performance levels. Each positive percentage point indicates that 1% more students met performance levels than in the past.

[2] The base year for all indicators is 1987-88 except CAP direct writing which is 1988-89.

[3] The relative rank is the rank a school achieved when compared to other schools with similar background factors.

Attachment 1

Final Student Portfolio*		Individual/ Formative	Individual/ Summative	Group/ Program
• Grade 11/12 CAP • End of course test results • Apprenticeship results	• SAT • AP • Community service • Senior project			

12	• Additional end of course tests
	• Results of apprenticeships,
	  work experience
	• Results of SAT, AP, etc.
	• Results of retake of grade 11 CAP
	• Results of community service,
	  senior projects, etc.
		X	X	X

11	• 11th grade CAP**
	  (if passed at appropriate level,
	  qualifies students for CC program
	  without remediation or entry-level
	  job; if not passed, remediation
	  planned for grade 12)
	• Additional end of course tests
	• Results of apprenticeships,
	  work experience
		X	X	X

10
 	
9
	• Interim portfolio
	  (results of end of course tests
	  taken to date and diagnostic
	  data)
	• School diagnostic tests
	• End of course tests
	  (Golden State)
		X	X	

8	• 8th grade CAP
	  (summative assessment of K-8
	  plus entry assessment into
	  high school)
		X	X	X

* Can be forwarded to employers and schools, through electronic means.
** May be taken and passed between grades 10 and 12.

Attachment 2

ON THE HOME FRONT

Reform Comes Home: Policies to Encourage Parental Involvement in Children's Education

Gene I. Maeroff

The problems of the public schools are not easily separated from America's other ills. Throughout its history this country has lurched from crisis to crisis, and so the mere emergence of another difficult period, as now exists, may not be particularly remarkable or perhaps even worrisome. However, current education troubles differ from those of the past not only in magnitude but also in the ways that the social milieu impinges on the schools. Trends in several areas illustrate this point and redound with serious consequences for parents who are raising children.

- *Values.* The United States is lost and drifting, appearing unable to regain control of its moral rudder. Materialism and bad taste have come to dominate life at many levels. Too many people are driven only by pursuit of money and not by deeper concerns. A small number are making so much money that soon the income disparities will likely start demoralizing the rest. A swindle of the enormity of the savings-and-loan scandal is emblematic of greed and poor judgment at their worst. Inevitably, there will be some fallout in shaping the thinking and attitudes of the young.
- *Poverty.* There is no prospect of coming close to wiping out poverty in this country. One of every five children in the United States is poor, many of them desperately so (U.S. Bureau of the Census 1990b). In urban school systems this percentage soars as high as 80

157

percent of the entire enrollment (Council of the Great City Schools, in press). These youngsters are afflicted by a host of problems that seriously impede the ability of schools to make a difference in their lives.

- *Family breakdown.* Single-parent families have always existed, but often in the past there was an extended family or neighborhood network that provided a safety net if the lone parent—usually a widow or widower—could not. Support structures are weakened today, a time when 25 percent of all families with children are headed by single parents—those who are divorced and widowed as well as those who never wed (U.S. Bureau of the Census 1990a). Fifty-nine percent of all black children live with one parent (U.S. Bureau of the Census 1990), and the portion will be even higher in the future because three out of four black women under thirty who have babies are unwed (U.S. Bureau of the Census 1988).

- *Drugs.* How will this terrible blight be lifted? Drugs feed on the emptiness within so many Americans, both poor and affluent. The nation looks to its borders and to the countries where narcotics originate to squelch the problem, but Americans should be looking inside themselves. Drugs compound all of our other problems. Hundreds of children are born as drug addicts each day, and even if they are weaned they are apt to be permanently damaged. How will the schools ever cope with this?

- *The inner city.* The nation has a Third World in its midst, yet few voices of alarm are being heard. A large and growing portion of the population—made up disproportionately of poor, uneducated people of color—is entirely alienated from middle-class America. The children who pass into adulthood in these settings have little prospect of attaining education beyond high school or ever holding a meaningful job.

This dismal scenario is the context for the subject at hand: parents and their role in the education of children. How can schools best work with parents in the prevailing climate? What can government do to help this process?

It is widely felt in this country that many parents are not responsibly preparing their children for school and are not reinforcing education once those children get to school. There is wide agreement about the desirability of continuity between home and school and between school and home, but in all too many cases—and always to the detriment of children—this circle of cooperation is broken. Asked how well the parents of children in their schools are "performing their roles," 60 percent of the nation's teachers rate the job as only fair or poor (Carnegie Foundation for the Advancement of Teaching 1990).

Nine out of 10 members of the public say that more parent involvement would benefit the schools (U.S. Chamber of Commerce 1990). Given this widespread conviction, it is worth trying to identify its possible forms. Such an examination might view the parental role in terms of three distinct parts, each of which has implications for public policy.

The first part contains everything that happens out of school, at home and elsewhere, that ultimately affects the child's formal schooling in an indirect way—"indirect" only because these are not activities explicitly linked to the curriculum in the way that, say, homework is.

What is at stake in the first part is the educational foundation that parents build in the home in the years leading up to school, as well as the continuing attitudinal reinforcement by parents once children attend school. This includes everything from providing for an infant's healthy physical development to the experiences that lead to intellectual readiness for schooling to the feelings about education that parents overtly or inadvertently plant in the minds of their children. The actions and activities of parents from the very moment their children are born—even during the prenatal period, some say—are at issue. Whether parents take children to pediatricians and whether they read books to their children, for example, are such matters.

The second part of involvement revolves around what parents do outside school that is linked directly to the education of their children once they are enrolled in school. These are the connections that parents make with schoolwork. The most obvious activity of this sort is being supportive of homework—for instance, making certain that a child has a quiet, private place to study or helping a child with assignments.

That is not the end of it. Parents can make it their business to become familiar with the curriculum, learning what is being taught in school, subject by subject. This sort of knowledge allows parents to both help their children academically in specific ways and to monitor their children's progress, a task of which most parents are more or less incapable because they lack the necessary information.

The third part of involvement is actual parent participation in the life of the school. This might be viewed along a continuum. At one end, where involvement is least, it could simply mean paying dues to parents' organizations or showing up for parent-teacher conferences a couple of times a year. At an intermediate point on the continuum, parents might volunteer to participate in school activities. At the other end, where involvement is most intense, we see something like what is now happening in Chicago, where parents sit on councils that govern individual schools.

In any of these three areas, the state might assist parents in carrying out their roles. A closer examination of each of the three parts will show how public policy could promote and abet involvement.

Indirect Reinforcement

What happens outside school has a profound impact on a child's learning in school. The attitudes and behavior of parents have much to do with a child's preparation for formal learning. Also affected are the child's aspirations, which tend to reflect this conditioning. Certainly the ability of a student to do schoolwork is an outgrowth of experiences in the home. Children who are intellectually stimulated outside school have advantages in school. According to the International Reading Association, "A language-rich environment in the child's early years is the foundation for reading and subsequent learning" (Maeroff 1989).

Parents who read to their children regularly from the time they are young, for example, give their youngsters intellectual nourishment for school. When they engage their children in quality conversation and answer their questions, parents further aid their development. Where they take their children and what activities are made available to them have much to do with the foundation for learning that children bring to school. Even the influence of the surrounding neighborhood is a factor.

This first part of parent involvement inculcates habits of mind. Depending on what they know and how they deport themselves, children will approach schoolwork in different ways. Herbert J. Walberg calls these interactions between parent and child the "curriculum of the home" (Walberg 1986).

If parents value education, chances are greater that their children will value education. If children learn at home that some of what is worth having takes effort and requires the delay of gratification, chances are greater that children will be willing to work hard in school. If parents do not impart such beliefs to their children, it might be possible to do so through programs that provide mentors and role models, but it will be more difficult that way—especially if a child lives in surroundings that are not supportive of academic achievement.

"Reinstilling the value of education in our community is an important thing," said Marion Wright Edelman, head of the Children's Defense Fund, recalling her childhood in a poor Mississippi town where high standards were set for the children. "We must bring back a sense of community expectations. We must provide a countervoice for black children that says 'You are worth something. You can make it' " (Miller 1986, p.2).

The first part of parent involvement mainly concerns parenting itself. More and more attention is being given to parenting as local, state, and national agencies and organizations sponsor what are called "parent enabling" programs. A precursor of this trend was the child study movement, aimed mostly at middle-class families, which gained momentum in the 1920s and 1930s as a way of educating parents and future parents. By 1932 parent education courses were offered in at least twenty-five states (Brim 1965). Most parenting instruction today is concentrated on those with newborns and preschoolers, but increasingly attention is also directed toward parents of school-age children.

Although the idea of teaching adults to be parents may at first seem farfetched, it is worth remembering that most people get more instruction in how to drive an automobile than they do on how to be a parent. Moreover, a person must take a test to get a driver's license.

A local community-based program to teach parenting might resemble Family Place, created in 1981 in Washington, DC, to serve disadvantaged mothers, some of them immigrants. Participants were guided in child-rearing in settings where they could seek advice from experts, as well as discuss mutual problems of parenting. Another local effort for disadvantaged families, the Mother-Child Home Program in Freeport, NY, focused on promoting habits of good conversation between mothers and their preschool children. Evidence of significant IQ gains by the children lasted for up to three years after the intervention ended (*Building Concepts Through Verbal Interaction* 1979).

Perhaps the nation's most comprehensive local effort at parent enabling exists today on Chicago's impoverished South Side. It serves mothers of preschool children whose residence in the same housing project, the Robert Taylor Homes, places their children in the catchment district of a single public school. Funded by $6.9 million from the Harris Foundation, the program offers women, from the outset of pregnancy, a wide range of assistance to help them become proficient mothers who can provide their infants with stimulating environments. The provision of health services is included. This support continues up until the children enter kindergarten at the Beethoven School.

Not just nongovernmental agencies, but states, as well, are sponsoring parenting programs. Leading models are found in Minnesota and Missouri. Early Childhood Family Education in Minnesota is aimed at boosting the competence of parents to provide the best possible environment for the healthy growth of their children during the formative years between birth and kindergarten. Participants gather weekly for two-hour sessions. During the first hour, parents play with their children while a teacher-observer offers "developmental tips." During the second hour, while the children are being cared for by others, the groups of parents talk with the teacher-observers, sharing ideas and advice.

Missouri's Parents as Teachers program involves visits to the homes of preschool children by specially trained parent educators, hired by local school districts with help from the state. Health and developmental screening is also part of this program. Every four to six weeks, groups of parents in the same neighborhood gather in the living room of one of their homes along with their children. The parent educator, meeting with the small group, leads a discussion on child-rearing and describes and demonstrates stimulating activities in which parents can engage with their children. At regular intervals the parents also assemble in larger groups at neighborhood schools for additional education.

The fact that the home is the site for parent education in the Missouri model is significant. Programs in which parents are visited in their homes were most successful, according to a review of evaluations of more than two hundred early parenting interventions by the Center for the Child of the National Council of Jewish Women (Gray 1990). The impact of Missouri's Parents as Teachers program on early intervention planning nationally is seen in the inspiration that it provided for US West Corporation's $10-million grant in 1991 to set up similar ventures in fourteen western states.

Other states have also sought to help parents of preschool youngsters give their children a firmer foundation for school. Arkansas has its Home Instruction Program for Preschool Youngsters, known by its acronym as HIPPY, which trains parents to better prepare their children for school. Also, there are such programs as Education for Parenting, in which Alaska has tried to teach parenting and caring skills to parents of children through the eighth grade.

Another approach that belongs to the first part of parent involvement is the effort to help parents who are less educated lift their own levels of schooling. The idea is that adults who feel the impact of education in their own lives might be more likely to appreciate, support, and promote the schooling of their offspring. Presumably the atmosphere in the home will change if parents themselves change.

Two notable vehicles for pursuing this goal are adult literacy programs and the GED programs that prepare dropouts for the high-school diploma. Such projects constitute one of the least-explored facets of the first part of parent involvement and would be a natural progression in places where parent enabling has made inroads among disadvantaged families.

Creating such programs may mean making the school a site for family education, not just an institution that teaches children. At times convenient to the schedules of adults, they might go to the school themselves and get instruction—usually in basic skills—that will allow them, too, to be learners. In McAllen, Texas, for instance, the school system had three Family Literacy Centers operating twice a week.

Parenting instruction need not end when children enter school. Twenty-five schools around the country are part of a network called the League of Schools Reaching Out, which was created by the Institute for Responsive Education in Boston. The institute holds video conferences in which league schools participate by satellite and telephone linkup. Typical of League members is School Number 5 in Perth Amboy, N.J., where many families are poor and Spanish-speaking. There are classes to teach parents English as a second language, breakfasts for parents, and family counseling arranged by the school. There have also been classes to teach basic math and science to parents and children (Haydon 1990).

The desired result, whether from "parent enabling" programs or efforts to teach basic skills, is that parents will end up better able and more inclined to support the development of their children. This approach can help establish the home as a place where behavior and values are supportive of education.

Reinforcing the Efforts of the Schools

The second way in which parents can connect with the education of their children is through specific efforts made at home to support the academic program. This can be aided by a flow of communication between school and home. It may include notes and reports that are sent home and phone calls to parents by teachers. "The school has an obligation to inform parents about school programs and their children's progress," says Joyce Epstein of the Center for Social Organization of Schools at Johns Hopkins University (Epstein 1987).

An example of a teacher who takes this responsibility seriously is Lucille C. Baca, who teaches in an elementary school in Albuquerque, NM. Through a series of newsletters written on a word processor, run off on a printer, and then photocopied for all the parents, she provides such advice and observations as the following:

> We began studying nutrition. We will also work on charting, place value and three-digit addition and subtraction. We will be doing a great deal of science in coming months to prepare for our Science Fair. . . . Your child writes stories daily in his/her journal and at least once a week we write a class story on the board. One child will give me the title, another child will give me the opening line, and other children will embellish the story and bring it to a close.

In Great Britain the government's Department of Education and Science instituted a requirement beginning in 1990 that each secondary school must have a prospectus—available for inspection by parents—that includes information about what is taught, how it is taught, and for how much time. Such a measure might be helpful to parents in the United States.

In the absence of this kind of support from the government, there are still steps that American parents can take to reinforce the school program in the home. Encouraging children to do homework, for example, is a start. Because youngsters tend to believe that learning is supposed to stop at the schoolhouse door, they are naturally inclined to object to any exercise outside of school that bears an academic aura.

Some critics argue that homework is useless, even when students are diligent about doing it, and that it ought to be abandoned by the schools. Rather than debate the merits of homework, let us assume that as long as the schools assign it, parents ought to do all they can to reinforce it.

Yet schools do not do as much as they might to underpin the efforts of parents in this respect. Few programs teach parents about their role in connection with homework and what they should expect of their children. This is especially true at the middle and high-school levels; it seems that the older the students, the less schools do to make parents partners in their education. Certainly policymakers might want to consider what interventions would be appropriate.

One positive development is the spread of Homework Hotlines, telephone numbers that students and parents can call for assistance with homework assignments. Sometimes, teachers get overtime pay to handle such calls, providing them with extra income. In such cities as New York, homework help is available by telephone in several languages.

Bolstering the ability of parents to assist children with homework, however, is only the beginning of bringing parents closer to the curriculum. A relatively untapped area has to do with making them more conversant with the curriculum and with specific academic expectations. A locality or state that moves in this direction will be charting virgin territory and, in the process, providing a model for others to follow.

This might mean holding periodic meetings about the curriculum or sending home materials that describe what is happening in each subject at a given time. Right now, parents who would like to engage their children in discussion of what they are learning often have no starting point except to ask the youngster "What did you do in school today?" We all know the answer to that one.

One approach might resemble an effort carried out some years ago by the Catholic schools of St. Paul, Minnesota. The Catholic school system, which was instituting a unit on sex education, wanted to forestall controversy. Classes were held first for parents, to offer the same material that was to be taught to the children, with each lesson being presented to parents before being presented to students. Thus, parents knew what was ahead and rumors could not undermine this well-intentioned but potentially explosive curriculum.

Something similar could be done for parents everywhere in connection with various subjects. Parents ought to get abundant information about what their children are studying. Besides making parents better informed, such an approach allows them to monitor the school more closely and gives them a basis for discovering whether their children are learning what is being taught.

It is remarkable how little parents know about what their children study in school. More states and local school systems ought to follow the lead of California's State Education Department, which has published subject-by-subject handbooks for parents in English and Spanish that trace the curriculum from kindergarten through twelfth grade. Each school district in California decides whether or not to distribute the pamphlets.

Under most circumstances, parents find it difficult to assist and monitor their children's work in school. Unfortunately, some parents seem unwilling to make the effort to find out about the content of their children's schooling, even when such programs are offered. In a survey sponsored by *Newsweek* magazine, Chrysler Corporation, and the National PTA, most parents said that they were too busy to devote much time to learning about the schooling of their children, even though they felt supportive of that schooling (PTA/Dodge National Parent Survey 1990).

For parents who *are* willing to give the time, some programs are available outside the school even if the school itself provides no such assistance. These outside ventures are aimed at equipping parents with knowledge and skills that will enable them to aid their children and monitor their progress. Material conveyed through this approach is less connected to the curriculum than it might be if the information were provided by the school itself, but it is valuable in the general sense that sooner or later it is apt to be relevant.

One of the best of these efforts is the Family Math Program, sponsored by the Lawrence Hall of Science at the University of California at Berkeley. Information and materials are available by mail so that the program can be used throughout the country. Workshops are organized by grade levels— one, for instance, for parents of second- and third-graders and another perhaps for parents of fourth-, fifth-, and sixth-graders. These workshops typically meet for an hour or two once a week for at least a month. The heart of the program, once parents have been through the workshops, is contained in a thick volume of math problems that parents can tackle with their children. A school district anywhere in the country could buy the materials and sponsor the workshops for parents.

Another way to inform parents in a general way about the curriculum is found in Hayward, California, where the Child Development Project—an outside agency—about twice a month provides homes with "family homework," tasks for students and parents to do together. These academically oriented exercises have the added feature of fostering communication between parents and children.

Also operating outside the schools is the National Committee for Citizens in Education, based in Columbia, Maryland. This organization, through its many reports and publications, arms parents with weapons they need to be knowledgeable advocates for their children on matters related to what takes place in the school.

At a time when parental choice in schooling is widely discussed, there is a serious need for parents to understand the curriculum. Only then can they choose the best educational settings for their children. What good to families is the right to choose schools if they don't know how to choose and cannot even tell when they have made the wrong choice? Even in the absence of a formal choice plan that lets them select the schools their children attend, parents are obligated to ensure that their children are well-served by the schools they are directed to attend.

Participation in School

The third and final part of involvement has to do with the actual operation of the school. Parent involvement in this area ranges from attending PTA meetings and teacher conferences to serving as a volunteer or teacher's aide to being a member of a governance council.

Some observers believe that getting parents more deeply involved is essential if poor and minority children are going to succeed in school. If these parents feel linked to the school, according to this line of reasoning, they will be more supportive of the education of their children. This argument implies that children from more affluent families do well in school because their parents are active in the school itself.

This is a myth. Advantaged parents are not necessarily extensively involved in their children's schools. Their influence on the schooling of their children arises primarily from what they do outside the schools, not from serving on governing councils or even as classroom volunteers. They are involved with their children, but not necessarily with the school. The attitudes and values—tacit and spoken—and the experiences of children in such families are largely what accounts for scholastic success. The schooling of children from all backgrounds would benefit from such attitudes, values, and experiences whether or not their parents actually participate in the life of the school.

Advantaged parents are more apt to have contact with the school over questions involving the progress of their children and policies affecting their children, such as teacher-pupil assignments. This is quite different, however, from being involved in the operations of the school.

Poor and minority parents may feel a sense of separation from schools that is difficult for others to appreciate. Such alienation—on top of not quite knowing what measures to take to boost academic achievement—may prevent these parents from doing all they might to aid their children. Thus, it may be that extraordinary forms of involvement in the school are needed to overcome the sense of separation that poor and minority parents feel.

Some researchers theorize that even in Japan, where reinforcement of schooling by the home is stronger than in the United States, differences in pupil achievement seem to arise from the perceptions of the parents of children of different social classes. In studying white and minority parents of fourth- and fifth-graders in a single American school, Raymond L. Calabrese found that minority parents were more alienated from the school than white parents. He discovered that most minority parents felt that they lacked the personal knowledge or confidence to confront a large bureaucratic institution and that they saw the school as unfriendly. "If school officials only contact minority parents to report negative occurrences or to enlist their cooperation in applying sanctions, then those parents rightfully may view with suspicion any other invitations to participate in school affairs," Calabrese concluded (1990).

James Comer's program, which has received so much attention, is predicated on parental involvement in the schools. Parents play roles in classrooms and are members of the School Governance and Management Team that is at the center of the Comer program. Ideally, the atmosphere in the school and the conduct of students are affected by the presence of parents in the building.

Comer said that a good relationship between parents and school personnel arose more freely in a simpler bygone era. He maintains that new mechanisms are needed to bring about similar contacts today if trust and mutual respect between school and home are to flourish. His approach puts parents into schools in various roles so that children can observe their parents and other adults interacting in a cooperative way with teachers (Comer 1986).

Head Start was among the earliest attempts to achieve such involvement. Parents served as assistant teachers and in other paid and volunteer roles. Title I of the original Elementary and Secondary Education Act also mandated the creation of parent advisory councils, which were supposed to put parents closer to policymaking in individual schools. When Title I became Chapter 1 in 1981, that mandate was weakened so that parents only had to be "consulted."

Research findings demonstrate that disadvantaged students whose parents are "involved" in their education benefit academically. However, almost all of these studies compared such students with other low-income students whose parents are not "involved." Seldom has a study addressed whether, and what kinds of, parent involvement work for these students to the extent that they can achieve at levels expected of middle-class children (Henderson 1987). It would be helpful to gather this sort of information.

Regardless of a family's economic circumstances, it is important to recognize the shortage of opportunity for parents to take on roles of authority in the children's classrooms. Most kinds of involvement give parents the chance neither to make significant contributions in the classroom nor to shape school policies on matters of teaching and learning. While endorsement of the concept of parent involvement may be fashionable in educational circles, schools continue to provide few outlets for parents to become real partners in the education mission.

The time is fast approaching when some clarification will be needed of what is intended when it is said that parents should be "involved" in the education of their children. The phrase has many meanings, and for that reason it has been analyzed here in terms of three separate aspects. Perhaps this analysis will help others to make sense of this important topic, where piety often takes the place of clarity. Too often one senses that even when people agree on the desirability of parent involvement, they are not talking about the same thing.

Some proponents are not satisfied that parent involvement has any meaning unless parents are actually setting school policies. Indeed, the Council of Chief State School Officers has urged schools to promote parent involvement in school decision-making (Council of Chief State School Officers 1989). In Chicago such parent involvement now means six parents on the eleven-member council that runs each school. This trend toward participation in governance is not limited to the United States. Under Great Britain's new education law, a governing council, including parents as members, is to be established at each school.

Involvement of this sort is sometimes controversial. It brings parents into schools in roles that could pose a threat to those who have traditionally been in charge. If policymakers and educators believe there are valid reasons for limiting parent participation in schools, they should make those reasons known instead of implying that there are no bounds to parent involvement. Given that parent involvement outside the school has been sufficient to ensure the successful education of so many children, perhaps a case can be made for limiting their role in school governance.

One must understand, though, that one reason the role of parents is restricted in terms of governance is because some teachers and principals prefer it that way. Educators cannot have it both ways. They cannot, on the one hand, criticize parents for not being involved in their children's education and, on the other, slam the door in the faces of those who want to get "too" involved. Annette Lareau theorizes that it is not a partnership that some teachers want with parents but a professional-client relationship, in which "both parents and children are seen as clients" (Lareau 1989).

If educators want parents to be more supportive of schools, then they probably will have to be more accommodating to all three models of parent involvement. Interestingly, this prospect arises at the very time that teachers, too, are on the verge of gaining more power in running schools. Might there be clashes ahead? Is there a zero-sum game in which "power" for one stakeholder group inevitably means less for others?

Teacher-parent cooperation could be hastened by training teachers to work with parents. One hesitates to add yet another task to the professional development of teachers, but this is a step worth considering. A possible prototype for this sort of training has been created by the Southwest Educational Development Laboratory (Williams & Feyl Chavkin 1986).

State officials, too, could begin to explore ways that schools might be assisted in reaching out to parents. One method has been demonstrated in Arizona, where the state education department provided annual seminars for administrators, teachers, and parent advisory council members at the request of school principals on "Planning for Parent Involvement." Such seminars, if carried out with good intentions, might be forums in which parents and educators, working together, could frame new agendas for cooperation.

So much is happening in forms of parent involvement that one can scarcely imagine what forms it might take by decade's end. Whatever happens, school and society ought to ease the way for parents to become more tightly connected to the education of their children.

However much or little parents are allowed to help operate the schools, more ought to be done to make it clear to parents that they are welcome in the schools. Some schools have done this by setting up a parents' room in an unused classroom or office. Such a place, with a supply of coffee and a rack of educational pamphlets, can be a gathering spot, even if only when dropping off and picking up children at an elementary school. Parents and teachers find it easier to keep in touch with each other where such rooms exist.

Among other initiatives, it is very helpful for employers to grant time to employees to go to their children's schools for various kinds of involvement. Employees are released for jury duty; surely involvement in the schooling of children is as important as judging the guilt of alleged criminals.

"If I were king of the world, I'd make a law that required every employer to grant every working parent time off once a month to attend school functions," said Jane Manring, a teacher in Maryland. "Parents would come to school for conferences, performances and to observe their children in the classroom. Being better informed, they could work with the school to encourage and support students" (Manring 1990).

It should be remembered that there is no choice for children when it comes to parents. Policymakers ought to view support for parent involvement not so much in terms of helping parents as of helping kids. After all, it is the future of the children that is at stake in parent involvement.

References

"Building Concepts Through Verbal Interaction: The Key to Future Success in School? 1979. *Carnegie Quarterly* 27 (Winter).

BRIM, O. *Education for Child Rearing*. New York: Free Press.

CALABRESE, RAYMOND L. 1990. "The Public School: A Source of Alienation for Minority Parents." *Journal of Negro Education* 59: 148–154.

CARNEGIE FOUNDATION FOR THE ADVANCEMENT OF TEACHING. 1990. *The Condition of Teaching*. Princeton, N.J.: Carnegie Foundation for the Advancement of Teaching.

COMER, JAMES. 1986. "Parent Participation in the Schools." *Phi Delta Kappan* 67 442–46.

COUNCIL OF CHIEF STATE SCHOOL OFFICERS. (February: 1989). *Family Support Education, and Involvement: A Guide for State Action*. Washington, D.C.

COUNCIL OF THE GREAT CITY SCHOOLS. In Press. *Condition of Education in Great City Schools*. Washington, D.C.

EPSTEIN, JOYCE L. 1987. "What Principals Should Know About Parent Involvement." *Principal* (January): 6.

GRAY, ELLEN. 1990. "Helping Parents Do Their Job." *NCJW Journal* 13 (Spring): 10–11.

HAYDON, TOM. 1990. "Perth Amboy School Reaches out to Parents." *Star Ledger*, April 8: p. 45 (Section 1).

HENDERSON, ANNE. 1987. *The Evidence Continues to Grow: Parent Involvement Improves Student Achievement*. Columbia, Md.: National Committee for Citizens in Education.

LAREAU, ANETTE. 1989. *Home Advantage: Social Class and Parental Intervention in Elementary Education*. New York: Falmer Press.

MAEROFF, GENE. 1989. *The School Smart Parent*. New York: Times Books.

MANRING, JANE. 1990. "Business, Parents, and Schools [Letter to the editor]. *Washington Post*, July 16: A10.

MILLER, JULIE A. 1986. "Conference Creates Blueprint on Education of Black Children." *Educational Daily*, September 9: 2.

"PTA/DODGE NATIONAL PARENT SURVEY." 1990. *Newsweek*, March 12: p. 6 (special advertising section).

U.S. BUREAU OF THE CENSUS. 1988. *Fertility of American Women: June 1988* (Current Population Reports, Series P-20, No. 436). Washington, D.C.: Government Printing Office.

U.S. BUREAU OF THE CENSUS. 1990a. *Marital Status and Living Arrangements: March 1989* (Current Populations Reports, Series P-20, No. 445). Washington, D.C.: Government Printing Office.

U.S. BUREAU OF THE CENSUS. 1990b. *Statistical Abstract of the United States 1990, 110th edition.* Washington, D.C.: Government Printing Office.

U.S. CHAMBER OF COMMERCE. 1990. *Public Attitudes Toward Education.* Roper Poll, Center for Workforce Preparation and Quality Education. New York.

WALBERG, HERBERT J. 1988. "Creativity and Talent as Learning." In Robert J. Sternberg (ed.), *The Nature of Creativity: Contemporary Psychological Perspectives.* New York: Cambridge University Press.

WILLIAMS, DAVID L., AND FEYL CHAVKIN, NANCY. 1986. *Teacher/Parent Partnerships: Guidelines and Strategies for Training Teachers About Parent Involvement.* Austin, Tex.: Southwest Educational Development Lab.

NEW REFORMS,
NEW POLITICS

9

The Changing Politics of Education Reform

Chester E. Finn, Jr., and Theodor Rebarber

Chroniclers of American education sometimes present its saga in "cycles," whereby periods of heightened public attention, discontent, and change in the schools alternate with times of stability, consolidation, and popular satisfaction. Certainly any sentient observer of the events of the 1980s recognizes that we have been living through a textbook specimen of the former, an era of widespread unhappiness with the status quo and ever more ambitious efforts to change it.

We believe—and the earlier essays in this book supply added evidence —that what has been underway is actually more dramatic and portentous than a cyclical phase. No one can yet tell how it all will turn out, of course, and we have no credentials as seers. But there is already reason to suspect that what has been happening in education, at least since the United States was declared a "nation at risk," will in time be judged by historians as more akin to revolution than reform. In this chapter we explain what draws us to that view and point to some of the political dilemmas and uncertainties that characterize this—like any other—revolution.

A Great Awakening

There is no denying that the stirring April 1983 report of the National Commission on Excellence in Education symbolized and evoked the present era of criticism and change in U.S. education. Yet a strong case can be made that the period started earlier, perhaps with the 1975 revelation by the College Board that average Scholastic Aptitude Test scores had been declining for a decade, with media attention to "illiterate" high-school graduates and with the "back to basics" movement that began in the late

1970s, a movement most explicitly embodied in the minimum competency tests that many states decreed must be passed by students before they could receive diplomas. By 1983, we would suggest, the "excellence movement" was already well underway, although it had no name, coherent theme, or well-articulated rationale until the commission asserted that the "educational foundations of our society are presently being eroded by a rising tide of mediocrity that threatens our very future as a Nation and a people" (National Commission on Excellence in Education 1983, p. 5).

That report burst upon a society already anxious about quickening economic challenges from other nations. Weak education was seen as a major impediment to our international competitiveness, a threat to our standard of living and our place in the world. Deepening this anxiety were results of international tests that showed U.S. students performing at levels well below their agemates in other industrial nations.

Echoed in dozens of other studies, reports, and pronouncements by blue ribbon groups, such concerns brought unprecedented pressure on politicians and policymakers to improve educational performance. Public confidence in the schools was weak—and declining. In the annual Gallup survey of attitudes toward education, local public schools earned an average grade of "B−" in 1974 but just "C−" in 1983 (Elam and Brodinsky 1989). Most worrisome of all, it did not appear likely that the education system would repair itself without external leadership and leverage. But where was that to come from?

The Primacy of the States

The answer that emerged, for the first time in U.S. history, was from the states. This was an extraordinary development. For as long as anyone could remember, local control had been the byword of U.S. education policy, and for several decades Washington had been widely regarded as the main source of innovation and change. States had not been that important. They bore the constitutional responsibility for education, to be sure, and their bureaucracies kept records, licensed teachers, distributed a great deal of money according to complex formulas, and sometimes approved textbooks. Yet most important decisions had long since been delegated to local boards and superintendents, who, after all, actually had schools to run. And if there were large education problems facing the nation—teacher shortages, let us say, archaic science curricula, enduring racial segregation, or worrisome Soviet technological advances—the federal government would shoulder the burden of solving them.

All this has now changed dramatically. Although some local educators welcomed the excellence movement and a few took the initiative in reforming their schools, and although Washington officials cranked up a few new programs and took fuller advantage of the bully pulpit, the 1980s was a decade in which states became the main engines of change in education policymaking.

It turned out that they were already the senior partners in financing the enterprise. The state portion of the public-school dollar (now 50 percent) crept past the local share (now 44 percent) in the late 1970s. It continues to rise, and, as property tax limitation referenda and school finance equalization lawsuits proliferate, it seems inevitable that fiscal decisions made in state capitals will increasingly matter most in public education. That many state budgets are extraordinarily tight today will make such decisions more difficult but no less determinative of what happens in the schools.

States are also where most of the action has been with respect to policy innovation. One can cite a handful of exceptions (Rochester, Chelsea, Chicago, and suchlike) where the main impetus was local, but these pale alongside such statewide reform efforts as those of Kentucky, South Carolina, California, New Jersey, Oregon and a dozen other jurisdictions. Moreover, large changes in high-school-graduation requirements, teacher qualifications, and student assessment have been made by virtually every state. Although it can be argued that such activism at the state level has increased rather than diminished the policy burden on local school managers, too (Fuhrman and Elmore 1990), it is hard to claim that decisions made locally are even half so pivotal as they were a decade or two ago in determining the main thrust of U.S. education.

Meanwhile, Washington stepped back. Deepening budget deficits, the "new federalism" philosophy of consecutive Republican administrations, and near-paralysis of the congressional policy process (as well as icy relations between the executive and legislative branches) meant declining influence—and a shrinking federal share of the education dollar, which inevitably reduces Uncle Sam's leverage still further. Although this could change under the influence of the dynamic leadership team that took charge of the Federal education department in 1991, at the present time Washington is very much the junior member of this partnership.

Lay Leadership

At least as momentous as the newfound dominance of the states was a marked shift in leadership and influence from the education profession and its peculiar governance structures—school boards, superintendents, commissioners, and the like—to the elected leaders of the general purpose government. Back at the turn of the century, in a time of general mistrust of politicians, patronage, and corruption, a period of mounting interest in civic reform and "clean government," and an era when some believed that important public functions should be guided by trustworthy, long-established elites rather than left to the unpredictable passions of new immigrants and the dubious folk they might elect to office, public education had acquired what amounted to its own separate governmental arrangements. Aldermen, legislators, mayors, and governors were to leave it alone. Experts and professionals would run it, subject to the supervision and policy guidance of specialized—and ostensibly nonpolitical—boards. This arrangement was installed at both state and local levels, and, in formal, structural terms, it continues today.

As the excellence movement gathered steam, however, it became clear that the traditional education governance scheme was not serving us very well anymore. It had permitted mediocrity to take root and spread. And there was no reason to expect it to do otherwise as long as it was insulated from public responsiveness and political influence. What might have looked like worrisome tampering by officialdom eighty years earlier had come to resemble an overdue restoration of accountability.

By now, the expanding role of the states in school and college finance had also caused education to become the largest single item in every state budget, ahead of welfare, ahead of public safety, ahead of transportation. It was unthinkable that elected state policymakers would forswear all involvement with these enormously costly decisions, particularly at a time of rising popular discontent with the performance of the education system.

What is more, as governors, legislators, and mayors intruded into policy domains heretofore entrusted to experts and specialized governing boards, no one rose up to smite them. This was due at least in part to the fact that their interest focused on educational quality rather than political patronage. The public's concern for improvement had created a leadership vacuum, and the failure of traditional structures to rise to that challenge allowed previously silent partners to speak up with little risk of retribution.

Thus governors and legislators began to make decisions that heretofore had been the province of school boards and superintendents. Although the general-purpose government still appointed no principals, evaluated no teachers, managed no schools, and awarded no diplomas, it wielded ever greater influence in such matters as the content of the curriculum, the standards by which students and teachers are judged, the terms for conferring licenses and diplomas, the pay scales and norms of school employees, the requirements for promotion in school and entry into college, the gauges of institutional performance and pupil progress, and so forth.

From Inputs to Results

State primacy and lay leadership went hand-in-hand with a fundamental shift in the criteria by which education "quality" was coming to be judged. The Excellence Commission, let us recall, had not complained that our investments were stingy, our intentions evil, or our efforts insincere; rather, it had faulted U.S. education for inadequate outcomes. Simply put, the students were not learning enough.

For a long time we had construed education in terms of intentions and efforts, plans and inputs, institutions and services. As long as we spent enough, tried hard enough, and cared enough, we believed we would have a good education system. In recent years, however, we have been moving, albeit fitfully, to redefine education in terms of how much people actually learn. One day we will say of a person that he had no education, however long he may have spent in school, if in fact he has not attained a satisfactory level of knowledge and skills.

A preoccupation with results implies that someone must be held responsible for producing them. This, too, is not something that the education system, left to its own devices, was apt to impose upon itself. But as we have seen in several earlier chapters, the press for accountability is a major component of the reforms that characterize American education today.

Waves of Reform

The major changes discussed in this book—the issues, ideas, and strategies that invigorate policy debates in the early 1990s—are sometimes referred to as "second wave" reforms in order to contrast them with those undertaken in the mid-1980s. The distinction has some merit.

In its early stages, the excellence movement concentrated on raising academic standards through new norms, requirements, and regulations for students and teachers and on adding programs and services in an effort to do more of—and presumably be better at—what was already underway.

Although higher standards drew criticism from some on egalitarian grounds, and there was predictable resistance to raising taxes to augment school offerings, in the main the reform initiatives of the first wave threatened few established interests and encountered little opposition from powerful political groups. With a handful of exceptions, basic interests and operating procedures remained undisturbed. The ground rules of American educational practice were not rewritten. Power relationships within the system were sometimes modified but not fundamentally disrupted. Hence requirements proliferated, taxes rose, school spending soared (by 33 percent in "constant" dollars from 1980 to 1990), and a great deal of legislation was passed (U.S. Department of Education 1990).

The main problem with these efforts, we can now see, is that they accomplished far too little. Our education results have not significantly improved. The first wave of reform washed over the schools and colleges without much visible impact on their outcomes. In 1990 SAT verbal scores were as low as they have ever been, and mathematics results were flat—for the fourth year in a row. The National Assessment of Educational Progress (NAEP), which surveys a nationwide student sample, revealed general stagnation over the past decade, and each new release of international comparisons confirmed that U.S. students were still learning far less than their counterparts in other lands.

There is some good news. The score gaps between minority and white students have narrowed somewhat. High-school completion rates are up a bit. And the "back to basics" movement has been remarkably successful; according to NAEP data, just about everyone who sticks with formal education through high-school graduation now acquires rudimentary literacy and numeracy. At those very modest levels, we are now doing satisfactorily. It is when we look at the levels we *ought* to be reaching that our performance remains so lackluster. Here is a single example from a recent math assessment:

"Christine borrows $850 for one year from the Friendly Finance Company. If she pays 12% simple interest on the loan, what will be the total amount that Christine repays?" (Dossey et al. 1988, p. 43).

This problem is not very difficult. It can be solved several different ways. It requires a bit of thought, but nothing fancy. It typifies what NAEP calls "level 350," however, and today that is a level of mathematics performance being reached by only *6 percent* of our eleventh-graders. If just 6 out of 100 high-school juniors can solve problems of this level of difficulty, that means 94 cannot (and this omits those who have dropped out of school by eleventh grade!).

Similar examples can be seen in reading, writing, science, history, and geography. What this reveals is that, while our schools are not producing new adult illiterates, they are graduating an enormous number of people with mediocre skills and knowledge, and that, above all, is why the nation is still "at risk" in 1991, notwithstanding many sincere efforts to correct the situation.

Vanilla—and Rocky Road

As we began to see that the "first wave" reforms were not getting the job done, people began to challenge previously unquestioned assumptions underlying the current system and to consider more drastic interventions in the educational status quo. Some critics and analysts said that what was necessary was fundamental reconstruction, perhaps even replacement, not more tinkering at the margins. The old system could not be made significantly more productive, they argued; a new one was needed.

We do not have a new education system yet, of course. But the three broad (and overlapping) categories of "second wave" reforms examined in earlier chapters of this book are important examples of changes with the potential to overturn the old education cart and send us in search of a new mode of transportation.

The categories are a bit deceptive, however; the label may exaggerate the reality. Each of these genres of reform comes in a range of flavors, from the mildest of vanilla to the sourest of lemon and most biting of peppermint. Some versions are indeed radical—and upsetting to vested interests; others are so bland that nobody is much threatened by them. The important question is which will make more difference when it comes to results. Disruption *per se* is no virtue; only if student outcomes improve is it worth the agony. Yet the painlessness of incrementalism has little value, either, if it yields no significant learning gains. These, above all, are the lessons that the reforms of the 1980s have to teach policymakers of the 1990s. Ends are what matter. The means, whether delicate or robust, are important only insofar as results improve.

How do we steer safely between ineffectual incrementalism and feckless radicalism? The experience of reform in the 1980s leads us to believe that the more innocuous versions of school restructuring, accountability, and parent enabling, although politically palatable and hence easier to enact, will change so little that their results can not be significant. However, those who travel the rockier political roads, in pursuit of bolder interventions and more dramatic policy formulations may encounter so much hostility and passive resistance among affected interests that their efforts will be frustrated too, albeit for different reasons.

This, it seems to us, poses perhaps the most difficult conundrum that legislators and other key education policymakers face as they weigh competing versions of "wave two" education reforms.

School Restructuring

Although perhaps the least clearly defined term in the entire education reform lexicon, "restructuring" commonly implies basic changes in ground rules and power relationships. Characteristic of these is decentralization of control and decision-making from system-wide central offices to the people involved with individual schools. This is a reversal of decades of district consolidation and policy centralization. But it is also quite different from earlier forms of decentralization, such as those New York City undertook in 1969, when a number of semiautonomous, medium-sized, multischool districts were created within massive metropolitan systems. Decentralization today means devolution of authority right down to the school building. Dade County, Florida, and Rochester, New York, are frequently cited examples of this approach, although important variations are also found in San Diego, Memphis, Hammond (Indiana), and Los Angeles.

This sounds radical, indeed, and it surely has that potential. Yet in most instances, building-level decision-makers gain only limited control over such important variables as curriculum, budget, and personnel. Even that can be too much for some. Many teachers and principals would just as soon *not* assume the additional burden of managerial decisions; hence it is common in "restructuring" systems to find some schools exercising wide discretion, others uncertain and fumbling as they seek to delineate their duties and reach agreement on issues, and some wholly untouched by the change. Nor can it be automatically assumed that shifting the locus of decisions from one level to another will lead to markedly *different* decisions being made. If people at the building level do not have alternative visions of how their school ought to operate, or lack an overpowering impulse to improve, giving them the authority to make such choices is no sure path to increased knowledge and skill levels among their students.

Chicago is an interesting case in point. The city practically declared war on its public-school system, which former U.S. education secretary William Bennett had termed the nation's worst. As Fred Hess recounts in Chapter 4, sweeping devolution of authority to the building level was the alternative that the city demanded and won from the Illinois legislature. What makes the Chicago plan different from other urban restructuring schemes, however, is that most of that rechanneled power flows to parents rather than professional educators. Parents have a majority on the eleven-member councils that govern each school.

This and other changes—including reduced job security and heightened accountability for school results—angered the Chicago principals' association, which, after finding little sympathy among elected officials, took their grievances to the courts. The result, in November 1990, was temporary invalidation of the reform law by the Illinois state supreme court. Reflecting continued strong political support for the reforms, however, the Illinois legislature passed in July 1991 a lightly-revised version of the law that addressed the issues raised by the court and included additional provisions favored by Chicago reformers. (For details, see Chapter 4.)

Chelsea, Massachusetts, poses another example of the uncertainties of school restructuring. That small city's school board, despite strong opposition from the teachers' union (and considerable disquiet in the Hispanic community), handed near-total authority over its school system to Boston University (a private institution) and its outspoken president, John Silber. This was not a decentralization plan—Chelsea has just a half dozen schools—but it certainly qualifies as a monumental rewriting of authority relationships. However will it work? Will it last long enough to yield valid evidence? The contract with Boston University is supposed to run for an entire decade, but the city can abrogate it at any time, and changes on the school board have already led to considerable uncertainty about the durability of this arrangement. Chelsea's ever-graver fiscal situation also introduces serious handicaps into the relationship. It is no more reasonable in Chelsea than in Chicago (or elsewhere) to expect rapid improvements in school results, yet policymakers' patience may not last, especially as aggrieved devotees of the old ways criticize and seek to revise the changes now underway.

Other heroic restructuring plans are so new that they have had no real opportunity to get into trouble—or to show results. Kentucky is probably the best example of a statewide scheme that, if it works as designed, will alter just about all the old assumptions, incentive structures, and power relationships. We cannot know whether the legislature and governor would have gone so far had the courts not voided the entire statutory framework of public education in the state. It was a most unusual circumstance, and this time policymakers took full advantage of it, displaying real imagination, vision, and courage in crafting what amounts to a whole new education system for the Bluegrass State. But how will it work? As people find they must really alter their ingrained behavior patterns, habits, and attitudes to accommodate it, will it even last?

Assessment and Accountability

Assessment may evoke strong sentiments among those wary of testing, but it almost never becomes a major political issue at the state or local level until it is joined to accountability. Then the trouble starts!

Assessment, as we see it, is the middle of a three-layer accountability "sandwich." Any serious education accountability plan consists, first, of clear goals and outcomes that make it apparent what one is hoping to accomplish and what the system would look like if it were succeeding. Second, it is essential to have trustworthy information feedback mechanisms by which to monitor how well those goals are being achieved. (Assessment of student performance is ordinarily a major element, but probably not the entirety, of such an information system.) Third, consequences need to follow, such that rewards and plaudits come to people and institutions that are achieving the desired results and interventions and changes afflict those who are failing. It's the prospect of consequences of course, in education as in other human endeavors, that alarms people who think they may be adversely affected. That is a source of friction—and often of political resistance.

In Rochester, New York, home of perhaps the most widely acclaimed community-wide restructuring plan, a dispute about teacher accountability has jeopardized the entire reform effort. In a city where close cooperation and trust between labor and management have been cited as important features of reform efforts, teachers voted in 1990 to reject an accountability plan designed jointly by their union leader and the school superintendent, notwithstanding that average teacher salaries would rise to $50,000 under terms of the same contract and that the most senior teachers could earn as much as $80,000.

A watered-down version was then approved by the superintendent and the union but rejected by unanimous vote of the school board amid widespread feeling in the community that teachers were taking undue advantage of the city's generosity and abjuring responsibility for whether their students actually learned more.

Similarly, it was the accountability—and vulnerability—of Chicago's principals under the 1988 reform law that led them into court to fight the legislation. Goals, tests, standards, and measures are relatively innocuous in themselves—"low stakes" in the jargon of the school reform community. When consequences follow, when rewards and bonuses are to be conferred or—especially—when sanctions, uncertainties, and threats to one's own position loom, the stakes rise and the long knives come out.

Yet Kentucky has built potent accountability features into its school reform plan, and, as Terry Peterson recounts in Chapter 6, South Carolina did much the same a few years earlier. This suggests that accountability systems need not always bring insuperable political resistance—a very important observation inasmuch as such systems could well turn out to be the indispensable elements of effective wave-two education reforms.

Elected state officials have begun to understand the very important role accountability has to play. After school finance, accountability is the issue most often mentioned by state legislators as uppermost on their education agendas (National Conference of State Legislatures 1991). In a period of painful fiscal austerity, taxpayers are no longer content to hand over their wallets and ask no questions. Inspired, perhaps, by business's interest in the "bottom line," the general public and elected officials increasingly focus on holding educators and educational institutions to account for their *results*.

Parent Enabling

Parent involvement strategies also range from mild to potent, and the politics associated with them vary from dull to disruptive. No one objects to showing mom and dad how to become more effective partners, to stepped-up home-school communication, or to kindred efforts designed to engage parents more successfully in the education of their daughters and sons. All the more when such programs are voluntary. And new government outlays and jobs for program staffers rarely engender substantial political opposition, at least so long as funds to pay for them can be found.

It is different, however, when parents gain decision-making power, either through participation in governance structures such as Chicago's school councils or when they acquire the right to select their children's school through choice policies.

Choice

Empowering parents to choose the schools their children will attend at government expense is one of the most hotly debated of the new reforms. Yet we admit to being slightly perplexed about how choice ever came to be so "controversial" in elementary-secondary education, considering how much it is taken for granted in almost every other domain of American life. Education Secretary Lamar Alexander wondered aloud at his 1991 confirmation hearing how we had ever abandoned the assumption that of course parents would select their child's school. But lose it we did, and choice now ranks up there with accountability and restructuring on the list of prickly dilemmas for policymakers eager to boost the efficiency of the nation's schools but wary of alienating the powerful interests of the status quo.

Today the most common type of choice plan confines parents' power of selection to various public schools, either within a local district or across the entire state. Sometimes the confines are tighter, such as when racial desegregation requirements are superimposed, turning the arrangement into what Charles Glenn (1989) terms "controlled choice." Even this can anger some of the stodgier professional groups although more and more of them are accommodating themselves to the idea of "public school choice." Far more controversial in their eyes is "supply side" choice, which menaces the monopoly of public education providers and includes private schools or other rival deliverers of education services. Yet proponents of supply side choice, such as John Chubb and Terry Moe, insist that restricting choice to similar schools run by a single complacent supplier sharply limits the potential benefits of the marketplace.

At first blush, choice looks like a pure "parent enabling" policy, but in fact it also touches on the themes of restructuring and accountability and thus fits into all three categories. It obviously strengthens the involvement of parents by giving them power over decisions affecting the education of their children, decisions that are virtually certain to engage their attention and increase their level of responsibility. Choice also fosters institutional accountability by causing resources to flow to schools on the basis of voluntary enrollment in them, thus creating a market that rewards successful vendors and penalizes the ineffective. Choice encourages restructuring, too, since decentralized authority is a prerequisite for the kind of school variety and competition that choice envisions—and because choice inevitably leads to more differentiation and specialization among suppliers.

Because it's been branded "controversial," choice is never plain vanilla from the standpoint of policymakers. For a really tingling flavor sensation, however, legislators may want to hold a hearing on the possible inclusion of private schools. In recent years only a few jurisdictions have seriously considered this, and to our knowledge just one state has enacted such a plan. At the behest of State Representative Annette (Polly) Williams and Governor Tommy Thompson, Wisconsin passed a law permitting up to one thousand low-income children to move from the Milwaukee public schools to (secular) private schools at state expense. This stirred a hornet's nest, of course, and the plan faces sustained opposition by the state superintendent, his department of education, and all the major public school lobbies in Wisconsin. Though a second year of the program is expected to begin in the fall of 1991, it is currently under challenge in state courts and its future is in doubt.

An initiative to create a complete choice "market," including all public and private schools in the state (and home schooling options as well), made it onto the Oregon ballot in 1990. A perception among many Oregonians that such radical change was unnecessary, however, combined with mistakes by proponents, resulted in the measure's defeat at the hands of a broad coalition led by the state superintendent and including all the major public education groups. Though this revolutionary proposal ultimately failed to convince the voters, it certainly heightened attention to education reform and may even have provided the necessary jolt to those interests comfortable with the status quo that made more palatable the sweeping reforms enacted a few months later in 1991.

Another option being explored to address the need for "supply side" variety is to allow new entrants into the public system through "charter schools." Enterprising teachers or other educators are granted a charter to create a school from the ground up, including design of the instructional program and hiring of staff. A charter school would be responsible for recruiting—and maintaining—a student body (for which it would receive state and local funding on a per capita basis) but would be exempt from state and local constraints regarding its everyday operation.

Though some districts have experimented with versions of such a system, only one state has enacted a statewide policy. Minnesota, the first state to allow students a choice among public schools regardless of district boundaries, passed a law in 1991 allowing the creation of a limited number of what it calls "outcome-based schools." Under the Minnesota plan, such schools are exempt from all state and local regulations—except in the areas of health, safety and civil rights—as well as previous collective bargaining agreements (though employees may seek to bargain collectively with an individual school). After a period of several years, the state or district decides whether to renew or terminate a school's "charter" based on its success as measured by student outcomes.

Allowing families a choice among schools is a reform likely to spread as time passes. Surveys indicate that the public overwhelmingly supports educational choice and that its enthusiasm for this proposal has been increasing. The strongest support is found among parents, the young, those with lower incomes, and minorities. On the issue of including private schools, recent polls show that a majority of the public now supports policies that would extend choice to them as well. A NBC/Wall Street Journal poll conducted in July 1991 found 56 per cent of the public favors vouchers or tax credits that would allow parents to select private schools at public expense. (Richmond Times-Dispatch, July 10, 1991) A survey conducted for the National Association of Independent Schools (NAIS) in the same month similarly found 57 per cent approval for vouchers. Such levels of support denote a substantial increase since 1983, when a New York Times poll found only 44 per cent in favor of choice among private schools. (Innerst, July 24, 1991) Choice draws on fundamental American values of individual liberty and equity (that is, wealthy parents already have a choice) and, once experimentation has begun, it may well require evidence that it is actually *harmful* to retard its spread. Our federal system encourages just such experimentation.

All Three Branches

Governors were the most visible state-level education reformers during most of the 1980s. The solid—and high profile—work of the National Governors' Association, beginning around 1985, and the even-higher-profile "summit" that the governors and President George Bush held in Charlottesville in late 1989, symbolized the new era of leadership by elected state officials.

The executive branch can surely make noise, command attention, and advance proposals, but it cannot write laws, raise taxes, or appropriate funds. Real and durable reform must be embodied in statute, and legislatures are where those decisions finally get made. As the excellence movement proceeded through the 1980s, more and more legislators assumed educational leadership roles, and the choices they made, hearings they held, evidence they weighed, experts they consulted, and priorities they set began to be recognized as the real forges of education policy. The project from which this book springs was itself just one instance of the widening attention—and deference—that has come to be paid to the centrality of the legislature in the policy process.

State governments consist of three branches, however, and of late the judiciary has also resumed an influential role. After a period of activism with respect to school finance in the 1960s and 1970s, state courts moved to the side of the education policy stage. The federal judiciary remained quite active and visible, of course, particularly in school desegregation, but it was not until the late 1980s that state courts again became major actors.

Since the mid '80s the state courts have become the venues for dramatic change as a half dozen states have been ordered by their supreme courts to equalize the resources available for public education across the various communities of the state. (Such rulings are usually complicated, but that is their essential point.) Similar lawsuits are working their way through the courts of many other jurisdictions. Since it is obviously harder to reduce education spending in wealthy districts than to boost funding in poor communities, the result of school finance equalization rulings is always to increase total public outlays for education.

Although the lawsuits filed thus far under the rubric of "equity" have concentrated on dollars as the solution to unequal results, in Kentucky the court's sweeping decision seemed to take a broader view, perhaps in response to the many studies that have denied a direct link between increased spending and improved performance. Whether or not other courts choose to follow this new line of reasoning remains to be seen. However, events in Texas following the invalidation of that state's school finance system in 1990 seem to indicate that elected officials may take advantage of the opportunity provided even by such limited mandates to address other aspects of reform as well. (In the Lone Star State they have emphasized accountability.)

State courts have also become significant players in political dramas scripted by the executive and the legislature, although this sometimes serves to slow down changes that others want to make. Notable examples are the Chicago and Milwaukee education reform sagas, where lay sections or entire statutes have been voided by the judiciary. Although it is likely in these cases that the vital features can be restored in constitutionally acceptable forms, it is well to note that interests offended by certain reforms but unable to prevail in legislative chambers are apt to seek satisfaction in the courtroom. At the very least, this realization should encourage ardent reformers to pay close attention to other statutory and constitutional provisions that may clash with the changes they hope to make. Nor should we be surprised that the more radical those changes are, the more ingenious—and dogged—their opponents will be in the quest for grounds on which to invalidate them.

The Politics of Persistence

Reform-minded legislators and governors tend to assume that, once they have passed a law, they have fulfilled their responsibilities. Frequently this turns out to be an illusion. Perhaps especially in the field of education, which consists of ponderous systems, conservative institutions, ingrained habits, many tenured employees, and millions of children who still require twelve or thirteen years to pass through the schools, a new statute is only one marker along the reform highway. Officials who then turn to other matters, assuming that the new education law will be correctly interpreted and speedily implemented, are apt to be disappointed.

Implementation is slow, even under the best of circumstances. Results are still slower to accumulate. Those who opposed the change or are injured by it will persist in their efforts to undo it, whether by rushing into court for an injunction, biding their time for the next session of the legislature, dragging their heels or simply ignoring the new mandates.

How can policymakers with other issues on their agendas keep focused on education reform? Do they have satisfactory institutional mechanisms for monitoring, evaluating, and reporting back on progress, mechanisms whose routine functioning will serve to buttress key aspects of reform? Can they create a schedule for themselves that includes systematic oversight of implementation? Will they take the pains to enlist civic

organizations, business groups, and other more-or-less permanent enti-
ties, so that the short time horizons of elected officials are not the only
timelines and calendars that matter?

We have no magic that will strengthen the resolve of elected officials to
finish what they start or clear other issues from their dockets. We can
simply assert with confidence that much remains to be done even after the
bill passes.

The Changing Education Policy Arena

Education policy at the state level was once a fairly sedate sport played in a
small arena with relatively few participants. A dozen or so influential
interest groups, virtually all of them representing the employees or
managers of the schools themselves, worked out agreements with each
other, with a few key legislators, with the state education commissioner
and—on costly items—with the governor or his agent. It was all fairly
cozy; many important discussions occurred out of public earshot; few
outsiders intruded.

That may have been acceptable when we were generally content with
the performance of the education system and when most of the decisions
were made locally or in Washington; anyway, not in the state capital. It is
certainly not acceptable in many jurisdictions today, however, nor is the
old way of doing business apt to return soon. The education policy arena is
now full of clashing interests and boisterous observers, and very much
exposed to public scrutiny. Governors play prominent roles, as do much
larger numbers of legislators (and, in many states, specialized staff
members). The judiciary, as we have seen, is involved as well. But perhaps
the greatest change has been the entrance into that policy arena of
representatives of education's *consumers* (that is, students, their parents,
and their future employers). What had long been a private conversation
held mostly among producers is now a lively debate between producers
and consumers. As there are many more of the latter, they always had the
potential to dominate these debates. All that was necessary was for them
to speak up and to vote accordingly. It turns out, of course, that a number
of governors and legislators were ready to become consumer advocates.

That has now happened in a big way, and the politics of the education
policy arena have been transformed for the foreseeable future. What
remains to be seen is whether partisanship is going to rear its head. The
one significant remnant of the putatively "nonpolitical" era of education
policy-making in the United States has been the unusually modest role
that political party membership has played in these deliberations. Deci-

sions are usually bi- or nonpartisan. It has been hard to discern many systematic philosophical differences between Democrats and Republicans with respect to schooling. Although ideology has played a sizable role in contemporary education policy debates, party *per se* has not.

That situation could change in the future. Will the Democratic party tend to ally itself with "producer" interests in education while Republicans evolve into the party of the "consumers"? Will new fissures erupt in previously solid political alliances? As yet there are only hints of such partisanship, much of it rooted in the Democrats' long-standing kinship with the teachers' unions and the Republicans' traditional closeness to the business community. Events in Wisconsin, however, where a Republican governor and his allies joined forces with a prominent—and radical—black Democratic legislator to push through a reform plan opposed primarily by mainstream Democrats and the education establishment may be an early warning of potential tensions within the Democratic coalition. The race issue makes this particularly complicated. Although Democrats have had the votes of most minority group members, it is black and Hispanic youngsters, particularly in sprawling urban school systems, who have been least well served by the efforts of the education establishment. It is not wholly implausible to imagine an alliance forming among minority leaders, parents, business leaders, and other consumer interests demanding nonincremental changes in American education. If one political party champions that alliance while the other defends establishment and producer interests, the politics of education reform could become very interesting indeed.

Yet it is not clear that this would be entirely for the better. Opening up the arena to more participants has generally been a healthy development, despite the noisy hubbub that has ensued. Marshaling all the inhabitants of that arena into two opposing teams, however, while perhaps an improvement in terms of tidiness, is apt to turn everyone's attention to scoring points. It's better education we need in the fifty states, today, and everyone's attention should accordingly be rivetted onto the scoreboards that record gains in knowledge and skills, not on those that keep track of partisan wins and losses.

The Coming Years

Several factors converging at the national level suggest that the federal government may in the near future no longer limit its actions to cheerleading and goal-setting (although effective use of the bully pulpit is sure to remain an important federal role). First, the public seems increasingly impatient for action at the national level. Survey results indicate that huge majorities of Americans favor national education standards (70 percent), a national curriculum (69 percent), and national tests (77 percent) (Elam and Gallup 1989). Second, our self-proclaimed "education president" has until November 1992 to justify that label to the American public. Third, the new and highly respected education secretary, former Tennessee governor Lamar Alexander, has raised expectations for a new federal leadership standard in this field, which he is quite likely to achieve. Fourth, not only are we no closer to achieving the laudable national education goals proclaimed by the president and governors, but we do not yet even have satisfactory mechanisms to measure progress (or the lack of it!).

We anticipate an escalation of the already lively debate about new forms of tests and assessments to measure educational outcomes for the country as a whole and to permit interstate comparisons. Although an explicit national curriculum does not seem likely at this point, some kind of voluntary mechanism to measure student achievement (and perhaps other educational outcomes as well) in relation to national goals and world standards is probably a good bet. A nationwide system of *individual* exams is already the subject of lively discussion in Washington.

Even if greater activity ensues at the national level, however, primary responsibility for education remains with the states. It will be up to the states to participate in any new national assessment (or, if we are wrong, to design their own). And it will be up to the states to make use of this information to design effective accountability and governance systems that encourage educators and parents to do all they can to help improve the education of our country's youth. Such far-reaching action will require even greater quantities of courage and vision from elected officials in what is likely to be an increasingly tempestuous political climate.

References

DOSSEY, JOHN A., et al. (eds.). 1988. *The Mathematics Report Card: Are We Measuring Up?* (Report No. 17-M-01.) Princeton, N.J.: Educational Testing Service. 1988.

ELAM, STANLEY M. and BRODINSKY, BEN. 1989. *The Gallup/Phi Delta Kappan Polls of Attitudes Toward the Public Schools, 1968–88.* Bloomington, Ind.: Phi Delta Kappan Educational Foundation.

FUHRMAN, SUSAN H., and ELMORE, RICHARD. 1990. Understanding Local Control in the Wake of State Education Reform. *Educational Evaluation and Policy Analysis* 12(1): 82–96.

GLENN, CHARLES. "Parent Choice and American Values." In Joe Nathan (ed.),

Public Schools by Choice: Expanding Opportunities for Parents, Students, and Teachers. St. Paul, Minn.: The Institute for Teaching and Learning.

INNERST, CAROL. 1991. "Parents Prefer Private Schools." *The Washington Times.* July 24.

NATIONAL COMMISSION ON EXCELLENCE IN EDUCATION. 1983. Washington, D.C.: Government Printing Office.

NATIONAL CONFERENCE OF STATE LEGISLATURES. 1991. *NCSL State Issues.* Denver: The Conference.

Richmond Times-Dispatch. 1991. "Statists Against Choice." July 10.

U.S. DEPARTMENT OF EDUCATION. 1990. *U.S. Department of Education News: 1990 Back to School Forecast.* Washington, D.C.: Government Printing Office.

About the Authors

Francie Alexander is the Deputy Assistant Secretary at the U.S. Department of Education's Office of Educational Research and Improvement (OERI). Before that she was the Executive Director of the National Council on Standards and Testing. She had been the Associate Superintendent of Curriculum, Instruction, and Assessment for the California Department of Education. She served a four-year term on the California Curriculum Development and Supplemental Materials Commission. Alexander has been very involved in the state's recent efforts to upgrade textbook quality and in the well-publicized rejections of middle-school science texts and K–8 mathematics textbook series. She also serves on the National Assessment Governing Board. Her contribution to this volume was written in her private capacity. No official support or endorsement by the U.S. Department of Education is intended or should be inferred.

John E. Chubb, political scientist in the Governmental Studies Program at the Brookings Institution in Washington, DC, is the author of numerous articles and books on U.S. government and public policy. His most recent book, *Politics, Markets, and America's Schools,* is co-authored with Terry M. Moe.

Chester E. Finn, Jr., is a professor of education and public policy at Vanderbilt University, director of the Educational Excellence Network, and president of the Madison Center for Educational Affairs. In late 1988 he completed a 3½-year tenure as Assistant Secretary for Research and Improvement and Counselor to the Secretary of the U.S. Department of Education. Among his seven earlier books are *We Must Take Charge: Our Schools and Our Future; What Do Our 17-Year-Olds Know?,* written with Diane Ravitch; and *Challenges to the Humanities,* edited with Ravitch and P. Holley Roberts. He serves on the President's Education Policy Advisory Committee and the National Assessment Governing Board.

G. Alfred Hess, Jr., is Executive Director of the Chicago Panel on Public School Policy and Finance. The panel is a coalition of twenty civic organizations concerned with public education in Chicago. He was one of the leaders of the school reform movement in Chicago and the author of

195

several parts of the Chicago School Reform Act of 1988. He is the author of *School Restructuring: Chicago Style*. Hess has served on numerous advisory panels for the Chicago Board of Education, the State Superintendent of Schools, Senator Paul Simon, the mayor of Chicago, and others. Before coming to his present position, he spent nearly twenty years in community organizing and adult training for community development.

Michael W. Kirst is chair of the Department of Administration and Policy Analysis at Stanford University. He is a former president of the California State Board of Education. His most recent book is *Schools in Conflict*. Kirst is the Director of Policy Analysis for California Education (PACE), an independent, university-based policy research organization.

Gene I. Maeroff is a senior fellow at the Carnegie Foundation for the Advancement of Teaching in Princeton, NJ. His two most recent books are *The School-Smart Parent* and *The Empowerment of Teachers*. For fifteen years he was on the staff of *The New York Times*, where he was national education correspondent.

Terry M. Moe is a professor of political science at Stanford University. He is the author of many books on bureaucracy and public administration, including *Politics, Markets, and America's Schools*, co-authored with John E. Chubb.

Joseph Murphy is Chairman of the Department of Educational Leadership at Vanderbilt University. He is a senior research fellow at the National Center for Education Leadership. Murphy's most recent books are *Restructuring Schools: Capturing and Assessing the Phenomena* and *The Education Reform Movement of the 1980s* (ed.).

Thomas W. Payzant has been Superintendent of the San Diego City Schools since 1982. He is a member and past president of the Large City Schools Superintendents. Payzant is also Chairman of the Board of Directors of the Council for Basic Education and serves on the National Board for Professional Teaching Standards.

Terry K. Peterson is Executive Director of the South Carolina Business-Education Committee, a panel of state leaders in business, the legislature and education which monitors South Carolina's comprehensive education reforms; he is also the executive assistant for public policy to the president of Winthrop College. Peterson has been involved with task forces on educational reform with many national groups, in 1988 chairing the Task Force on Accountability and School Improvement for the U.S. Department of Education, and is frequently asked to advise states about education reform strategies.

Theodor Rebarber is an OERI Associate at the U.S. Department of Education. Before that, he was a research associate at Vanderbilt University's Educational Excellence Network. He is the author of three policy guides for state legislators, *Parent Enabling Policies for States, Accountability in Education,* and *Restructuring Education.* His contribution to this volume was written in his private capacity. No official support or endorsement by the U.S. Department of Education is intended or should be inferred.

Summer Institute Participants

Vanderbilt University (July 26–29, 1990)

I. STATE LEGISLATIVE DELEGATIONS

Colorado

Senate
Mike Bird, Chair, Joint Budget Committee
Dottie Wham, Chair, Judiciary Committee

House
Jeanne M. Adkins, Member, Education Committee
Jeanne Faatz, Chair, Education Committee
Paul D. Schauer, Chair, Finance Committee

Florida

Senate
Bob Johnson, Chair, Education Committee

House
Michael Friedman, Chair, Education Committee
Also attending:
Ann Levy, Analyst, Education Committee
Michael J. O'Farrell, Staff Director, Education Committee
Pat O'Connell, Legislative Affairs, Florida Department of
Education

Indiana

Senate

Maurice Doll, Member, Education Committee
Patricia Miller, Member, Education Committee
Richard Thompson, Member, Education Committee

House

Stephen Gabet, Ranking Minority, Education Committee
Douglas Kinser, Member, Education Committee
Paul Robertson, Co-chair, Education Committee
Philip Warner, Co-chair, Education Committee

Iowa

Senate

Willian Dieleman, Chair, Ways and Means Committee
Larry Murphy, Chair, Education Committee
Maggie Tinsman, Member, Education Committee

House

Janet Adams, Member, Education Committee
Ruhl Maulsby, Member, Ranking Minority, Education Appropriations Committee
Don Shoultz, Vice-chair, House Education Committee

Kansas

Senate

Jerry Karr, Member, Education Committee
Dave Kerr, Member, Education Committee
Audrey Langworthy, Member, Education Committee

House

Gene Amos, Member, Education Committee
Rick Bowden, Ranking Minority, Education Committee
James E. Lowther, Member, Education Committee

Maine

Senate

Stephen C. Estes, Chair, Education Committee

House

Omar T. Norton, Member, Education Committee
Judy Paradis, Member, Education Committee

Also attending:
David Elliot, Principal Analyst, Education Committee
Leanne Greeley-Bond, Maine Development Foundation
Bruce Pelletier, Legislative Aide, Speaker's Office

Minnesota

Senate

Tracy Beckman, Vice-chair, Education Committee
Dave Frederickson, Member, Education Committee
Also attending:
Maja Weidmann, Legislative Analyst, Senate Counsel and Research

Nebraska

Dennis Baack, Member, Education Committee
La Von Crosby, Member, Education Committee
David Bernard-Stevens, Vice-chair, Education Committee
Also attending:
C. K. Eberspacher, Legislative Aide, Representative Crosby
Polly Feis, Interdisciplinary coordinator, Nebraska Department of Education
Mary Ann Losh, Staff Development, Nebraska Department of Education

New Mexico

Senate

Carlos R. Cisneros, Chair, Education Committee; Chair, LESC
Fernando R. Macias, Chair, Judiciary Committee

House

Barbara Casey, Member, Education Committee
Ramon Huerta, Chair, Enrolling and Engrossing Committee
Also attending:
Guy Jacobus, Research Analyst, LESC
Pauline Rindone, Research Analyst, LESC

Pennsylvania

Senate

Jeanette F. Reibman, Member, Education Committee
James Rhoades, Vice-chair, Education Committee

House

Ronald R. Cowell, Chair, Education Committee
Paul Wass, Member, Education Committee

Also attending:
Don Francis, Legislative Aide, Senator Rhodes
Charles Greenawalt, Senate Policy Director
Steve Miller, (Counsel Staff, Speaker's Office)

South Carolina

Senate

Samuel Stilwell, Member, Education Committee

House

David Beasley, Chair, Education Committee
Mike Jaskwhich, Member, Education Committee
Also attending:
Melanie Barton, Assistant Director of Research, Senate Education Committee
Carol Stewart, director of Research, House Education Committee
Ellen Still, Director of Research, Senate Education Committee

Tennessee

Senate

Ray Albright, Chair, Education Committee
Leonard Dunavant, Member, Education Committee
Andy Womack, Vice-chair, Education Committee

House

Clint Callicott, Member, Education Committee
Joe Bell, Member Education Committee
Ronnie E. Davis, Member, Education Committee
Leslie Winningham, Vice-chair, Education Committee

Vermont

Senate

Michael Metcalf, Member, Education Committee
Jeb Spaulding, Chair, Education Committee

House

Barbara Grimes, Chair, Education Committee
David Larsen, Member, Education Committee
William Talbott, Member, Education Committee
Also attending:
Don Dickson, Legislative Counsel, Education Committee

Washington

Senate

Eleanor M. Lee, Vice-chair, Education Committee
Patty Murray, Member, Education Committee
  Also attending:
  Larry Davis, Senior Analyst/Supervisor (Senate Education Committee)

House

Greg Fisher, Vice-chair, Education Committee
Bill Brumsickle, Member, Education Committee
  Also attending:
  Robert Butts, Analyst, House Education Committee

Wyoming

Senate

Boyd Eddins, Co-chair, Education Committee
Allan Howard, Member, Education Committee

House

Mike Enzi, Member, Education Committee
Jim Hageman, Co-chair, Education Committee
  Also attending:
  Scott Farris, Administrative Assistant-Governor's Office
  David Nelson, Staff Counsel, Legislative Office

II. INSTITUTE STAFF

Educational Excellence Network
  Chester E. Finn, Jr., Director
  Theodor Rebarber, Research Associate
  Andrew C. Forsaith, Research Associate
  Matthew D. Gandal, Research Associate

National Conference of State Legislatures
  John L. Myers, Program Director, Education
  Tim Storey, Policy Associate, Education

III. OTHER ATTENDEES

Gene Bryant (*TEA News*)
Mark Hudson (Arkansas Legislative Council)
William S. McKersie (The Joyce Foundation, Senior Program Officer)
Peter Schmidt (*Education Week*)

Index